KU-254-988

RELATIVE FREEDOMS

Women and Leisure

EDITED BY
Erica Wimbush and
Margaret Talbot

Open University Press
MILTON KEYNES · PHILADELPHIA

Open University Press
12 Cofferidge Close
Stony Stratford
Milton Keynes MK11 1BY

and
242 Cherry Street
Philadelphia, PA 19106, USA

First Published 1988

Copyright © The Editors and Contributors 1988

All rights reserved. No part of this publication may be reproduced, stored in a retrieval system or transmitted in any form or by any means, without permission from the publisher.

British Library Cataloguing in Publication Data

Relative freedoms: women and leisure.
1. Women. Leisure. Social aspects
I. Wimbush, Erica   II. Talbot, Margaret
306'.48'088042

ISBN 0-335-15569-3
ISBN 0-335-15568-5 Pbk

Library of Congress Cataloging-in-Publication Data

Relative freedoms: women and leisure/edited by Erica Wimbush and
  Margaret Talbot.
     p.   cm.
  Includes index.
    1. Women—Recreation.   2. Leisure.   I. Wimbush, Erica.
II. Talbot, Margaret.
GV183.R43 1988
790.1'94—dc 19   88-12659   CIP
   ISBN 0-335-15569-3 ISBN 0-335-15568-5 (pbk.)

1589115

BIRMINGHAM UNIVERSITY LIBRARY

Typeset by Colset Pte Ltd, Singapore
Printed in Great Britain by Redwood Burn Ltd, Trowbridge, Wiltshire

RELATIVE FREEDOMS

This book is dedicated to the spirit of independence which our mothers passed on to us; may it continue to empower future generations of women.

Contents

List of contributors   ix
Acknowledgements   xi
Introduction   xiii

PART 1: APPROACHING LEISURE: Introduction   1
1   Feminism and leisure studies: opening up new directions
    ROSEMARY DEEM   5
2   Historical sources for studying work and leisure in women's lives
    LIZ STANLEY   18

PART 2: FACING CHANGES: Introduction   33
3   Leisure and male partners
    EILEEN GREEN AND SANDRA HEBRON   37
4   From 'playing out' to 'dossing out': young women and leisure
    VIVIENNE GRIFFITHS   48
5   Mothers meeting
    ERICA WIMBUSH   60
6   'No peace for the wicked': older married women and leisure
    JENNIFER MASON   75

PART 3: EXPLORING THE MYTHS: Introduction   87
7   'Eyes down': a study of bingo
    RACHAEL DIXEY   91
8   Beating them at our own game? Women's sports involvement
    MARGARET TALBOT   102
9   Stepping out: the importance of dancing for young women
    VIVIENNE GRIFFITHS   115

PART 4: THE POWER GAME? Introduction   127
10 'Not tonight, dear!' The social control of women's leisure
    DIANA WOODWARD AND EILEEN GREEN   131
11 Women in leisure service management
    JUDY WHITE   147

12 'Their own worst enemy'? Women and leisure provision
MARGARET TALBOT   161

Conclusions   177
Author index   185
Subject index   189

List of contributors

Rosemary Deem is a Senior Lecturer in the School of Education at the Open University. She has been working in the field of gender and leisure for several years and published *All Work and No Play: The Sociology of Women's Leisure* in 1986.

Rachael Dixey lectures at Trinity and All Saints College, an institution of higher education affiliated to Leeds University. She teaches health studies and social policy and is also involved in health education, guidance and counselling. Prior to carrying out research into women's leisure, she worked in Botswana and Papua New Guinea in the field of educational planning and provision. She is interested in walking, canoeing and ornithology.

Eileen Green teaches Sociology and Women's Studies at Sheffield City Polytechnic and is Director of the Women's Research and Resources Centre there. She has completed research on Working Mothers (with Janet Parry) and Gender and Leisure (with Sandra Hebron and Diana Woodward) and is currently co-directing research on Human Centred Office Systems involving a case study of women workers.

Vivienne Griffiths is a Lecturer in Education at the University of Sussex and has a particular interest in gender and education. Formerly a teacher, she has also worked in drama-in-education groups and is interested in using drama to explore gender issues. Her current research is on adolescent girls and their friends.

Sandra Hebron is now Media Officer at Cornerhouse, Greater Manchester's Arts Centre. Previously she worked as a Research Associate at Sheffield City Polytechnic where she also taught Women's Studies. She is currently researching and writing on the politics of representation and is active in the independent film and video sector.

Jennifer Mason is a Research Officer at Lancaster University working on an ESRC funded project investigating family obligations and kin support. She has conducted research on long term marriage and lifestyles in later life and published several articles on this topic.

Liz Stanley is working class by birth, a lesbian by luck and a northerner and a feminist by choice. Originally from Portsmouth, she now lives in Manchester and teaches in the Sociology Department at Manchester University. Her main writing interests concern feminist theory and research methods, men's sexual violence towards women, and, more recently, writing a feminist autobiography.

Margaret Talbot is the first woman to be appointed Head of the Carnegie Department, Leeds Polytechnic, one of the former men's physical education colleges. She has published widely in the area of women, leisure and sport, but perhaps most notable is her State of the Art Review on 'Women and Leisure' for the Sports Council/SSRC. She is a founder member of the Women's Sports Foundation.

Erica Wimbush is a Research Director at the Centre for Leisure Research in Moray House College in Edinburgh. As such, she contributes to a wide-ranging programme of externally-funded research on leisure, recreation, sport and tourism, with particular responsibility for developing the social and educational aspects of CLR's work. Principal researcher on the 'Women, Leisure and Wellbeing' project written about in this book.

Diana Woodward joined Sheffield City Polytechnic as a lecturer in Industrial Sociology, and has been there ever since, latterly teaching and researching gender, the sociology of heatlh and illness, and research methods. With Eileen Green and Sandra Hebron she worked on an ESRC/Sports Council funded study of gender and leisure, located in Sheffield, on which her paper is based. In 1987 she became Dean of the Faculty of Education, Health and Welfare with polytechnic-wide responsibility for Equal Opportunities.

Judy White has been a lecturer in the Department of Local Government and Development at the University of Birmingham for the past 15 years, she is currently concerned with issues of women managers and organizational change with a particular emphasis on leisure services. She is undertaking a major research project for the Local Government Training Board investigating the position of women in local government and their training needs.

Acknowledgements

We would like to thank all those individuals who have contributed to this book in their different ways. In particular, the nine other authors who have helped to pull this volume into shape by contributing not only their research work about other women's lives, but also their personal experiences and thoughts on the subject. Within our respective homes and institutions, the support and back-up of our partners and colleagues has played a vital part in facilitating our ability to carve out the time and space in which to write and think. In particular, we would like to thank our colleagues at the Centre for Leisure Research, Trinity and All Saints' College and the Carnegie Department, Leeds Polytechnic. We are especially indebted to the library staff at these three institutions for meeting our many and varied requests for references and information.

Erica Wimbush would also like to record her thanks to the Health Promotion Research Trust who have provided the financial support necessary to undertake this book as part of their broader commitment to supporting work on the dissemination of the 'Women, Leisure and Well-being' research project which they sponsored. HPRT have also contributed through their financial backing for the Weekend Workshop held in Edinburgh in April 1985 where the idea for this book first emanated.

Erica Wimbush and Margaret Talbot

Introduction

This book is an attempt to draw together some of the rich and varied material about women's and girls' experience of leisure as interpreted by female researchers working in different parts of Britain. The main impetus behind compiling this collection emanated from a weekend workshop held in Edinburgh in April 1985 for researchers working in and around the subject of women's leisure. Meeting to discuss our various approaches, problems and findings served to generate a supportive network among many of the women who took part; putting together this book has been a continuation of this collaborative process. The contributors to this volume have all tried to be open about their research, acknowledging the flaws and the fact that we are still only at an early stage in a long quest to find ways of analysing leisure that embrace the diversity of women's experiences.

While editing this book, we have been continually impressed by the enjoyment and excitement which many authors have conveyed in their work with women and in sharing their observations about women's friendships, passions and pastimes. For many of us, listening to the stories and experiences of other women has been part of a process of learning about our own lives as women. The positive and vibrant portrayals of women's leisure which stem from this enthusiasm are, we hope, a distinctive feature of these writings.

The contributions to this book are all written by women who broadly subscribe to a feminist perspective. As Rosemary Deem states in the first chapter, a distinctive feature of this approach is that the study of leisure is set within the context of 'women's oppression and gender relations and the concern to bring about positive changes in the social position of women'. But just as women constitute a diverse social group, so there are variations in the approaches adopted and strategies advocated within feminism. For Rosemary Deem, for example, feminist consciousness is shared by those who have 'explored the structures and ideological forces shaping women's oppression . . . and seek to find ways in which that subordination and oppression may be overcome'. Liz Stanley also identifies a political dimension to contemporary feminism, but her notion of feminism includes all women, being based on the idea of 'empowerment' – enabling women to find a voice so that we can 'speak with our own voices and be listened to by other women'.

In furthering the interests of women and feminist perspectives on society, sport and leisure have been considered to be largely irrelevant or peripheral since they only affect a minority of women. It is our view that not only do certain forms of sport and leisure hold enormous significance for female participants, but more generally women's right to regular time off or time free from paid and unpaid work is of fundamental importance for their general health and well-being. Yet it is an aspect of sexual inequality which has received relatively little attention from feminists or leisure scholars.

Furthermore, as a social institution sport and leisure has a social and political significance that extends far beyond the lives and interests of individual women. Mainstream sport and leisure activities affirm hegemonic values and represent the preferences and participation patterns of the dominant (white, male, middle class) groups; theoretical approaches within leisure studies have also tended to reflect these interests. In this book we have tried to counter the prevailing images of women in leisure studies as invisible, shadowy figures in the survey statistics on recreational participation, often shunted into the margins of cultural life as spectators and supporters of their families' leisure, doing nothing much at home or portrayed as passive objects at the mercy of the exploitative market-place of leisure-commodity production.

Looking beyond the male-stream of sport and leisure and beneath the surface imagery of 'fair play' and 'rational recreation', we see that leisure is not a social arena portraying a unified culture. It also provides an arena for the expression of different values and behaviours, particularly those of subordinate groups. In this sense we have wanted to highlight the many positive ways in which women have appropriated space and time for themselves, within and outside the mainstream of cultural life, and the meanings attributed to women's leisure that are constructed within, and in response to, patriarchal relations.

In countering fatalistic views of women's leisure as inevitably trapped within a web of constraints, we are not suggesting that women are by any means free agents, thereby conforming to the (mis)conception of leisure as an area of autonomous choice where time is unfettered by the obligations of the workplace. Historically, leisure did not develop in the same way for both sexes under industrial capitalism. Women's time differs from men's, being shaped by the sexual inequalities that structure participation in employment, domestic and caring work, the distribution of resources and participation in public social life. Women's lives do not therefore fit neatly into an historical framework that ignores the way patriarchal relations have divided women's and men's lives and consciousness. Women's leisure, particularly that of mothers and wives, tends not to be sharply differentiated from work, but is closely intertwined with kinship relations, the rhythms of domestic and waged labour and the localized contexts of the home, street and neighbourhood. Consequently, women's personal time and their family time have become systematically conflated by many social commentators.

Moreover, women's time and choices are closely circumscribed, primarily by their gender, but also by their age, ethnic origin and class; these in turn shape their employment status, income levels and household circumstances. The autonomy which women have to enjoy personal leisure is relative to these overarching structures. Leisure is thus one of women's 'relative freedoms.'

Throughout history, women have struggled to carve out times and spaces for themselves, having to overcome such obstacles as busy and often multiple-layered timetables, uncooperative partners, disapproving relatives, limited personal money and mobility and the fear of being harassed or attacked by men in public places. It has also been suggested that the time demanded by regular participation in recreational or sports programmes may be experienced by many women as more restricting than liberating (Lenskyj 1988). But for those women who have managed to secure a 'room of their own' or time for themselves, having manoeuvred around these barriers, the end goal may be that much more prized. For some women household and caring roles provide a sense of autonomy compared to the more alienating alternatives available on the labour market (Oakley 1974). Other women gain a sense of autonomy and individual worth through their paid jobs and by pursuing careers. Less often do we hear about the everyday endeavours of women who struggle to carve out spaces for themselves through their involvement in the many spheres of recreational and cultural life – through writing, sports, politics, voluntary work, adult education, dance, performing and so on.

In researching leisure in women's lives, it has become clear that one response from women to their subordination within patriarchal relations is to value highly those rare moments, those hard won spaces, where they can experience and enjoy a greater sense of autonomy and control. Examples of these are described in some of the following chapters.

The relationship of leisure to other spheres of life is complex, but the complexity is all the more apparent when examining women's lives. The first part of the book comprises two chapters which, in their different ways, address this issue and how feminists have approached it, both theoretically and methodologically. In Chapter 1 Rosemary Deem maps out the contribution which feminists have made to leisure studies. She emphasizes the insights gained from other areas of social science which do not specifically deal with leisure. Research which has focused on gender inequalities in areas like cultural studies, the sociology of work, education, health studies, community studies and historical research all help to enrich our understanding of leisure as integral to wider social institutions, rather than as a separate entity.

Related to this is the emphasis feminists put on the need to examine leisure within a broader social context, as part of life-styles as a whole rather than as a separate dimension – or to view it 'in the round' as Liz Stanley describes it. In Chapter 2 she explains the importance of 'putting context back in' to leisure studies:

> context consists of the interweaving of many strands within which 'work' and 'leisure', among other things, are located as part of the whole. That is work and leisure make sense only in relation to each other and to other parts of the whole. Leisure certainly does not make sense on its own; it has to be understood as part of a conjunction of interests, needs, skills, commitments and obligations in women's lives, most importantly including those of work.

By adopting an holistic perspective, feminism has helped to widen the conceptualization of leisure to include unpaid work as well as paid employment. This has contributed to our understanding of how the interrelationships between paid work, unpaid work and leisure change over the course of an individual's lifetime as well as across historical time. Liz Stanley stresses the importance of an historical comparative approach using a range of autobiographical data sources, in order to understand the influence of social change on individuals' lives and the shifting interaction between work and leisure.

The continuities and changes in women's experiences of leisure through different periods in the life-course are examined in Part 2 of the book. The four chapters are based on recent empirical studies and show clearly how the complex changes which women face in their work, leisure and social networks during significant transitional periods are socially constructed and maintained in order to 'simplify men's lives'.

Exploring women's leisure activities offers a window into the cultural management of gender, an aspect of women's oppression which is often obscured in other areas of economic and social life. As the chapters in Part 3 reveal, bingo clubs, sports pitches, community centres, discos and street corners are all social spaces in which gender relations are played out, where notions of sexuality, courtship, male power, female dependency and autonomy are expressed, legitimated or challenged. These three chapters look at the sense of fulfilment and satisfaction that women derive from their participation in bingo, sport and dance. At the same time the authors explore the 'myths' surrounding leisure activities which occur in primarily female contexts, thus undermining their value to participants and perpetuating gendered ideologies about femininity and appropriate female behaviour.

The primacy of gender relations in structuring inequalities in the experience of personal leisure for women and men is a central theme throughout this book. Patriarchal relations, like class relations, are culturally reproduced, even magnified, within leisure and recreation. They are legitimated and sustained by a complexity of ideological and material forces which help to shape our social institutions – the family unit, the media, the education system, the legal system and so on. The policies, provisions and professional practice promulgated by the institutions of leisure and sport are an integral part of this framework. The chapters in Part 4 address questions about the ways in which patriarchal power relations are translated in terms of gendered divisions in leisure – within families, public social spaces, different forms of sport and leisure provision and leisure management practice. These chapters illustrate the myriad of ways in which women's autonomy and ability to exercise real choice in leisure are circumscribed. The authors also give examples of ways women have found to manoeuvre around some of these barriers, sometimes challenging the status quo in the process and helping to reshape the cultural framework to suit better female interests, needs and values.

We are acutely aware that the collection of articles presented in this book represents only a sample of the possible range of literature on women's leisure. For this reason it is perhaps worth indicating some of the main gaps in what we have managed to include here.

All our contributors have been aware of the deficiencies in portraying a range of cultures, both in existing research and in our own studies, and have tried to compensate for the gap. For example, Vivienne Griffiths considers the cross-cultural dimension in exploring the significance of dancing for women and girls in Chapter 9, while Eileen Green and Diana Woodward examine the significance of ethnicity and racism in mediating the way in which women's access to leisure is constructed, defined and regulated (Chapter 10). Racial divisions in women's social and leisure outlets, the meanings attributed to these and constraints on participation have been examined here mainly through referral to the growing literature on black women's lives in Britain (e.g. Wilson 1978; Bryan, Dadzie and Scafe 1985).

Little is known about the extent to which gender inequalities in leisure are heightened or modified by ethnicity. There has been some research undertaken in the United States about black women athletes (e.g. Green *et al*. 1981; Bentley 1983; Prakasa Rao and Overman 1984, 1986) and a recent review of sports participation among Muslim women in Islamic countries (Sfeir 1985). Studies of sport and leisure among ethnic minority groups in Britain which examine gender relations are very limited. What research has been done has been carried out largely by white, male, middle-class researchers (Taylor and Hegarty 1985; Carrington, Chivers and Williams 1987). As such these studies display some of the problems of ethno- and andro-centricity in understanding the lives of ethnic minority women. They highlight a problem for all researchers, although it is one familiar to anthropologists: to what extent can we expect to 'get inside' the cultures of other social groups and interpret these in ways that make sense to them? The present dearth of research and literature which explores the richness of variations in the cultural forms and leisure pursuits among women from the range of ethnic groups living in Britain suggests that this should be a high priority for future research.

As Liz Stanley notes (Chapter 2), the patterns of change and continuity in the cultural handling of gender are accessible to us mainly through historical records of women's lives. Thanks to the commercial growth of women's publishing, we now have books appearing such as the reprinted work of Margaret Llewelyn Davies ([1904], 1977) on the Women's Co-operative Guild. There is little historical documentation specific to women's leisure. For the most part, published work on the history of leisure is a history of male leisure and is focused on the public worlds of institutionalized sport, recreation and popular amusements. In one of the most recent historical analyses of leisure in capitalist Britain, John Clarke and Chas Critcher (1985) were forced to accept these gaps in the historical records relevant to leisure and fell back on those sources written by men and about their concerns, where half the population form 'a missing dimension'. Perhaps leisure historians should take a leaf from Kathy Peiss's book (1986), which delves deep into an impressive range of public and voluntary association records, personal letters, archive material and literature to reveal a penetrating insight into working women's leisure in turn-of-the-century New York.

Competitive sport and physical education are areas where historical records on women's involvement have been more accessible. Sheila Fletcher (1984) has made a start in filling this gap with her account of the history of training for women teachers of physical education. There is already a large body of literature available on women in sport (see Shoebridge 1987) and it has not been possible to do justice to the full range of it here. Much of the literature in this area refers to the ways in which sport tends to polarize the sexes, with sport epitomizing masculine values

(Talbot 1979). Qualities associated with sport – competitiveness, aggression, instrumentality – are all qualities associated with contemporary notions of what is 'masculine' (Sabo and Runfola 1980; Theberge 1981), while opposite qualities are attributed to 'femininity'. Jennifer Hargreaves (1985) points out that this ideologically based polarization of the sexes leads to the 'logical' conclusion that men are 'naturally' better suited to sport. This belief persists despite the growing body of evidence to contradict the universal perception of female inferiority in sport (Dyer 1982).

The prevailing view of sport as a male endeavour is fostered and maintained not only through gendered ideologies but also through the power of our cultural institutions – through the media, sports promoters, the governing bodies of sport, government agencies and importantly through our education system. Sex segregation within the school subject of PE remains an anomaly within a curriculum which ostensibly promotes equal opportunities. Girls' and boys' segregated experience of PE at school plays an important part in the reproduction of sexual inequalities and the reaffirmation of stereotyped notions of masculinity and femininity during childhood and adolescence (Scraton 1986; Leaman 1984). However, the myriad of other cultural influences on the development of girls' and boys' patterns of play and recreation outside school have been the subject of less scrutiny.

For those women who do take part in sport, the enjoyment and sense of achievement derived are inevitably mediated by their contradictory position within an institution representing a heavily masculine image and ethos (Talbot 1984). Sheila Scraton (1985) has alerted us to the 'treble bind' which female PE teachers find themselves caught within if trying to motivate girls' interest in sport. How sportswomen cope with and attempt to resolve the anomalies of their position are discussed in this book by Margaret Talbot (see Chs. 8 and 12) and elsewhere by others (e.g. Graydon 1983).

Health studies is another area not represented within this collection but which has helped to illuminate women's involvement in physical recreation and access to 'free' time. For example, the reprinted work of Margery Spring-Rice ([1939] 1981) on the health records of working-class wives highlights the historical changes in women's scope for leisure as the extent of child-bearing years has diminished and the demands of domestic labour become less physically rigorous. On the other hand, for working-class wives the experience of physical exercise as primarily that of climbing stairs and fetching and carrying children and food has not changed so dramatically.

Despite the realities of women's working lives, since the mid-nineteenth century concerns about the health and fitness of the nation's workers have prompted the promotion of participation in physical activity and sport. However, as Linda Borish (1987) points out, the physical activities suggested for women and men are gender-specific. The problem of changing women's health behaviour and attitudes to physical exercise still tends to be seen as a matter remedied by more and better information. At best these health education strategies are politically and sociologically naïve since they ignore the socio-economic conditions and ideological forces which shape attitudes and constrain behaviour (Burrage 1985). They are also 'victim blaming' in that they define the problem as a matter of individual rather than collective responsibility. The tendency to regard women as 'their own worst enemy' is an attitude also prevalent among sports providers, as Margaret Talbot discusses in Chapter 12.

Holidays and day outings are the forms of leisure which working women have perhaps found the most attractive ever since the Victorian days of railway excursions to the seaside from the industrialized inland towns. Holidays are still the popular remedy prescribed for working women showing the strain of coping with the overload of managing multiple roles. However, in practice, for many people holidays away from home are out of reach. Forty per cent of British adults take no annual holiday (Central Statistical Office, 1987), leaving day trips, weekend outings and 'armchair travelling' as the main forms of break away from the routines and demands of home.

For women, holidays and outings away from home are only a relative freedom from the workaday surroundings and routines of daily life since much of women's work is compounded by the preparation and planning of holidays. For those taking families with them, caring and cleaning roles are continued on holiday, often under less convenient and more stressful conditions. For this reason, Rosemary Deem concludes that 'Holidays are not necessarily leisure for women unless they go alone or with other women, but may be an extension of their normal domestic and childcare responsibilities; nor are they necessarily a rest from tensions and conflicts within households or families.' (Deem 1986: 63).

While acknowledging gender differences in the experience of the family holiday for women and men, it has also been argued that the enjoyment of holidays for both sexes stems from the reversal, or at least modification, of those influences which structure our everyday existence (Clark and Critcher 1985: 71). Divisions of labour rigidly defined in family life may become more blurred on family holidays as men are more available to partners and children and the pressure of work and school timetables are temporarily suspended. For young single women on holiday there may be greater social and sexual freedoms away from home and the policing patterns of parents, although unwanted predatory properties of men may be similarly less constrained. For older women, holidays may combine the duty of taking elderly parents, company which may circumscribe the daughters' mobility and choices while away. There has been very little research undertaken to help illuminate the workings of gender in the holiday context and qualify the ample speculation about the possible heightening, suspension and reversal of everyday tensions, roles and regulations.

Within the field of cultural studies, a strong feminist critique has developed which has generated some rich material on women's leisure, but particularly that of young women and girls (e.g. Griffin 1985; CCCS 1978, 1981; McRobbie 1978, 1980). Some of these feminist studies have also examined how class, race, age and gender interact for different groups of young women (e.g. Amos and Parmar 1981; Sharpe 1976; Jamdagni 1980). The lack of a specific input to this book from the field of feminist cultural studies warrants a brief review of its contribution to the debates concerning women's relationship to commercial leisure and popular culture.

The widespread and continual popularity among women of commercial cultural products like television soap operas, romantic fiction and magazines has attracted a lot of debate among feminists. Mainstream feminist media criticism has condemned these commercial forms of leisure as an expression and instrument of patriarchal ideology. For example, some have argued that the planning and design of commercial leisure products and provision fail to grasp women's actual needs and interests, but cater for stereotyped needs and images of women as portrayed in the media, advertising and elsewhere (e.g. Deem 1986). Women consumers are perceived as trapped within subordinate positions by being presented with stereotyped and role-confirming images. But there is other evidence to suggest that the commercial leisure sector, in having to be sensitive to market demands in order to maximize economic gain, has had to adjust its stereotyped view of the female consumer. For example, the 'streetwise knowledge' promoted by some of the new magazines for young women (e.g. *Etcetera* and *Mizz*) actually draws on a feminist culture in which 'the conventions of gender and sexuality are . . . being actively tampered with' (Winship 1985: 25).

Discontent with the pessimistic views of a unidimensional relationship between women consumers and popular culture, has brought other feminist researchers to develop a dialectical account of the way women relate to these cultural forms. For example, Charlotte Brunsdon (1981) stressed the active role of the female viewer in interpreting the 'open' narrative of television soap opera programmes. Depending on the viewer's approach, these programmes can be read as critical or reinforcing of patriarchal ideology.

However, many such accounts are limited by their reliance on textual analysis alone, abstracted from the social contexts within which meanings are constructed by individuals. Other media researchers have built on the active viewer/reader approach but sought to ground their studies within the social context of the consumers' life-styles. For example, David Morley's (1986) research on television watching was framed within the context of family life. He demonstrated that men and women watch television in very distinct and different ways. In fact, the differences in men's and women's approaches to television watching were so contrary that they were a source of considerable tension when combined: several of the women said their husbands 'are always on at them to shut up'. For this reason, some women manoeuvred around male barriers to their enjoyment of television as a social activity and invited friends around to their houses to watch video tapes of their favourite fictional programmes when their husbands and sons were out of the way. They felt they enjoyed the programmes more in the company of other women who liked the television programmes in the same way.

Janice Radway's (1984) ethnographic research on dedicated romance readers is another example of this type of contextualized study of women's active relationship with popular cultural forms. She showed that the enjoyment women derive from reading these novels is connected to the fact that they address problems and desires seen to be characteristic of their lives. For Radway, romance reading is not necessarily the result of the success of patriarchal ideology, but an expression of the failure of patriarchal marriage to address women's basic emotional needs.

In reviewing feminist re-evaluations of popular fiction, Ien Ang (1987) considered the political consequences which they implicitly or explicitly endorse. She concludes that

The practice of consuming popular fiction may not be directly conducive to political radicalism (but then would that be too high an expectation anyway), it does not contribute to overthrowing the status quo, but as part of female existence within the status quo it helps make women's lives more cheerful, just as, for instance, music, dance or gossip do.

(Ang 1987: 657)

As feminists engaging with leisure studies, we have sought to emphasize in this book the positive roles which leisure can play in women's lives – bringing enjoyment, a sense of autonomy and fulfilment, having a laugh together, relaxation, a bit of peace and quiet – however limited or temporary these may be. As Ang suggests, the aim of feminist cultural politics in this area perhaps lies in changing women's largely private and home-based experience of leisure, thereby countering the social isolation which this exacerbates. Making possible women's enjoyment of leisure time as a more public experience and expanding the public places in which women can enjoy leisure activities and interests collectively would play a vital role in creating friendships between women and strengthening female solidarity and social networks. This is hardly a radical proposition; we take for granted that male bonding and solidarity is reinforced through public, collective forms of leisure – the pub, football, snooker and so on. But then, unlike 'the brotherhood of man', sisterhood is one of the best kept secrets of patriarchy . . .

References

Amos, V. and Parmar, P. (1981) 'Resistances and responses: the experiences of black girls in Britain', in Angela McRobbie and Trisha McCabe (eds.) *Feminism for Girls: An Adventure Story*, London, Routledge & Kegan Paul.

Ang, Ien (1987) 'Popular fiction and feminist cultural politics', *Theory, Culture and Society* 4(4): 651–8.

Bentley, K. (1983) *Going for Gold: The Story of Black Women in Sport*, Los Angeles, Carnation Company.

Borish, Linda (1987) 'The robust woman and the muscular christian', *International Journal of the History of Sport* 14(2): 139–54.

Brunsdon, Charlotte (1981) 'Crossroads: notes on soap opera', *Screen* 22(4).

Bryan, Beverley, Dadzie, Stella and Scafe, Suzanne (1985) *The Heart of the Race: Black Women's Lives in Britain*, London, Virago.

Burrage, Hilary (1985) *Health Education: The Androcentric Agenda*, Department of Sociology, University of Liverpool.

Carrington, Bruce, Chivers, Terry and Williams, Trevor (1987) 'Gender, leisure and sport: a case study of young people of South Asian descent', *Leisure Studies* 6(3): 265–79.

Central Statistical Office (1987) *Social Trends* 18 London, HMSO.

Centre for Contemporary Cultural Studies (1978) *Women Take Issue: Aspects of Women's Subordination*, London, Hutchinson.

—— (1981) 'Women and leisure', in Alan Tomlinson (ed.) *Leisure and Social Control*, Brighton, Brighton Polytechnic.

Clarke, John and Critcher, Chas (1985) *The Devil Makes Work: Leisure in Capitalist Britain*, London, Macmillan.

Deem, Rosemary (1986) *All Work and No Play: The Sociology of Women and Leisure*, Milton Keynes, Open University Press.

Dyer, Ken (1982) *Catching Up the Men: Women in Sport*, London, Junction Books.

Fletcher, Sheila (1984) *Women First: The Female Tradition in English Physical Education, 1880–1980*, London, Athlone Press.

Graydon, Jan (1983) 'But it's more than a game, it's an institution': feminist perspectives on sport', *Feminist Review* 13(spring): 5–16.

Green, T. S. *et al.* (1981) *Black Women in Sport*, Reston, Virginia, AAHPERD.

Griffin, Christine (1985) *Typical Girls?* London, Routledge & Kegan Paul.

Hargreaves, Jennifer (1985) 'Their own worst enemies', *Sport and Leisure*, July/August: 20–8.

Jamdagni Laxmi (1980) 'Hamari rangily zindagi (Our colourful lives)', research report, Leicester, National Association of Youth Clubs.

Leaman, Oliver (1984) *'Sit on the Sidelines and Watch the Boys Play': Sex Differentiation in Physical Education*, York, Longmans for Schools Council.

Lenskyj, Helen (1988) 'Measured time: women, sport and leisure', *Leisure Studies* (forthcoming).

Llewelyn-Davies, Margaret (ed.) [1904] (1977) *Life as We Have Known It — Co-operative Working Women*, London, Virago.

McRobbie, Angela (1978) 'Jackie: an ideology of femininity', CCCS stencilled paper, Birmingham, Birmingham University.

(1980) 'Settling accounts with subcultures: a feminist critique', *Screen Education* 34: 37–49.

Morley, David (1986) *Family Television: Cultural Power and Domestic Leisure*, London, Comedia.

Oakley, Anne (1974) *The Sociology of Housework*, Oxford, Martin Robertson.

Peiss, Kathy (1986) *Cheap Amusements: Working Women and Leisure in Turn-of-the-Century New York*, Philadelphia, Temple University Press.

Prakasa Rao, V. V. and Overman, S.J. (1984) 'Sex role perceptions among black female athletes and non-athletes', *Sex Roles* 11(7/8): 601–14.

(1986) 'Psychological well-being and body image: a comparison of black women athletes', *Journal of Sports Behaviour* 9(2):79–91.

Radway, Janice (1984) *Reading the Romance: Women, Patriarchy and Popular Literature*, London and Chapel Hill, North Carolina University Press.

Sabo, Donald and Runfola, Ross (1980) (eds.) *Jock: Sport and Male Identity*, Englewood Cliffs, NJ, Prentice-Hall.

Scraton, Sheila (1985) 'Boys muscle in where angels fear to tread: the relationship between physical education and young women's subcultures', paper presented at Leisure Studies Association Conference, Ilkley, April 12–14.

(1986) 'Images of femininity and the teaching of girls' physical education', in J. Evans (ed.) *Physical Education, Sport and Schooling*, Brighton, Falmer Press.

Sfeir, Leila (1985) 'The status of Muslim women in sport: conflict between cultural tradition and modernisation', *International Review of the Sociology of Sport* 20(4): 283–306.

Sharpe, Sue (1976) *Just Like a Girl: How Girls Learn to Be Women*, Harmondsworth, Penguin.

Shoebridge, Michele (1987) *Women in Sport: A Select Bibliography*, London and New York: Mansell.

Spring-Rice, Margery [1939] (1981) *Working-Class Wives*, London, Virago.

Talbot, Margaret (1979) *Women and Leisure: A State of the Art Review*, London, SSRC/Sports Council.

(1984) 'Women and sport: a gender contradiction in terms', in Alan Tomlinson (ed.) *Leisure: Politics, Planning and People*, London, Leisure Studies Association.

Taylor, M. J. and Hegarty, S. (1985) *The Best of Both Worlds? A Review of Research into the Education of Children of South Asian Origin*, Windsor, NFER/Nelson.

Theberge, Nancy (1981) 'A critique of critiques: radical and feminist writings on sport', *Social Forces* 60(2): 341–53.

Wilson, Amrit (1978) *Finding a Voice; Asian Women in Britain*, London, Virago.

Winship, Janice (1985) 'A girl needs to get street-wise: magazines for the 1980s', *Feminist Review* 21 (winter): 25–46.

PART 1

Approaching leisure

INTRODUCTION

Within the field of leisure studies it is now well known that for women and men the experience of leisure is of a different order. It is recognized that this 'difference' relates to both participation rates in sports and recreation activities as well as the ability to secure 'free time' or 'time off' from work (paid or unpaid). The way these differences between the sexes are understood theoretically and approached methodologically, however, can vary considerably. Reviews of the various theoretical perspectives on leisure can be found in the recent books by Rosemary Deem (1986), John Clarke and Chas. Critcher (1985) and Chris Rojek (1985).

Although the 'male-stream' of leisure studies has become increasingly aware of the significance of gender, it is more often regarded as one of a series of variables which inform distributional patterns of leisure, rather than as the primary force shaping social relations. It has been predominantly through the work of feminist writers that gender relations in leisure have been examined and their theoretical, social and political consequences exposed. According to Rosemary Deem's review of feminists' contributions to the study of sport and leisure (Ch. 1), what is distinctive about this approach is the setting of leisure 'firmly within the context of women's oppression and gender relations' combined with 'a concern to bring about positive change in the social position of women'. In this part we are concerned to look at the contributions made by feminists' approach to the study of leisure and the implications for methodology.

What does leisure mean for those who are not in full-time paid employment? Are conventional definitions of leisure valid, or even useful, in understanding women's experiences? Feminists' questioning of mainstream approaches to studying leisure has at least put the interaction between employment, unpaid work and leisure firmly on the agenda, even though methods of analysing their interrelationship are only slowly progressing. For example, crude time-budget diary methods are still used to measure the division and use of time even though we know that women's use of time is often multiple, with several activities being undertaken at the same time, making the usefulness of such techniques very limited. One of the major contributions of feminists' approach to leisure has been to apply more imaginative methods in order to find more appropriate and sensitive tools to explore the complexity of women's lives. These can also provide a more illuminating way to approach the study of people's leisure generally, but especially in the lives of those for whom employment does not provide the central pivot around which time and activities are structured.

Following the approach of anthropology and community studies, some feminists have argued that it is more revealing and fruitful to examine 'what women actually do' in a more grounded fashion, giving special attention to how they order and conceptualize time and activities. The emphasis on the need to examine leisure within the context of life-styles as a whole has meant that feminists' contributions to methodology have been largely in the area of qualitative research. For example, in Chapter 2 Liz Stanley's theoretical approach is to study women's lives 'in the round'. This informs her preference for using diaries and other autobiographical material (e.g. oral history, Mass-Observation Archive data) to understand the work–leisure dynamic in women's lives and examine how this differs between individual women as well as over time. This methodology also opens up a Pandora's box of possibilities to redress the relative invisibility of women in the history of sport and leisure. For those thinking of embarking on historical research about women's leisure, Liz Stanley's guide to historical sources will prove invaluable as well as inspirational.

The studies presented by Vivenne Griffiths (Chs. 4 and 9) and Jennifer Mason (Ch. 6) provide further examples of methodologies based on studying women's lives 'in the round', within the context of life-styles and communities. As an educationalist working for a year in a mixed-sex comprehensive school in West Yorkshire, Vivenne Griffiths followed a group of sixteen working-class girls through their second to third year of secondary schooling (Griffiths 1987). In doing this she adopted an anthropological approach whereby she managed to compile a detailed ethnography of the young women's lives and friendships within and outside school. Jennifer Mason, on the other hand, applied more formalized qualitative techniques in order to explore an agenda of issues related to the notion of 'structural disruption' (Mason 1987). She used a series of semi-structured interviews with eighteen long-married couples aged between 50 and 70 years, allowing discussion with the couple together as well as individual interviews. The discrepancies found by other feminist researchers (e.g. Pahl 1980) between the accounts of husbands and wives interviewed seperately and together not only says something about power and gender relations, but also it points to the need to follow theoretical understandings through into methodological practice.

Even though neither Griffiths nor Mason set out to examine the notion of leisure *per se*, their approaches have provided valuable insights concerning the role and meaning of leisure at different periods in people's lives. Erica Wimbush (Ch.5), on the other hand, did set out with 'leisure' on the research agenda, but she approached it by exploring the more generic notion of well-being, using in-depth interviews with seventy mothers of young children (Wimbush 1986). In adopting this approach, she was able to explore not only the possible link between leisure opportunities and mothers' general health but also the significance for women's well-being of the many blurred grey areas where work and leisure are interwoven. Exploring the boundaries between paid work, unpaid work and leisure, how the equation varies between different groups of women (and men) and at different times in people's lives, is another area where feminists have contributed to the study of leisure.

Although qualitative methods are often favoured by feminists on account of their greater flexibility and sensitivity, they are not always the ones adopted or necessarily the most appropriate. It can be argued, for example, that the adoption of alternative holistic approaches to studying leisure only serves to legitimate the view that women's and men's leisure is simply different, thereby perpetuating the status quo. Applying conventional categories of leisure and recreation to women's lives can also be valuable in exposing gender inequalities: in access to personal free time separate from work obligations; in access to public social spaces and in opportunities for recreational participation.

Quantitative survey techniques were used in both the study of bingo (Dixey and Talbot 1982; see also Ch.7) to provide a national profile of bingo players and in the Sheffield study of leisure and gender (Green, Hebron and Woodward 1987; see also Chs.3 and 10). These surveys have provided valuable quantitative data on women's leisure in contemporary Britain. They have allowed generalizable statements to be made about the influence of structural factors upon the quantity and quality of leisure time and activities which different ages, races and classes of women experience; the variations between women employed, those unemployed and those working at home; between childless women and those with dependent children; and between single women and women living with male partners. In furnishing these facts the surveys have of course revealed more clearly the different nature and level of constraints acting on women's leisure compared to men's.

What is distinctive about the use of survey methods in these studies is the fact that the empirical data generated do not stand alone but have been contextualized by their combination with smaller scale qualitative studies of leisure in women's lives. For example, information from Dixey and Talbot's national survey of bingo players was supported by a community study of a working-class area in Leeds in order to get a better understanding of the significance of bingo in the lives of the players.

Without the support of qualitative research (in whatever form) to provide an understanding of the contexts in which meanings are constructed, purely quantitative approaches can have major shortcomings. For example, in a recent study of the meaning of leisure where purely quantitative techniques were applied (Stockdale 1986), the findings were meaningless, having been so abstracted from lives of the individuals who had constructed them! There is also a danger that stand-alone recreation surveys are prone to measure implicitly the lives and popular leisure pursuits of subordinate groups against hegemonic norms, standards and values. For example, the conventional categories of sport and leisure activities used in the General Household Survey omit leisure pursuits which many women regard as relaxing, pleasurable or fun (e.g. having a bath, chatting with friends, reading fiction, coffee mornings), while including others which may well not be considered as leisure by women (e.g. escorting children, driving lessons, church-going).

In acknowledging the contribution of feminists' approaches to the study of leisure, we do not intend to dismiss the value of inputs from other academics and writers. The approaches adopted within cultural studies, for example, have contributed much to the theoretical debates around popular culture and the social control of women's leisure (e.g. CCCS 1981). Their methodologies reflect the concerns of Rosemary Deem and Liz Stanley, to look at life-styles 'in the round' and to place leisure within 'the context of community and region as well as class, race and gender'.

References

Centre for Contemporary Cultural Studies (1981) 'Women and leisure', in Alan Tomlinson (ed.) *Leisure and Social Control*, Brighton, Brighton Polytechnic.

Clarke, John and Critcher, Chas (1985) *The Devil Makes Work: Leisure in Capitalist Britain*, London, Macmillan.

Deem, Rosemary (1986) *All Work and No Play: The Sociology of Women and Leisure*, Milton Keynes, Open University Press.

Dixey, Rachael and Talbot, Margaret (1982) *Women, Leisure and Bingo*, Leeds, Trinity and All Saints' College.

Green, Eileen, Hebron, Sandra and Woodward, Diana (1987) *Leisure and Gender: A Study of Sheffield Women's Leisure Experiences*, Final Report to ESRC/Sports Council Joint Panel on Leisure Research, London, Sports Council.

Griffiths, Vivienne (1987) 'Adolescent Girls: transition from girlfriends to boyfriends', in Pat Allat, Teresa Keil, Alan Bryman and Bill Bytheway (eds.) *Women and the Life-Cycle: Transitions and Turning Points*, London, Macmillan.

Mason, Jennifer (1987) 'A bed of roses? women, marriage and inequality in later life', in Pat Allat, Teresa Keil, Alan Bryman and Bill Bytheway (eds.) *Women and the Life-Cycle: Transitions and Turning Points*, London, Macmillan.

Pahl, Jan (1980) 'Patterns of money management within marriage', *Journal of Social Policy* 9(3): 313–35.

Rojek, Chris (1985) *Capitalism and Leisure Theory*, London, Tavistock.

Stockdale, Janet (1986) *What Is Leisure?*, London, Sports Council/ESRC.

Wimbush, Erica (1986) *Women, Leisure and Well-being* Edinburgh, Centre for Leisure Research.

1

Feminism and leisure studies: opening up new directions

ROSEMARY DEEM

What I want to explore in this paper is the contribution which feminists have made and continue to make to the study of leisure. It is necessary to make clear that when I say 'feminist contributions' I mean those which have explored the structures and ideological forces shaping women's oppression, taking into account women's life-styles in general and their experiences of leisure in particular. Women's subordination to men in society is seen by feminists as problematic and they seek to find ways in which that oppression and subordination may be overcome. Thus those studies and writers who have analysed women's leisure but do not share this perspective are not the main focus of my argument.

Contribution of feminism to leisure studies

Much conventional sociology of leisure has taken as its starting-point the boundaries between paid employment and leisure. Almost all the work on the history of leisure has concerned itself with how men have spent their leisure time and what connections there have been between that and their main form of work or employment. A great deal of time has been devoted to studying how the male working class has wrested leisure time away from work time over the course of industrialization, through things like the Ten Hour Act and paid holidays (Thompson 1967; Burns 1973). Although a few writers (e.g. Parker 1983) have pointed out that in some circumstances paid work and leisure are so blended together that they are difficult to disentangle (vicars or residential social workers, for instance), this has been regarded as the exception rather than the norm.

The sociology of leisure and the sociology of work have at times been very closely linked; they have had in common the sharp focus on paid employment versus leisure. Recently both these fields have been forced to explore other kinds of work than paid full-time employment. One important example of this refocus is to be found in Ray Pahl's (1985) study of the informal economy on the Isle of Sheppey. He and Claire Wallace looked at the extent to which unemployment and disengagement from the formal economy tend to increase involvement in the household economy and communal economies where goods and services are produced for barter, informal cash transactions or simply for household use.

Housework has also had its status raised to that of work proper (Malos 1980; Maynard 1985), although the reluctance of most male leisure researchers to follow through the implications of this reorientation for men and households in general is quite remarkable.

Looking at forms of work outside the formal economy has consequences well beyond that of providing new areas for research. Feminist analyses of housework, home working and other forms of unpaid work, like care of children and adult dependants, have shown that the notion of time being set aside only for leisure is very difficult to achieve for those outside full-time paid employment. The problems are enhanced for those with domestic responsibilities because such work is not highly structured, is often contingent on the actions of others and cannot simply be stopped or forgotten about at the end of the day (Deem 1986; Graham 1984). Leisure, for many women, is of a quite different order from that experienced by most men. It is feminist writings which have so sharply exposed this contrast and its theoretical, social and political consequences.

In tracing some of the contributions which feminists and feminism have made to the study of leisure, I want to make clear that feminists have not worked in a vacuum. Just as feminism has had some, though regrettably so far small, impact on mainstream leisure studies, so more general developments in social science have where appropriate been taken on board by feminism, as in the need to consider class and age alongside gender. Hence not all the territory marked out here should or can be seen as the exclusive terrain of feminists. It is clear, for example, that the field of cultural studies has been one which has contributed quite significantly to the development of approaches to sport and leisure which take gender seriously (Hall and Jefferson 1975; CCCS 1977; Clarke, Critcher and Johnson 1979). Similarly, for instance not only feminists have found it worthwhile to study the life-cycle and life-course (Rapoport and Rapoport 1975).

But at the same time, feminist approaches to sport and leisure have not just confined themselves to studying women's leisure or even incorporating gender into their analyses of leisure experiences. What is distinctive about the feminist contribution is the endeavour to set the study of leisure firmly in the context of women's oppression and gender relations and the concern to bring about a positive change in the social position of women. So feminism has not just looked at what women's lives are like but has also examined the connections between those life-styles and femininity. There is almost no counterpart to this in the study of male lives and leisure. Thus, despite the massive attention paid by leisure studies to male leisure and sport, little of that research looks at how masculinity and the role of men in gender power relations has shaped and influenced that form of leisure. There is, for instance, only one study of football hooliganism which claims to do this (Dunning and Murphy 1982).

Feminists have also made significant contributions to social science methodology. This has been mostly, although not exclusively, in the field of qualitative research (see Bowles and Duelli Klein 1983). Some of this headway has been made by studies of women's leisure. Few feminists would identify with the exclusive use of quantitative methods and data as a means to explore leisure. Hence considerable emphasis has been laid on the need to study leisure qualitatively as part of life-styles as a whole rather than as separate aspects of an individual's life (Stanley

1980; Griffin 1985; Wimbush 1986; Deem 1986).

Other contributions have been both empirical and theoretical. In the next chapter Liz Stanley looks at the use of historical sources in understanding the work–leisure relationship in women's lives. There is as yet little work published in this area, although Sheila Fletcher (1984) provides an excellent account of the development of the female tradition in physical education. But the discovery of women's history by feminist historians has been an important catalyst to historical studies in general (Lewis 1984; Liddington and Norris 1978; Vicinus 1985; Llewelyn Davies 1904; Rowbotham 1977) and a useful source of data for those interested in how women's lives and leisure have developed.

Feminists have questioned conventional notions of leisure which are constructed around a separation of paid work from leisure (Green, Hebron and Woodward 1985, 1987a; McIntosh *et al.* 1981). The impact of others, especially men and children, on women's leisure has been closely studied (Wimbush 1986; Deem 1986; Green, Hebron and Woodward 1987a), and there has been some exploration of the impact of sexuality on sport and leisure participation by women (Scraton 1986, 1987). Feminists have begun to analyse how male social control over women has constrained the where, when and how of women's leisure (see Ch. 11, and Green, Hebron and Woodward 1987b). In the process of doing all this feminists have also shown how important it is that women should be involved in sport and leisure because of the potentially liberating effects such involvement can bring (Scraton 1987; Graydon 1983; Talbot 1981, 1984). Later in this volume Margaret Talbot presents a full discussion on women's involvement in sport.

The development of feminist studies of leisure

During the 1970s most mainstream leisure studies texts considered women either not at all or only in so far as they took into account institutions like the family (Dumazedier 1974; Cheek and Burch 1976; Roberts 1978; Kaplan 1975). For example, one textbook (Smith, Parker and Smith 1973) made significant mention of women in only two of its twenty-two chapters, one on the family and one on adult education. It constantly refers to 'man', 'he' and 'his' in connection with leisure, and the only mention of women in the Introduction is the intriguing sentence that 'the housewife can escape from the triviality of being a domestic servant by taking an Open University degree' (p. 5). Knowing the problems that married women OU students often have in leaving their domestic responsibilities and persuading their husbands to allow them to attend tutorials and summer schools, I wonder what the authors actually meant by that statement!

At the behest of the SSRC/Sports Council Joint Panel on Sport and Leisure research, in 1979 Margaret Talbot produced a report setting out the 'state of the art' in the study of women's leisure. This review uncovered a considerable amount of relevant studies and findings, linked them together in a logical way and posed a number of important questions for future research. So the necessity to look carefully at women's leisure and to take seriously the analysis of gender relations was beginning to appear on the leisure studies agenda by the beginning of the 1980s.

In 1980 itself, another important contribution was made at a joint British

Sociological Association and Leisure Studies Association seminar on Leisure and Social Control by a group of researchers from the Birmingham-based Centre for Contemporary Cultural Studies. They developed a critique of male-centred leisure studies and pointed to important researches of their own about girls, young women, and housewives (McIntosh *et.al.* 1981). Another major input was made by Liz Stanley (1980) who stressed the necessity to explore the meaning of leisure, the fact that women were not just deviant men and that women are a heterogeneous group with many different interests. Rachael Dixey and Margaret Talbot's (1982) researches on bingo revealed the game to be a leisure activity dominated by women and valued by them not just for its own sake but because it provided somewhere out of the home where unaccompanied women could go without being harassed or policed by men.

In 1982 the SSRC/Sports Council Joint Panel finally launched a research initiative on women and leisure, although the panel which interviewed the shortlisted applicants was all-male! The funding was awarded to two Sheffield Polytechnic researchers, Eileen Green and Diana Woodward, who subsequently were joined by Sandra Hebron. Their project ran from 1983 to 1986 and uncovered a wealth of data about women and leisure in Sheffield, material which also has a much wider applicability (Green, Hebron and Woodward 1985; 1987a). Two other projects funded by the Joint Panel have also looked at women's leisure – the Leisure in the Home study headed by Sue Glyptis at Loughborough University (Glyptis, McInnes and Patmore, 1987) and the study of shift work at Liverpool University (see Chambers 1986) – although neither project has taken a feminist approach as its main standpoint. Contributions have also been made by non-ESRC funded research. For example, in Edinburgh Erica Wimbush has done important work linking the study of health and well-being to considerations about women and leisure in a study of young mothers (Wimbush 1986).

The 1980s have also seen important developments in the field of women and sport (see Green *et al.* 1985; Graydon 1983; Talbot 1984; Ferris 1981; Brackenridge 1987). Amongst the issues which they have explored have been the growing success of women in competitive sport, the continuing barriers to wider female sports participation, the problems faced by women in sports leadership, the ways in which men have tried to exclude women from certain sports as well as the benefits of sport to women. On a practical level, Celia Brackenridge and others set up the Women's Sports Foundation in 1984, with the intention of promoting women's sports and ensuring equal opportunities and options for women across all sports, recognizing that the latter requires a shift of power in sport away from vested male interests. So far as more academic analyses of sport by feminists is concerned, M. Ann Hall (1986) has noted an important shift in this field from concern with the distributional aspects of women in sport (where women are and what sports they do) to the relational aspects (how patriarchal relations exclude or limit women's participation in sport). Until the arrival of feminist interventions, the study of sport within leisure studies might have been more appropriately renamed Football Studies. The focus of attention for feminists interested in sport and leisure has not been limited to adult women. Sheila Scraton has drawn our attention to what is happening to girls in school-based physical education (Scraton 1986, 1987) and Chris Griffin to the ways in which female school-leavers organize and perceive their lives and leisure (Griffin 1985).

Non-feminist contributions to gender and leisure

It is of course perfectly possible to study women and leisure without doing so from a feminist perspective. Indeed, mainstream leisure studies has not so much neglected women altogether, as treated them within limited contexts. For example, women are considered as part of family leisure or as housewives who have little in common with paid and by implication male workers; women are viewed as of only slight significance to the analysis of leisure as an aspect of male experience. Another mainstream approach, noted by Liz Stanley (1980), has been to view women as the problem, rather than seeing women's experiences of leisure as something of importance because it directs our attentions to new aspects and dimensions of leisure in ways which the study of men does not.

With the development of feminist analyses of leisure, there are signs that the male-stream of leisure studies has at least noticed that it might be necessary to mention gender occasionally, even if it has not entirely shifted the preoccupation with class, capitalism and paid employment as determinants of leisure. Thus more recent books like Stan Parker (1983) and Ken Roberts (1981, 1982) have tried harder than before to use non-sexist language. At the same time, their inclusion of gender has produced a series of even more pluralistic analyses which treat class, age, race and gender as though they were similar and cumulative factors. This view is particularly problematic because it implies that gender itself, and more importantly gender relations of power between men and women, are not of major importance in determining leisure choices and experiences. Feminists, on the other hand, have argued strongly for the crucial importance of gender and gender relations to leisure, irrespective of other important factors like class or age. To say otherwise is to argue, for example, that men's leisure is as much affected by fears of sexual harassment, assault and violence as is women's leisure, a standpoint which is patently not supported by the evidence.

Not all the analyses which have taken gender on board the lower decks are necessarily pluralist though. Chris Rojek's theoretical treatise on leisure published in 1985 does not exclude women's leisure and even has index categories for sexism, although it does not fully incorporate gender into its analysis. The improvement is not across the board however. Tony Veal (1987) manages to use both sexist language and minimize references to women in his latest book.

But there are gender-aware analyses of leisure beginning to appear from non-feminists. This is particularly true of John Clarke's and Chas Critcher's work (Critcher 1986; Clark and Critcher 1979, 1985) and the study of sex differentiation in physical education by Oliver Leaman (1984). John Clarke and Chas Critcher (1985) make a serious and sustained attempt to incorporate a gender analysis in their recent study of leisure in capitalist Britain. In reviewing radical theories of sport, Chas Critcher (1986) suggests that recovering gender relations is one of three crucial directions in which the sociology of sport has to move. Why I do not refer to such analyses as feminist is because none of these writers fully accept that women are oppressed primarily by gender relations and patriarchy rather than by class relations and a capitalist mode of production. Moreover, none are fully committed to a theoretical and political analysis which will point to ways of overcoming the subordinating effects of gender relations and patriarchy.

New directions for the sociology of leisure

Exploring the boundaries of work and leisure

I have already drawn attention to the ways in which feminism has both widened the concept of leisure beyond the point at which it is only applicable to those in full-time employment and brought in an analysis which looks at the effects of unpaid work on leisure. These are important developments which have also begun to be taken on board by more mainstream analyses (Deem and Salaman 1985).

Paradoxically, however, some feminist analyses have also shown that for those women who are in employment, the kind of compartmentalization practised by many men for their leisure is more likely to be possible (Deem 1986). This is despite women's dual role in the home and in employment. Indeed, studies of women who have been made redundant or otherwise become unemployed say they find it difficult to reorganize their lives so that either unpaid work or leisure are again possible (Coyle 1984; Martin and Wallace 1984).

Ironically, the idea of paid work being crucial to life and leisure is one that some leisure theorists have begun to reject in discussing the possibilities of a leisured society (Jenkins and Sherman 1981). To argue that women may be more able to claim leisure time and rights when they are in paid employment is neither to say that women are not often exploited in employment, nor that they need to become like men if they are to have equal access to leisure. In a differently organized society there might be other kinds of boundaries drawn around paid and unpaid work and leisure and the sexual division of labour might be such that women who work at home are not disadvantaged in leisure terms by that situation. But at present we live in a society where the sexual division of labour, although shifting (Gershuny and Jones 1987), is not disappearing, and where paid work, despite unemployment, is still seen as very important. It gives access to money, friendships, status and legitimate claims to leisure to an extent that unpaid work does not. Furthermore, the number of women spending the majority of their adult lives in paid employment is continuing to rise (Martin and Roberts 1984).

Our knowledge of what happens to women in paid work is much greater than our knowledge about women in unpaid work, because unpaid work is less visible and harder to research, as well as being an area which is less likely to attract research funds. Hence, despite a considerable amount of research into unpaid work already, there is still much more scope for expanding further how unpaid work affects and relates to leisure. For example, the extent to which those who do only unpaid work think themselves less worthy of leisure than those in paid employment, where unpaid work includes not just domestic work and childcare (Wimbush 1986) but also the care of sick, elderly and disabled dependants and a wide range of community and voluntary work. There is also much to be done exploring why and how women and men attach different priorities to paid work, unpaid work and leisure. So for example, Debbie Chambers shows that because of their domestic commitments, women find shift work more attractive than men do (Chambers 1986). They are less concerned about shift work's affects on their leisure because they are already used to unpaid commitments disrupting their leisure.

Leisure and time

Stan Parker has drawn my attention to my understating of the importance of time (Deem 1986). Other feminist researchers have begun to consider the importance of time to leisure, as indeed have some non-feminist time-budget researchers as well as John Clarke and Chas Critcher (1985). The ways in which time is important to leisure have of course already been pointed out to us on numerous occasions by social historians (e.g. Thompson 1967). But such analyses have focused almost exclusively on how the switch from agricultural work to industrial employment affected the male working class. Women's conceptions of time and the ways in which time organizes their days is still very much underresearched. But Graham notes that the peaks of women's personal timetables are usually very different from those of the men they live with, and that the main time periods devoted to leisure by men and children are often those least available to women for leisure (Graham 1984). In my own research I found this particularly true of holidays, which for women, especially if they are on so-called self-catering holidays, can involve more time committed to work than if they were at home. When the male working class fought for holiday time, they did not have in mind their wives' rights to leisure as well as their own.

Many definitions of leisure talk about leisure taking place at times when other activities do not – in other words, when there are periods of choice and actual spaces. But much of the research on women suggests that the quality of women's time is such that several things are done at once (Sharpe 1984; Wyatt 1985) and leisure is combined with other activities. Wimbush (1986) suggests that this doubling up of work and leisure may actually be a way that women help to legitimate having time off:

> It's purely the idea of sitting and relaxing, watching television. Knitting's just another dimension. It means I'm not sitting doing absolutely nothing. So if anyone comes in and asks 'What are you doing?', 'Oh, I'm knitting'. I tend to keep it for the evenings when the kids aren't around.
>
> (quoted in Wimbush 1986: 61)

Everyone including the woman herself, may feel that this doubling up is acceptable, whereas just sitting, relaxing and watching television might make her feel guilty and invoke comments about laziness from her husband. Enjoyment and relaxation often has to be snatched by women houseworkers from other activities like taking children to their leisure activities.

Women's experiences of time, then, are much more fragmented than are those of many men, particularly for women not in any form of paid employment. This points the way to the need to explore time in different ways, and perhaps not always through the diaries so beloved of time-budget researchers, because this method is not always sensitive enough to record multiple use of time.

Life-styles and leisure

Leisure studies has for a long time operated in an empirical (and sometimes also theoretical) vacuum separated from research on other aspects of social life. What feminist contributions to the sociology of leisure have done is to stress the importance of analysing leisure in the context of individuals' lives as a whole. It is not possible to understand why, for instance, women have far more leisure at home than men unless the rest of their lives are explored too. For women the home is a workplace, even if they also have a job outside it, and their responsibilities for others, their relationship with their children and male partners, the community they live in and their friends as well as their living standards are all crucial to an understanding of why they do what they do in their leisure. Hence Rachael Dixey and Margaret Talbot, in their study of bingo, also undertook a community study of a working-class area of Leeds so that they could better understand the significance of bingo in the lives of women (Dixey and Talbot 1982). Erica Wimbush (1986) has explored the connections between well-being and leisure for mothers; in terms of women's life-styles as mothers, she shows the significance of leisure for developing and maintaining women's support systems (Wimbush 1986; see Ch. 5 below). Studies of women with children in paid and unpaid jobs suggest that tiredness is a constant problem which may prevent leisure even when time is available (Yeandle 1984; Sharpe 1984; Wimbush 1986).

Only the cultural studies strand of leisure research seems fully to have understood the same necessity to place and study leisure in the context of life-styles and communities, although an older tradition of community studies made similar points over two decades ago (Stacey 1960). Such contextualization is particularly apposite in the study of women's leisure. Some non-feminists have argued that women's life-styles are enviable compared to those of men, for their ability to blend work and leisure together in a holistic way (Gregory 1982). The other side of this, however, is the strains and stress women may suffer through having forcibly to blend their lives together in this way, leaving them with no space, time or inclination to just reflect (Yeandle 1984; Sharpe 1984; Wimbush 1986). Not every woman enjoys having a life-style in which it is impossible to untangle work and play (Deem 1986).

The lesson here is that we must look at life-styles as a whole and try to utilize methods of research which will allow us to place leisure within the context of community and region as well as class, race and gender.

Context and meaning

Context itself is an important aspect of whether women gain enjoyment and relaxation from activities – going for a drink in a pub with two women friends is very different from going to a wine bar with a husband to meet his work colleagues. It is crucial that such nuances are detected. That women may sometimes enjoy cooking or sewing or looking after children is often adduced as evidence that women 'enjoy' housework, whereas more careful analysis shows that it is only certain aspects of cooking or sewing or children which are enjoyable – for example, baking cakes when no one is at home, or playing with children in the park when you don't have to hurry back to get a meal and do the washing. Activities are not in themselves necessarily pleasurable or relaxing. My own Milton Keynes research found that many women enjoyed cooking meals for friends, but did not enjoy entertaining their husbands' work colleagues or fellow football players (Deem 1986).

Meaning and context are very closely linked. Although mainstream leisure studies has paid some attention to the meaning of leisure, this has often been a theoretical debate detached from the groups and individuals who construct those meanings. It has been feminist analyses which have drawn particular attention to the ways in which leisure and sport can provide women with a sense of liberation if they are doing something they choose to do and over which they have some control. Margaret Talbot (1984) has suggested that sport can be particularly rewarding to women because it gives them control over their own bodies, rather than women seeing their bodies as objects for men to admire and control. The meaning of leisure as something chosen and individual may be more important to women than men because women are more likely to find themselves in a wide variety of situations where they lack control and power.

Gender relations and power

As I said earlier, more recent mainstream analyses of leisure have begun to take on board the importance of analysing gender as a dimension of leisure. But it is not always evident that the full import of this is understood. Taking gender seriously means much more than noticing the existence of women. Gender relations involve studying relations of power, ideologies and other mechanisms whereby one gender wields power over the other, just as accusations of sexism involve relations of power and not simply mentioning one sex to the exclusion of the other. Women are constrained by patriarchal relations of male dominance to a much greater extent than many male researchers realize (see Part 4). Liz Stanley has pointed out the ways in which men 'police' many public places such as pubs and clubs where women on their own or with other women are not welcome (Stanley 1980). More recently, Eileen Green, Sandra Hebron and Diana Woodward have drawn attention in their Sheffield research to the reluctance of most women to go on their own to city centre leisure venues ranging from cinemas to pubs (Green, Hebron and Woodward 1985). Even travelling on public transport can be problematic for women, whether at night or by day. In my Milton Keynes research I found many women who were frightened of using the city's cycle and footpath network because of previous sexual attacks on women during daylight hours (Deem 1986). It is scarcely surprising that so much women's leisure takes place in the home, although, even there, little guarantee of peace exists, because violence is as likely to be experienced by women in their own homes as outside them (Hanmer and Maynard 1987).

Inside the household gender power-relations continue to exert their influence. Although it is often claimed that the sexual division of labour in the household is becoming less rigid (Gershuny and Jones 1987), there is little evidence to suggest it is disappearing altogether and much to suggest that it remains the responsibility of women to do housework and provide childcare (Maynard 1985; Malos 1980;

Mason 1986; Yeandle 1984). It is not in men's interests to disturb these arrange-ments, because it would decrease the support for their own leisure. Even where men are unemployed they are not always willing to take on more domestic work and may inhibit women's social spaces for leisure by hanging around the house (McKee and Bell 1984). The research on women's leisure in Sheffield and Edinburgh (Green, Hebron and Woodward 1985; Wimbush 1986) found that women had to spend a good deal of time negotiating with male partners over leisure entitlement and going out, although no equivalent negotiations usually take place over male leisure time away from home. Men are often heard to complain about having to babysit – for their own children! The Sheffield researchers also found that men were reluctant to allow women to go where alcohol was to be found. Yet if a similar control were enforced by women over their husbands, pubs would long ago have ceased trading! Women are in general the facilitators of others' leisure – husbands, children, male relatives – rather than the recipients of leisure. In my research I found that few women thought of themselves as having a right to leisure (Deem 1986); many men do see themselves as having such a right.

But how many mainstream studies of leisure or sport have looked at the power struggles over leisure which take place in households every day? How many have thought beyond the 'they are individuals and they choose not to do . . .' aspects of women's failure to participate in many male-dominated sports? Having seen the way male members of my cycling club provide their wives and girlfriends with the heaviest and most difficult-to-ride bikes they can find and then complain about how slow the women are on touring rides, it is difficult not to believe in male conspiracy theories. But it is easy to see much scope for further research in the sociology of sport well removed from the sphere of football hooligans and schemes for the young unemployed.

There is, however, a more general point here, concerned with the necessity of directing feminists' attention not only to the existence of power relations but also to how and why those power relations are sustained by ideological and material factors. There is much discussion about the importance, for example, of gender ideologies but little attempt to explore how these actually work in the field of leisure.

Conclusions

A good many gaps to fill?

What I have tried to do in this paper is to show how feminist analyses of leisure and sport have begun to rectify some of the deficiencies in conventional approaches to leisure studies. This, however is not to say that there are no other non-feminist attempts to do the same (e.g. Clarke and Critcher 1985). The major difference, however, is that these parallel endeavours do not take gender relations as central to their enterprise. There are many other issues which could have been included here, some of which are taken up by other contributors. For example, feminist researchers are on the whole much more sensitive to other social divisions like age and race than are non-feminist researchers.

While not pioneering the life-cycle approach (see Rapoport and Rapoport 1975) feminists have been more ready to utilize life-cycle approaches to leisure and sport. It is of course also true that feminist approaches to leisure studies have not always learnt from more conventional approaches – for example, in the treatment of class. But the significance of taking gender relations seriously is inescapable, and it is high time that male leisure researchers began to examine carefully the connections between male leisure, male power and socially constructed notions of masculine gender identity as well as considering some of the other new directions which I have sketched out here. As Debbie Chambers says in her study of shift workers, 'Men appear better able to preserve normal life-styles irrespective of their work schedules; women are a central part of men's resources to overcome [these] . . . women do not have equivalent resources' (Chambers 1986: 321). It is up to all leisure researchers, not just feminist ones, to find ways in which women can enjoy such resources and support too.

References

Bowles, Gloria and Duelli Klein, Renate (1983) *Theories of Women's Studies*, London, Routledge and Kegan Paul.

Brackenridge, Celia (1987) 'Gender inequalities in sports leadership', paper given to the 'Future of Adult Life' conference, Leeunwenhorst, Netherlands, April.

Burns, Tom (1973) 'Leisure in industrial society', in Mike Smith, Stan Parker and Cyril Smith (eds.) *Leisure and Society in Britain*, London, Allen Lane, Penguin.

Centre for Contemporary Cultural Studies (1977) *On Ideology*, London, Hutchinson.

(1981) 'Women and leisure', in Alan Tomlinson (ed.) *Leisure and Social Control*, Eastbourne, Brighton Polytechnic, Chelsea School of Human Movement.

Chambers, Debbie (1986) 'The constraints of work and domestic schedules on women's leisure', *Leisure Studies* 5(3): 309–25.

Cheek, N. and Burch, W. R. (1976) *The Social Organisation of Leisure in Human Society*, New York, Harper & Row.

Clarke, John and Critcher, Chas (1985) *The Devil Makes Work*, London, Macmillan.

Clarke, John, Critcher, Chas and Johnson, Richard (1979) *Working Class Culture*, London, Hutchinson.

Coyle, Angela (1984) *Redundant Workers*, London, Women's Press.

Critcher, Chas (1986) 'Radical theories of sport: the state of play', *Sociology of Sport Journal* 3: 337–43.

Deem, Rosemary (1986) *All Work and No Play: The Sociology of Women and Leisure*, Milton Keynes, Open University Press.

(1987) 'The politics of women's leisure', in David Jary, Jim Horne and Alan Tomlinson (eds.) *Sport, Leisure and Social Relations*, Sociological Review Monograph 33, London and Keele, Routledge & Kegan Paul.

Deem, Rosemary and Salaman, Graeme (eds.) (1985) *Work, Culture and Society*, Milton Keynes, Open University Press.

Dixey, Rachael and Talbot, Margaret (1982) *Women, Leisure and Bingo*, Leeds, Trinity and All Saints' College.

Dumazedier, John (1974) *The Sociology of Leisure*, Amsterdam, Elsevier.

Dunning, Eric and Murphy, Philip (1982) 'Working class social bonding and the socio-genesis of football hooliganism', University of Leicester, Department of Sociology.

Ferris, Liz (1981) 'Attitudes to women in sport; prolegomena towards a sociological theory', *Equal Opportunities International* 1(2): 32–9.

Fletcher, Sheila (1984) *Women First: The Female Tradition in English Physical Education 1880–1980*, London, Athlone Press.

Gershuny, Jay and Jones, Sally (1987) 'The changing work/leisure balance in Britain: 1961–1984', in John Horne, David Jary and Alan Tomlinson (eds.) *Sport, Leisure and Social Relations*, Sociological Review Monograph 33, London and Keele, Routledge & Kegan Paul.

Glyptis, Sue, McInnes, Hamish and Patmore, Alan (1987) *Leisure and the Home*, Sports Council/ESRC, London.

Graham, Hilary (1984) *Women, Health and the Family*, Brighton, Harvester Press.

Graydon, Jan (1983) 'But it's more than a game. It's an institution. Feminist perspectives on sport', *Feminist Review* 2.

Green, Eileen, Hebron, Sandra and Woodward, Diana (1985) 'A woman's work . . . is never done', *Sport and Leisure*, July/August, pp. 36–8.

  (1987a) *Leisure and Gender*, final report to Sports Council/ESRC, London, Sports Council.

  (1987b) 'Women, leisure and social control' in Jalna Hanmer and Mary Maynard (eds.) *Women, Violence and Social Control*, London, Macmillan.

Gregory, Sarah (1982) 'Women among others: another view', *Leisure Studies* 1(1): 47a–52.

Griffin, Chris (1985) *Typical Girls*, London, Routledge & Kegan Paul.

Hall, M. Ann (1986) 'How should we theorise gender in the context of sport?', paper presented to 'Sport, Sex and Gender' Conference, Lillehammer, Norway, 12–14 November.

Hall, Stuart and Jefferson, Tony (eds.) (1975) *Resistance through Ritual*, London, Hutchinson.

Hanmer, Jalna and Maynard, Mary (1987) (eds.) *Women, Violence and Social Control*, London, Macmillan.

Jenkins, Clive and Sherman, Barrie (1981) *The Leisure Shock*, London, Eyre Methuen.

Kaplan, Max (1975) *Leisure Theory and Policy*, New York, John Wiley.

Leaman, Oliver (1984) *Sit on the Sidelines and Watch the Boys Play: Sex Differentiation in Physical Education*, London, Longmans for the Schools Council.

Lewis, Jane (1984) *Women in England 1870–1950*, Brighton, Wheatsheaf.

Liddington, Jill and Norris, Jill (1978) *One Hand Tied Behind Us*, London, Virago.

Llewelyn Davies, Margaret (ed.) [1904] (1977) *Life as We Have Known It – Co-operative Working Women*, London, Virago.

McIntosh, Sue, Griffin, Chris, McCabe, Trish and Hobson, Dorothy (1981) 'Women and Leisure', in Alan Tomlinson (ed) *Leisure and Social Control*, Eastbourne, Brighton Polytechnic, Chelsea School of Human Movement.

McKee, Lorna and Bell, Collin (1984) 'His unemployment; her problem', paper given to British Sociological Association Conference, April.

Malos, Ellen (1980) *The Politics of Housework*, London, Allison & Busby.

Martin, Jean and Roberts, Ceridwen (1984) *Women and Employment: A Lifetime Perspective*, London, HMSO.

Martin, Robert and Wallace, Jean (1984) *Working Women in the Recession*, Oxford, Oxford University Press.

Mason, Jennifer (1986) 'Gender inequality in long-term marriage', paper presented to British Sociological Association Conference, University of Loughborough, March.

Maynard, Mary (1985) 'Houseworkers and their work', in Rosemary Deem and Graeme Salaman, (eds.) *Work, Culture and Society*, Milton Keynes, Open University Press.

Pahl, Ray (1985) *Divisions of Labour*, Oxford, Blackwell.

Parker, Stan (1983) *Work and Leisure*, London, Allen & Unwin.

Rapoport, Rhona and Rapoport, Robert (1975) *Leisure and the Family Life Cycle*, London, Routledge & Kegan Paul.

Roberts, Ken (1978) *Contemporary Society and the Growth of Leisure*, London, Longmans.

(1981) *Leisure*, London, Longmans.

(1982) *Youth and Leisure*, London, Allen & Unwin.

Rojek, Chris (1985) *Capitalism and Leisure Theory*, London, Tavistock.

Rowbotham, Sheila (1977) *Hidden from History*, 3rd edn, London, Pluto Press.

Scraton, Sheila (1986) 'Images of femininity and the teaching of girls' physical education', in John Evans (ed.) *Physical Education, Sport and Schooling*, Barcombe, Lewes, Falmer Press.

(1987) 'Boys muscle in where angels fear to tread: the relationship between physical education and young women's subcultures', in David Jary, Jim Horne and Alan Tomlinson (eds.) *Sport, Leisure and Social Relations*, Sociological Review Monograph 33, London and Keele, Routledge & Kegan Paul.

Sharpe, Sue (1984) *Double Identity*, Harmondsworth, Penguin.

Smith, Mike, Parker, Stan and Smith, Cyril (1973) *Leisure and Society in Britain*, London, Allen Lane.

Stacey, Margaret (1960) *Tradition and Change: A Study of Banbury*, Oxford, Oxford University Press.

Stanley, Liz (1980) 'The problem of women and leisure: an ideological construct and a radical feminist alternative', paper given to the 'Leisure in the 80s' Forum, Capital Radio, 26–8 September.

Talbot, Margaret (1979) *Women and Leisure: A State of the Art Review*, London, SSRC/Sports Council.

(1981) 'Women and sport: biosocial aspects', *Journal of Biosocial Science*, Supplement 7: 33–47.

(1984) 'Women and sport; a gender contradiction in terms?', paper presented to International Conference of Leisure Studies Association, Brighton, Sussex, July.

Thompson, Edward P. (1967) 'Time, work-discipline and industrial capitalism', *Past and Present* 38.

Veal, Tony (1987) *Leisure and the Future*, London, Allen & Unwin.

Vicinus, Martha (1985) *Independent Women: Work and Community for Single Women 1850–1920*, London, Virago.

Wimbush, Erica (1986) *Women, Leisure and Well-being*, Edinburgh, Centre for Leisure Research.

(1988) 'Transitions in work, leisure and health experiences in motherhood', in Pat Allatt, Teresa Keil, Alan Bryman and Bill Bytheway (eds.) *Women and the Life Cycle: Transitions and Turning Points*, London, Macmillan.

Wyatt, Sally (1985) 'Science Policy Research Unit time-budget studies', paper given to 'Women, Leisure and Well-being' Workshop, Dunfermline College of Physical Education, Edinburgh, April.

Yeandle, Susan (1984) *Women's Working Lives*, London, Tavistock.

2

Historical sources for studying work and leisure in women's lives

LIZ STANLEY

Studying women's life and leisure 'in the round'

The concepts of women's 'work' and 'leisure' cannot be adequately understood in the abstract. Conventional social science theorizing is of course no stranger to abstraction. After all, according to the *Oxford English Dictionary*, 'theory' consists of abstractions abstractly related. Interesting on one level (although a past student of mine referred to it, very graphically, as 'plaiting sand'), an abstracted approach to exploring work and leisure does not help one whit in understanding their complex co-presence in people's lives in the real world. To gain this understanding we need to examine actual work and leisure in actual everyday lives. This means eschewing gross generalizations about 'people' and instead teasing out some of the different work–leisure relationships that are experienced by the young and old, by white and black people, by women and men, by gay people and hetero-sexuals, and so on.

Much leisure studies, including feminist leisure studies, consists of research which focuses on particular leisure activities or particular leisure dimensions of people's lives. This entails importing researcher-defined categories of what con-stitutes 'leisure'. Even more sensitive work typically starts from people's own categories but then strips these of their particular personal context by adding them to other responses by yet other people and producing generalizations about many such responses.

Problems with this kind of approach to data collection and use centre on its rigorous removal of 'context': the removal of the fabric of people's lives. To continue the 'fabric' analogy, context consists of the interweaving of many strands within which 'work' and 'leisure', among other things, are located as a part of the whole. That is, work and leisure make sense only in relation to each other and to other parts of the whole. 'Leisure' certainly does not make sense on its own; it has to be understood as part of a conjunction of interests, needs, skills, commitments and obligations in women's lives, most importantly including those of 'work'.

There are various ways of 'putting context back in'. Feminist leisure studies research which looks at women's lives much more 'in the round' in a contemporary setting is to be welcomed[1]. However, this needs to be matched by an *historical* examination of women's lives and experiences. Neither 'leisure' nor 'work' are static features of women's lives. 'Social change' is of the essence because work and leisure themselves – and the relationship between them – change over a historical period and also over the course of someone's lifetime. 'Social change' can be looked at in generalized collective terms – or, as I show in this paper, it can be looked at in the context of individual lives. I stress the need for a historical comparative approach: we cannot adequately understand 'now' if we do not know something about its relationship with 'then' and about how the one became the other.

In the previous paragraph I referred to 'individuals'. Often this term is used in a psychologistic and reductionist sense: the unique individual who is composed by their 'inner' psychological selves. In complete contrast, I use the term in the sociological sense that individual people are members of, are indeed products of, particular cultures. We are social beings through and through, and because of this it is possible to examine general social processes in the context of particular individual lives. This is the basis for using autobiographical materials in exploring women's work and leisure historically.

The classic example of this approach is Thomas and Znaniecki's *The Polish Peasant in Europe and America* (1918). Here 'the' Polish peasant was precisely that – one particular male Polish peasant whose life was looked at to come to theoretical and substantive grips with 'social change', 'emigration', 'family' and other conceptual schemes. The premise here was that 'theory' must work adequately at the level of individual as well as of group experience – and that if it doesn't, then something is wrong and it must be changed. The premise behind this paper is a similar one: theory should be derived from, rather than being concerned to obliterate, individual difference. In terms of the work–leisure relationship in women's lives, our theoretical understanding of this must recognize that there are work–leisure relationships: rather than one such relationship, many possible conjunctions of work and leisure are possible, and these multiple conjunctions need to be at the heart of our understanding of what it is to be a woman.

I became concerned with studying women's work and leisure in this way in a serendipitous fashion. I had been interested in the founding of a distinct 'leisure studies' while at the University of Salford in the early 1970s and at the same time involved in feminist ideas and activities. Then by chance I bought Derek Hudson's (1972) edited version of the diaries of Arthur Munby (1828–1910) and these introduced me to the diaries of Hannah Cullwick.

Hannah Cullwick (1833–1909) was a working-class woman who worked throughout her life, from age 8 until old age. Emotionally entangled with upper-class Munby, Hannah consistently refused 'ladyhood' except on an occasional basis. Also for a lengthy period of her life from 1854 to 1874 she wrote a diary (Stanley 1984). Hannah Cullwick's diary is an atypical one and all the more remarkable for being so. It consists not of the diary staple of the psychological reworking of persons and events but, rather, detailed descriptions of the minutiae of her working life and of moments of 'less work' and 'more leisure' within it. It comprises the most detailed single source that exists for studying the life, work and leisure of a Victorian working-class woman in that most typical of all Victorian occupations, domestic service.

The most compelling feature of the Cullwick diaries is that they show work and leisure 'in the round'. They demonstrate vividly that her 'work–leisure relationship' was very complex and that it changed in structured ways – from situation to situation over the time spent in a particular place of employment, between different places, between 'work' and the same activities done for Munby, and also over her life-course. There were compensations to be set against the demanding and exhausting work she engaged in, coming in part from emotional ties not only to Munby but also to friends, to fellow servants in a particular place, to her sisters and brothers. Importantly, compensations also came from the nature of the work itself. Then as now, domestic work was both less regimented and more constraining than paid employment outside the home, for it does not take place in a 'capsule' of time with a specified beginning and end and it is not (usually) supervised. This permits domestic labourers like Hannah to experience 'work' and 'leisure' in a free-flowing fashion. And for Hannah, work itself, the exertion of physical strength and effort, was pleasurable, not least because of her great pride in her body and its abilities.

I am most definitely not saying that these or any other diaries constitute 'the truth'. All autobiographies are highly selective *accounts* produced around particular (and often changing, as Hannah Cullwick's diaries so amply show) motives and intentions. This of course makes them more interesting and not less, for it makes very apparent the conundrum that historians frequently fail to acknowledge: that historical accounts are all, without exception, filtered to us through the particular accounts of particular persons. This is no less so with parliamentary papers and the reports of royal commissions than with diaries and letters: the fact is simply less easy to ignore with the latter.

Through working on the Cullwick diaries I became a convert to a 'whole life' way of looking at leisure: not separating it off from other activities, nor researching it outside of naturally occurring situations and the records of these that exist, but instead studying it 'in the round' as a totality. Various research projects have looked at women's lives in a more rounded fashion but with a particular eye to the work–leisure dynamic (see Fletcher 1985 and, in a different way, Green, Hebron and Woodward 1985, 1987) and it will be interesting to see where such a line of exploration in feminist leisure studies leads. However, such research focuses on contemporary settings and requires a high level of funding; and extensive data sources already exist which are underutilized in exploring women's leisure concerns. The particular underused sources I am concerned with here are historical in nature. Because they deal with times past, these sources enable us to gain analytic purchase on *changing* ideas about 'work' and 'leisure' and how these intersect in women's lives in complexly variant ways: they permit comparisons between 'then' and 'now'. Also the passing of time opens up sources which were, contemporaneously, 'private' in nature, such as diaries; these permit comparisons between different individual women and their social settings as well as between time periods.

I discuss three interrelated sources which illuminate historically changing work–leisure relationships in women's lives, using basically autobiographical means. My aim is briefly to discuss particular examples, show what can be gained conceptually from using such sources and suggest where other similar materials may be found. My discussion is intended as a spring-board, for readers to move out from it to their own particular investigations. The three types of source I discuss are: (1) diaries and autobiographies; (2) the Mass-Observation Archive at the University of Sussex; and (3) oral history writing projects.

Diaries and autobiographies

Generally written in the immediacy of the moment, diaries can show much about the management of time, of competing demands and commitments in women's (and indeed men's) lives at a particular historical period, and at different junctures within the life of a particular diary-writer. A brief comparison of some different kinds of diaries – the 'companion' diaries of Arthur Munby and Hannah Cullwick, and the diaries of Virginia Woolf – demonstrates this very well.

Although there are exceptions,[2] most diaries record the lives of individuals rather than of social groups. They provide that individual's view of their life and activities and so construct a highly particular 'world'. Only rarely do the 'worlds' of two diary writers overlap and intertwine; even more rarely do they overlap in such radically contrasting ways as do those of Arthur Munby and Hannah Cullwick.

Munby was born into the well-to-do professional class; Cambridge followed public school; he trained as a barrister, then worked until retirement for the Ecclesiastical Commission as a quasi-legal clerk. His work routine was a (flexible) 10 to 4 five-day week with generously long holidays. His leisure time was clearly demarcated and combined maintaining family links, involvement with the Working Men's College, friendship with many of its Christian socialist – and like him, ex-Trinity College – teachers, and much socializing, including on the fringes of 'polite' but artistic society. His leisure also importantly included Munby's interest in 'collecting' the lives and work histories of working-class women: his diary is an accurate and rare source of information about Victorian working women. He carefully notes dress, appearance, demeanour and speech, the job itself, pay and conditions, and a multiplicity of other aspects of these women's working lives. His diary is an enthralling document, urbane and courteous in style, and beneath the surface obsessive about 'collecting' working women, an activity which took up the major part of Munby's leisure and 'work-related' time.[3]

In great contrast, Hannah Cullwick was born into a working-class Shropshire rural and mining community, and started work at the age of 8 after a brief introduction to reading, writing and scripture at a local charity school. Thereafter, she worked in London in a succession of servant's places, mainly as kitchen maid and maid-of-all work. Her work was highly skilled. Her working-day lasted from about 6 a.m. until late at night, seven days a week and often fifty-two weeks a year (holidays were unpaid, thus a luxury). Days, afternoons and evenings off were rarely routinized: each one had to be separately asked for and could be withdrawn at whim at the last moment. Hannah's 'leisure', then, came mainly in the form of 'less work' and in the context of her working-day: errands for her 'missis', kitchen visiting, meals and talks with fellow servants. Outside of this her main 'time off' was spent with Munby; and gradually this became 'less leisure' as she took on more of his domestic tasks. Munby relied on servants to get him through: Hannah, like many women since, provided exemplary service because it was carried out meticulously through love.

Hannah's diary is unique in its detail of a servant's working-day, week, year, and its punctuations by 'less work' and 'more leisure' activities (visiting, theatres and music halls, fairs, walks). Much more could be said about its relationship to Munby's diary, and what the two together suggest about contrastive work–leisure relationships in different sections of mid-Victorian society. But for space reasons I outline features of her diary which are interestingly compared with women's domestic labour now.

'Kitchen visiting' was the practice whereby servants who had often in the past worked together took their leisure together by visiting each other's 'places'. Hannah Cullwick was clear there was no point in waiting for a fellow servant who failed to arrive on time, for if their master or mistress wanted anything, their own needs had to go by the board. She laments the appallingly long and hard extra work required of her and other servants when her employers decided to have an extra-sociable Christmas. The 'family holidays' of her employers occur with little warning in the midst of her work routines. During 'holidays' Hannah experienced the same work but reconstituted in different seaside locations and made more difficult by cramped surroundings, unaccustomed working conditions and insufficient cooking and cleaning devices. Also the sporadic presence in her work space of her mistress, arriving to release household stores and to check on the use of these, caused both resentment and disturbance to work routines.

This is interesting in itself for what it says about work and leisure in Hannah's life. It also throws into sharp relief comparable features of the domestic relations of men and women now: the unaccustomed presence of a male partner (on holiday, unemployed, retired) that drives out visiting female friends; public holidays like Christmas and Easter that require women to service male partners and children even more thoroughly and 'festively'; the increased labour caused by self-catering family holidays; an occasional male presence which insists on 'better' ways of spending money, preparing food and so forth.

As an upper-class woman with an income of her own, and later as a publicly acknowledged writer, Virginia Woolf's life was very different from Hannah Cullwick's. Interestingly, as she grew, the more her life came to share a similar work-oriented structure and punctuation of a long working-day by 'less work' rather than by any distinctively 'leisure' activities. A 'typical' Woolfian day would include a morning spent writing, an afternoon typing then reading, pre-dinner diary writing, and when well visits to and from friends who shared her writing trade or an associated one in painting or music. Work, then, dominated Virginia Woolf's life as certainly as it did Hannah Cullwick's. Virginia Woolf did little domestic labour until later in her life, when she came to realize how much the pattern of her life had been dominated by the working-day of rigidly trained Victorian servants who insisted upon formal many-course meals, fellow servants and all the appurtenances of a 'good place' (an interesting case of the 'work of subordinates' determining the 'leisure of superordinates'). In middle age she elected to dispense with much of this.

Virginia Woolf's is one of the great British diaries – literate, detailed, scrupulous, aware, self-reflecting and sensitive, organized around her very being as a writer, and filled with the professional artistic, feminist and radical upper-middle classes of her day. Her diary together with her letters, essays and novels, ensures that Virginia Woolf's is one of the best-documented working lives. Many aspects of her diary could be discussed to examine features of the work–leisure relationship. Because of space considerations I deal with one only, the complex ties between the work and leisure of Virginia Woolf and the work of the servants whom she employed.

Among her friends and acquaintances much 'work' was put into establishing and maintaining friendships, for friendship was highly valued and extensively engaged in. It also acted as an essential 'leisure' support to the working lives of this group of people, for they tended to share a working involvement in 'literature' in one or other of its forms. And their 'work' and 'leisure' were supported by servants who shopped, cooked and cleaned and by doing so enabled both the leisure *and* the work of their employers.

It must be emphasized that this was no peculiar unawareness of 'Bloomsbury', no demonstration of its élitist iniquities. As the discussion of Naomi Mitchison's diary below suggests, more overtly radical people than Virginia Woolf could be much less aware of the constraining and distorting effects of 'service' on employees and employers alike. Woolf was aware of and alarmed by the extent to which the necessary subservience of servants distorted their behaviour, led to dishonesty and secrecy, and even if temporarily, changed her basic respect for these women to something close to despising them. Also she was very aware of her dependency on servants as well as vice versa.

It has been claimed that the diary form is class-biased: the form of the literate middle and upper classes only. What has given rise to this false mythology is not that working-class people – and women in particular – have failed to write diaries but rather that their diaries are less likely to be preserved, and preserved in places where they are classified, appear in bibliographies and thus become widely known about. However, that women's class is complex and ambiguous and by no means simply connected with that of their fathers/husbands is a truism generally accepted. Thus in fact 'middle class' and 'working class' women actually share many dimensions of inequality, oppression and exploitation in their lives. A comparison of women's lives even between the diaries of Cullwick and Woolf confirms this argument and extends our grounds for making it.

Thus many of the 'ladies' who figure in Hannah Cullwick's diaries are as controlled and confined in their freedom of movement and ability to change their lives as working-class women. The forms that this control and confinement took might have been somewhat different, but the consequences were remarkably similar. Although incomparably more free in some ways, Virginia Woolf was as subject to the vagaries and dictates of Leonard Woolf as Hannah Cullwick was to Munby, for he exercised strict controls over the management of her health/illness and thus over the time–work dimension in her life. And in doing so, as both Vita Sackville West and Ethel Smyth ruefully noted, Leonard Woolf also controlled the dynamics of love and friendship as effectively as any working-class male driving out visitors of his wife's. He also completely controlled their household purse strings, including her independent earnings.

Diaries are a 'private' form: generally they are not written with publication in mind. In spite of this, only very rarely can we read about the day-to-day life of lesbian women (Whitbread, 1988): either writing is 'laundered' by the writer to obscure this fact in her life, or family and friends make sure it never sees publication. Recently a number of interesting and indeed scandalous diaries by homosexual men have been published – for example, Joe Orton (Lahr 1986) and Tom Driberg (1977). However, these reflect the lives of gay males, and a very particular kind of gay male at that – London-based, sexually predatory and sexually obsessed. In this regard, the diary of Virginia Woolf is probably a better guide to the life of lesbian women of her time: her sexual relationship and lasting friendship with Vita Sackville West was deeply embedded in shared literary concerns and woven around her life with her husband.[4]

As yet the Woolf diaries are one of the very few accounts of the everyday life of the married lesbian woman in the 1920s and 1930s. Even more rare is information about historical diaries written by women of colour. Certainly these *do* exist, but they are more likely to exist in the natural language of the writer and to be unpublished. One exception to this, an autobiography rather than a diary, is the *Wonderful Adventures of Mrs Seacole in Many Lands* (Seacole [1857] 1984). This is the story of a Jamaican woman who came to Britain and became involved, as an unofficial nurse and general provisioner, in the Crimean War. By its end she was a national heroine, although one quickly forgotten and inadequately rewarded. Given the present burgeoning of the feminist publication of biographies, it is certainly to be hoped that many more of these will deal with the lives of women other than the white, middle class and heterosexual.

Important sources for using diaries for research purposes include Arthur Ponsonby's *English Diaries* (1923) and William Matthews's *British Diaries* (1950). Many working-class people have provided written testimony in the form of autobiography. The most complete and up-to-date guide to working-class diaries and autobiographies is formed by John Burnett's two collections, *Useful Toil* (1974) and *Destiny Obscure* (1982), together with John Burnett, David Vincent and David Mayall's three-volume edited collection on *The Autobiography of the Working Class* (1985, 1986, 1987).

While often useful for leisure researchers, as well as intrinsically interesting, it is important to note significant differences between diaries and autobiographies. The latter are retrospective reworkings; the former (and with some notable 'retouched' examples, such as political diaries) are the product of the actual moment they speak to. This has consequences for those interested in using such materials to investigate the work–leisure relationship for women historically. Retrospectively provided information is not inferior to that provided at the time, but it is certainly different. Retrospectively, we *summarize*, we gloss a set of events rather than *describe*. What this omits of course is detail, and it is precisely with detail, of particular aspects of 'work', of particular features of 'leisure' and of particular interminglings of the two, that feminist leisure researchers such as myself are concerned. This frequent lack of daily routine detail in autobiographies needs to be kept in mind when interpreting the material they contain. A discussion of autobiographical materials is contained in the section on oral history writing projects below. What follows is a discussion of a different form of diary materials.

The Mass-Observation Archive

The Mass Observation Archive at the University of Sussex holds an extensive collection of materials from the period 1937 to 1949. All the major events of that time were researched by Mass-Observation (M-O) using diaries and 'special directives' to record particular events. Events covered include unemployment, the growth of fascism, shifts in British foreign policy, Coronation Day 1937, the outbreak of war, the Blitz, and the Labour victory in the 1945 general election. Many more aspects of everyday life were also researched by M-O, including the use of public houses, 'totemism' in rural life, Blackpool holidays and the 'Lambeth Walk' among much else.

In 1949 the original M-O dissolved, and its rump became a still-existent survey organization, Mass-Observation Ltd. The original M-O, however, is best known for ethnographic research of various kinds carried out by ordinary people within and on their own local communities, and also for its diaries. These diaries were of two main kinds: the long-term war diaries and the 'day surveys' completed by M-O's volunteer observers. These day surveys were one-day diaries in which observers recorded everything they felt relevant, interesting or useful, each person in their own distinctive fashion.

Two diaries produced for M-O during the Second World War, by Naomi Mitchison (1985) and Nella Last (1981), deal with the vicissitudes of war, worry for self and others, responses to 'the enemy' and their own nation, and the daily round of activities. But each diarist does so in very different ways. In addition, both reveal fascinating differences in work–leisure relationships as compared with each other and also for each woman over the six years of the war. These diaries were each written by a 'middle class' woman, but women whose lives, thoughts and feelings were so different as to emphasize the gross oversimplification of the supposedly unitary category 'middle class'.

Naomi Mitchison knew the founders of M-O well, and before the war had participated in various of its activities. When war was declared in 1939 she, like many observers, undertook to keep a diary for its duration. Then, as now, a well-known writer and involved as a feminist in radical-left politics of the day, her war diary shows how Naomi Mitchison's writing, politics, family, and life on her and her husband's Scottish estate, were supported by a network of servants and employed artisans. 'The kitchen' only rarely surfaces into the diary. Lying in bed in the morning reading *Tribune*, Naomi Mitchison lamented the government's suppression of various radical papers; we hear the pages of *Tribune* turn, but not the sound of servants cleaning, cooking and ensuring all is well with the household. However, local working people appear extensively around 'Big House' social activities and Naomi Mitchison's political work.

Work and leisure intertwine in complex ways in Naomi Mitchison's life. She 'manages' the household rather than does domestic labour herself. Outside of this, there is less of a dominance of the rhythms of any one activity here than in the lives of Hannah Cullwick and Virginia Woolf: writing, farming, reading, talking, children, social and political life, all have their ebbs and flows and no one sphere of activity becomes superordinate.

Nella Last's diary is a very different record by a very different woman. Less easy to place in class terms, she was an 'ordinary woman' from the northern shipbuilding town of Barrow-in-Furness. Her husband was of the skilled and employing artisan class, and her two sons were becoming part of the professional middle classes. A stalwart of the Women's Voluntary Service (WVS, now the WRVS), Nella Last's concerns were local without being parochial, and her activities in this organization were undoubtedly war work of a useful and important kind.

In a different way from Naomi Mitchison, Nella Last's day is a complex blend of work and leisure activities organized by the events and ups and downs of the war itself. The war is differently 'present' in this diary, for her horizons were those of the everyday flow of boys and men away from the area, their deaths and imprisonments and, above all, the everyday life of those – primarily women – who were left and who faced the Blitz in a shipbuilding town. Much more involved as a domestic labourer – though with a daily 'help' with whom she shared housework – Nella Last cooks, looks after hens, makes items for the hospital and the WVS and serves regularly in its canteen. She also looks after her husband and sons, supports relatives and friends and, as she herself remarks, transforms herself from the retiring headachey woman she used to be. Noting that her husband's constant keeping her at his side 'stifled' her, the war in some ways considerably frees her while restricting her in others. The war robbed Nella Last of 'time', free and unfettered time, but through the work it occasioned it enabled her to find herself. Thus as the war draws to a close in 1945 she notes that everything was 'slipping and changing', like it did when the war started. Everyday routines were being broken up: 'The little pattern of life . . . is quickly dissolving into memories. The leisure left is not altogether desirable; the change-over has gaps' (Last 1981: 294). 'Leisure', her diary makes clear, was time on her hands, the lack of useful purpose; and it was leisure in this sense that the war had put a welcome end to and peace threatened to reconstitute.

M-O had a particular, coherent and radical approach to methodological issues. Observations of *any* kind, and no matter by whom, cannot be separated from the observer: *somebody* sees, observes, records. M-O was concerned to make this understanding explicit within its brand of social science, not disguise it beneath a rhetoric of 'science' and 'objectivity'. It referred to its observers as 'subjective cameras', and its founders were almost as interested in *how* its observers saw as they were in *what* they saw. With benefit of hindsight – and as hopefully the accounts of the contrasting approaches of Nella Last and Naomi Mitchison have demonstrated – this has paid enormous dividends. Through its work we can explore how different kinds of people experienced in sometimes similar and sometimes different ways the 'same' events. Closely associated with its radicalism of method, M-O was concerned that its radical democratizing form of social science should 'observe' the relevancies of everyday life and experience, not produce esoteric research designed only for other researchers. And thus its approach to 'method', to the diaries, the day surveys and the special directives as key means of recording everyday life in Britain.

For example, eschewing the 'Oxbridge, London and Home Counties' focus of most British social science then and even now, one of its major data-gathering projects focused on Northern England, on 'Worktown' (Bolton) and all aspects of life within it – Remembrance Day, work, politics, unemployment, religion, annual Blackpool holidays and the incidence of illicit holiday sex. Another example – and one which shows the great importance of this combination of method and content for feminists – concerns the 'day survey' diaries. The majority of volunteers were female and provided the bulk of these diaries. One such is by Phyllis Waldon of Keston in Kent (Calder and Sheridan 1984: 6–8). It shows the complex combinations of work and leisure in her life, as in many other women's lives, and in doing so says much about differences between women and men. Thus Phyllis Waldon wakes up one Sunday morning remembering amusing scenes from a film and goes to sleep thinking of work involved in the day ahead. She makes tea and biscuits for her husband and self in bed; he asks what is for breakfast and 'Says he'll have his in bed. Very glad about this, as . . . he does find fault with the children's table manners so' (quoted in Calder and Sheridan 1984: 7).

The data which results from this extraordinary venture has been criticized by the methodologically and politically respectable as pseudo-science and naïve subjectivity. In the 1980s and with a resurgence of methodological radicalism, a different and positive re-evaluation has become possible. This archive holds a wealth of information about the lives and experiences of ordinary people of the period from 1936 to 1949. For feminist leisure researchers especially, there are immense riches here. Concerned with all kinds of social phenomena whilst also recognizing the primacy of work in most people's lives, M-O data contains much of importance for discussing women's work–leisure relationships 'then and now'. Some has been used for discussing women's leisure in Rochdale in the 1930s and 1940s (Abenstern 1985). Much more remains as a greatly underused resource for feminist leisure researchers.

Earlier I stressed the importance of a strong historical perspective in feminist discussion of women's work and leisure. There is both continuity and change in women's work and leisure and in the material conditions within which these are located. And as M-O's work conveys so well, there is also continuity and change in 'perspective' – in how we see and what we see and what importance we accord it. Like 'Joanna Field's' (1937) *Experiment in Leisure*, material in the M-O Archive reminds us that other women thought about 'leisure' and its relationship to 'work' sometimes much as we do, sometimes in astoundingly different ways. We need to know about and take account of both.

Oral-history writing projects

This section does not deal with 'oral history' as such, for like leisure studies oral history now exists as a substantial subdiscipline. It deals instead with a body of oral-history writing which has come into existence largely outside of an academic framework and which can be described as 'a people's autobiography'. That is, people writing about their own working lives and experiences and by doing so extending our understanding of what the concepts 'history' and 'work' actually mean. In this discussion I refer to various oral-history writing projects; and then focus on some themes dealt with in these, showing how and in what ways they can illuminate our understanding of the work–leisure relationship in women's lives.

The Sistren Theatre Collective is based in Jamaica and was founded to give space to explore the lived experience of black women's working lives. It has since expanded into other media like screen-printing and publishing and also by taking its theatre work to black women outside of the Caribbean, including to Britain. It draws on an indigenous black feminism as well as recent contemporary variants. Its specific purpose is to locate political analysis within a firmly experiential framework. Along the way it explores many facets of the historical and present-day experiences of black women and importantly includes a strong tradition of women's storytelling.

Lionheart Gal (Sistren 1986) contains life-stories of Collective members. As well as speaking to each woman's particular experiences, these life-stories deal with 'development' in the Caribbean area from the time of slavery on, particularly within living memory as many people emigrated to 'better' lives elsewhere. As the editor of the collection, Honor Ford Smith notes:

> The stories can be read individually . . . However, within each story there are different emphases such as work, housing, relations with men and children, so that taken together, they are a composite woman's story . . . All of the testimonies are underscored by a movement from girlhood to adulthood, country to city, isolated individual experience to more politicised collective awareness.
>
> (Ford Smith 1986: xiii)

These life-stories explore very different images of black women: the mythological woman warrior and the proverbial black mammy. And as many of the contributors suggest, these are not so dissimilar from each other as may appear on first sight. The important role of mythology in enabling women's social and political survival shown here has also been explored in other emigrant women's writing, with one well-known example being Maxine Hong Kinston's *Woman Warrior* (1977).

One of the first explorations of immigrant women's lives in Britain was Amrit Wilson's *Finding a Voice* (1978). This similarly eschews a conventional 'academic' generalized approach in favour of enabling particular Asian women to speak more for themselves (and the interviews conducted as a part of the book were adapted for teaching English as a second language). This kind of writing conveys a political message directly and powerfully; more importantly, it empowers the women who speak. This I take to be one of the most fundamental tenets of contemporary feminism, that we should speak with our own voices and be listened to by other women.

The Gatehouse Project publishes local community writing, and like other community publishers it also engages in all aspects of the process from 'having an idea' through to 'publishing a book'. Gatehouse is particularly concerned with the experience of adults with reading and writing difficulties and with helping people to surmount particular writing problems. It gives special emphasis to writing by women, people of colour, beginning readers, and more recently the elderly (Gatehouse 1980, 1983, 1985a, 1985b). In doing this, many of its projects and publications have been focused on people's work and leisure experiences within a local community (Wilson 1980; Fulcher 1981; Gatehouse 1980). Its publications show that paid employment takes particular local forms, and so too does leisure. It also shows in a very vivid way how complexly gendered leisure and local traditions are.

The 'big sister' of oral-history writing projects is A People's Autobiography of Hackney (London). Its first and perhaps most famous publications are the two collections on *Working Lives* (A People's Autobiography of Hackney 1977a, 1977b), which contain tape-recorded, transcribed and edited accounts of people's experience of paid employment, as well as some written directly. Combined with these written accounts are photographs of people at work. The result is a fascinating and detailed account of varieties of paid employment in Hackney from 1905 to 1977, showing the varied ways in which people not only moved in and out of paid employment or changed jobs, but also managed the competing demands and attractions of other kinds of work commitments and of leisure.

Oral-history writing projects[5] demonstrate the extraordinarily complex relationships that exist between a 'community of place' and a 'community of people' and show how changes in one can lead to an entirely different dynamic between them. The work of the Sistren Collective is particularly relevant here, but so too is that of A People's Autobiography, for change can be wrought by 'development' of a different kind from that of mass emigration. They also show clearly that 'community' is a sexed, raced, aged and classed phenomenon, experienced in radically different ways by females and by males, by people of colour, of different ages, and with different material and social resources at their disposal.

Some communities have experienced large-scale change over the course of the century, some in a relatively short period of time, like Caribbean societies or some areas in Britain during the Blitz, others over a longer time-scale, like many British inner-city areas. Although not usually thought of in such terms, ageing itself is a momentous social change in and an essential part of the life-course of an individual. The autobiographical materials produced by such projects enable us not only to understand but also to appreciate better and re-evaluate age and experience.

Ageing is something which – if we are lucky enough – happens to us all. To grow older is to accumulate years and so experiences of change of different kinds, including expectations concerning 'fit and proper' paid employment, work outside of employment, leisure, for different groups of people. To accumulate experience is to accumulate knowledge, and knowledge is one of the fundamental means that people have for empowering themselves.

For working-class people, to have achieved age is to have survived, to have 'come through' in spite of many barriers and difficulties. In some ways to 'tell the tale' of one's own past is comparable to telling tales of myth and legend within particular ethnic communities. In this sense 'myth' is indispensable to women's survival, for it enables a transformation and transcending of the everyday as well as a re-evaluation of it, and thus it helps fuel social change in women's lives.

Oral-history writing projects show us that a focus on women's 'leisure' or 'work' that does not take full account of the particular and individual location of these, and the way they are shaped by local community circumstance, is immensely problematic. To ignore such things is to strip from the concepts of work and leisure the very features that give them relevance and meaning in women's lives. These projects show the exact form that particular conjunctions of work and leisure take in people's lives over time and through changing circumstance. They also demonstrate how the 'local and personal' can be caught up in and transformed by the international, as with mass emigration from the Caribbean, or by the impact of the decline of empire and markets on local British economies and communities.

Conclusions?

Obviously 'conclusions' in the conventional sense are not an appropriate end to a paper concerned with describing sources rather than presenting 'findings'. Given that this description of sources has been located within an argument concerning the useful role of historical data sources in exploring women's work and leisure, I conclude by briefly reiterating the main reasons why I think that historical sources are so important.

Neither 'work' nor 'leisure' are unchanging absolutes, nor are they to be adequately understood in isolation from each other. To more adequately understand and conceptualize women's work and leisure we need to understand not only change but also the shape that changing work and leisure takes in the totality of someone's life. This does not mean through a 'snapshot' approach, which takes a thin slice out of someone's life at one particular moment, but rather developing means by which we can see the relationship of particular 'moments' to the whole. Historical autobiographical materials provide such means; they also provide the ability to compare the details of different people's lives around the changing and complex totality of these.

Notes

1. I do not deal in this paper with the nature and shape of the feminist contribution to leisure studies, as other papers in this collection do so. In addition to these, a useful and comprehensive guide is contained in Deem (1986).
2. See here the Spotland poorhouse diaries (Cole 1984) for a record of the life of an institution over the period 1836 to 1845. Rochdale held out the longest of any area against the 1834 Poor Law Amendment Act with its requirement to form large-scale 'union' workhouses to deal with destitute persons: the Spotland poorhouse continued dispensing a pre-1834 amalgam of outdoor relief and a much more humane small-scale local poorhouse.
3. That is, travelling to and from work, breaks for meals, preparing for work, and so on.
4. Many people might object to this dubbing of Virginia Woolf as a lesbian. I recognize that defining just what is 'lesbian' is immensely complex and problematic (is it what one has done, what one feels, what other people think . . . ?): however, I take it as axiomatic that defining Virginia Woolf as 'heterosexual' is at least as problematic –·indeed, I would argue, more so.
5. The Gatehouse Project and A People's Autobiography are members of the Federation of Worker Writers and Community Publishers: and a full list of the autobiographies and other publications of the projects involved in the Federation is available. The address for this is Federation of Worker Writers & Community Publishers, c/o Gatehouse Project, St Lukes, Sawley Road, Miles Platting, Manchester M10 3LY.

References

Abenstern, Michelle (1985) 'Women's leisure in Rochdale in the 1920s and 30s', paper given at the Social History Society Annual Conference on 'Sex and Gender', Reading.

Burnett, John (1977) *Useful Toil: Autobiographies of Working People from the 1820s to the 1920s*, Harmondsworth, Penguin.

(1982) *Destiny Obscure: Autobiographies of Childhood, Education and Family from the 1820s to the 1920s*, Harmondsworth, Penguin.

Burnett, John, Vincent, David and Mayall, David (1985, 1986, 1987) *The Autobiography of the Working Class*, Vols. 1, 2 and 3, Brighton, Harvester Press.

Calder, Angus and Sheridan, Dorothy (1984) *Speak for Yourself*, London, Jonathan Cape.

Cole, John (1984) *Down Poorhouse Lane*, Littleborough, George Kelsall Publishing.

Deem, Rosemary (1986) *All Work and No Play? The Sociology of Women and Leisure*, Milton Keynes, Open University Press.

Driberg, Tom (1977) *Ruling Passions*, London, Jonathan Cape.

Field, Joanna, (1934) *A Life of One's Own*, London, Virago Press.

(1937) *An Experiment in Leisure*, London, Virago Press.

Fletcher, Anne (1985) 'Women and leisure', unpublished M. Phil thesis, University of Birmingham.

Ford Smith, Honor (1986) 'Introduction', in Sistren, *Lionheart Gal*, London, The Women's Press.

Fulcher, Margaret (1981) *A Woman on Her Own*, Manchester, Gatehouse.

Gatehouse (1980) *Tip of My Tongue: Women's Experiences at Home and at Work*, Manchester, Gatehouse.

(1983) *Where Do We Go from Here? Adult Lives without Literacy*, Manchester, Gatehouse.

(1985a) *Just Lately I Realise: Stories from West Indian Lives*, Manchester, Gatehouse.

(1985b) *Day In, Day Out: Memories of North Manchester from Women in Monsall Hospital*, Manchester, Gatehouse.

Green, Eileen, Hebron, Sandra and Woodward, Diana (1985) 'A woman's work', *Sport and Leisure*, July/August, pp. 36–8.

(1987) *Leisure and Gender*, final report to ESRC/Sports Council, London, Sports Council.

Harrison, Tom (ed.) (1943) *The Pub and the People*, London, Cressett Library.

Hong Kingston, Maxine (1977) *Woman Warrior*, London, Picador.

Hudson, Derek (ed.) (1972) *Munby: Man of Two Worlds*, London, John Murray.

Jennings, Humphrey and Madge, Charles (eds.) (1937) *Mass-Obversation Day Survey May 12 1937*, London, Faber & Faber.

Lahr, John (1986) *The Diaries of Joe Orton*, Harmondsworth, Penguin.

Last, Nella (1981) *Nella Last's War*, London, Sphere.

Mass-Observation (1939) *Britain*, London, Cresset Library.

Matthews, William (1950) *British Diaries*, Berkeley, University of California Press.

Michison, Naomi (1985) *Among You Taking Notes*, Oxford, Oxford University Press.

A People's Autobiography of Hackney (1977a) *Working Lives 1900–1945*, London, Centerprise.

(1977b) *Working Lives 1945–1977*, London, Centerprise.

Ponsonby, Arthur (1923) *English Diaries*, London, Methuen.

Seacole, Mrs ([1857] 1984) *Wonderful Adventures of Mrs Seacole in Many Lands*, London, Falling Wall Press.

Sistren (1986) *Lionheart Gal*, London, The Women's Press.

Stanley, Liz (ed.) (1984) *The Diaries of Hannah Cullwick*, London, Virago Press.

(1987) *Essays on Women's Work and Leisure and 'Hidden' Work*, Studies in Sexual Politics No. 18, Sociology Department, University of Manchester.

Thomas, W. I. and Znaniecki, Florian (1918) *The Polish Peasant in Europe and America*, 2 vols., New York, Dover Publications.

Whitbread, Helena (1988) *I Know My Own Heart: The Diaries of Anne Lister*, London, Virago Press.

Wilson, Amrit (1978) *Finding a Voice*, London, Virago Press.

Wilson, Paul (1980) *Fun at Fine Fare*, Manchester, Gatehouse.

Woolf, Virginia, (1977, 1978, 1980, 1982, 1984) *Diaries*, London, Hogarth Press.

PART 2

Facing changes

In this part of the book we explore the continuities and changes in women's leisure experiences by focusing on some of the critical periods of transition in women's lives – the forming and undoing of heterosexual partnerships, the turbulent changes around adolescence, the confinements associated with becoming a mother, and the gradual adjustments to life in later years. These transitional periods, commonly referred to as life-cycle stages, are often multi-layered, incorporating a complex web of changes in women's lives. These may include biological processes, such as ageing, pregnancy and childbirth, culturally defined status transitions denoted by, for example, motherhood and retirement, and the socio-economic adjustments that accompany severances like redundancy, divorce or leaving home.

One of the main attempts to map out how leisure changes over women's and men's lives is in the context of family leisure and the family life-cycle (Rapoport and Rapoport 1975). Although transitional periods often encompass changes within both private and public domains, all too often conceptualizations of turning-points in women's lives focus on the private sphere, or family life-cycle. This ignores the fact that there is an increasing number of women spending the majority of their adult lives in paid employment (Martin and Roberts 1984) so that life-cycle transitions are likely to have repercussions for women in public *and* private domains.

Another problem with the life-cycle approach as a way of conceptualizing the individual's progression through life is the tendency to conflate biological and social life-events. In the study of women's lives this creates a scenario of socio-biological inevitability and suggests a sequential path through the 'ages and stages' of family formation – adolescence, courtship, marriage, childrearing, 'empty nest' – regardless of individual differences (e.g. single and childless women). Women and men are increasingly unlikely to follow this unilinear progression. For example, the dynamics of family life are such that parents (and children) are now more likely to move in and out of marriages and in and out of poverty (Graham 1984). Although only a minority of women are lone parents at any one time, many more have experienced, or will experience, being a single mother before their children leave school. Furthermore, the employment profiles of women and men through the life-course are changing (Hakim 1979). For women, a two-phase work profile has emerged which relates to a rise in the employment of married women coupled with a continuing responsibility for domestic labour (Martin and Roberts 1984).

These historical changes have repercussions for women's experience of leisure during their lifetime. Both the recent survey of women's leisure in Sheffield (Green, Hebron and Woodward 1987) and Rosemary Deem's book (1986) emphasize the considerable diversity in women's leisure patterns and the meanings it has for them at different stages in their lives. In general terms, it is single, childless and employed women who enjoy the most 'free' time while married women with young children are the most constrained. Between these extremes there are many interesting variations however. For example, lone mothers are found to enjoy a greater sense of independence and freedom in their social lives than their married counterparts, even though their material resources are often tighter (Wimbush 1986).

Whether looking at the family, employment or leisure, the matrix of changes which women encounter at different periods in their lives reveals a complexity that is gender-specific. During transitional periods, the adjustments that women have to make are far more wide-ranging than those encountered by men at the equivalent periods in their lives. Indeed, it is just this relative complexity that has prompted some researchers to exclude women from studies of leisure around life-cycle transitions, such as retirement. Introducing a set of articles about transitions and turning points in women's lives, Patricia Allat and Teresa Keil observed that:

> Although we lack similar documentation of men's lives, the overwhelming impression of the empirical material on the life course of women is of a complexity that contrasts with that of men. From the evidence here, this complexity is, moreover, structurally and culturally created and maintained in order to simplify men's lives.
>
> (in Allat *et al*. 1987: 3)

Thus, to 'simplify men's lives' part of women's customary caring role is to support and cushion male partners during critical turning-points in their lives (e.g. retirement, unemployment, redundancy, strikes). The social construction of retirement as primarily a male transition, for example, means that there is little recognition of the attendant tensions, frictions and sacrifices that women experience during this period in later life; loss of privacy and personal leisure time may also be compounded by a loss of independent employment and income.

In analysing the usefulness of the life-cycle approach in understanding the changing patterns and meanings of leisure through women's lives, Rosemary Deem (1987) stresses that the impact of ethnicity, social class and employment status can have as much, if not more, impact on women's leisure as life-cycle stages. Moreover, as the chapters within this section clearly illustrate, the overarching structures and ideology of patriarchy act as continuous constraints at all stages in the life-cycle, circumscribing women's access and right to personal leisure and, in the process, facilitating men's.

In common with the 'life-course' perspective, the writers in this part emphasize the context of historical change and the notion of 'agency' – the active response of individuals to structural and ideological constraints. The strong influence of male power on women's leisure opportunities, friendships and social networks throughout their lives is thus a continuing theme in the following chapters. Women's response to this aspect of gender relations is considered in terms of negotiations with parents, male partners and others about appropriate recreational activities and, more generally, about their access to resources for, and their right to, personal leisure.

Starting from the point that most women in heterosexual partnerships share common personal experiences of male control and influence on their leisure, Eileen Green and Sandra Hebron (Ch.3) begin this part with an analysis of the influence of male partners on women's free time and leisure participation. They draw mainly on the study of women's leisure in Sheffield (Green, Hebron and Woodward 1987) to explore how and why women's leisure patterns become shaped within heterosexual partnerships. They examine three particular phases of coupledom: courtship, cohabitation and splitting up. The power of men's influence is explained in terms of the ideological construction of coupledom and family life and the inequitable division of labour and material resources between partners.

Vivienne Griffiths (Ch.4) and Jennifer Mason (Ch.6) continue the theme of how women manage heterosexual relationships, the former in relation to young single women facing the transitions to adulthood, boyfriends and work or unemployment. Mason looks at how older married women face the many adjustments that are focused around retirement and their repercussions for established personal, marital and domestic routines. For both Griffiths and Mason, leisure is seen as an important arena in which gender relations are expressed, legitimated and challenged.

Viv Griffiths describes young women's struggle to maintain their established girlfriends at the conventional changeover time from girlfriends to boyfriends. In comparison, the older women described by Jennifer Mason seem to find it more difficult to renegotiate their husbands' long-established behaviour patterns and attitudes. Particularly entrenched are ideas about the sexual division of labour, where the husband's role is that of 'helper'. Assumptions about the desirability of 'togetherness' and spending more time together as a couple once the man retires have differing consequences for women's and men's personal leisure interests and friendships.

Viv Griffiths' emphasis on the value of female friendships for support and company in negotiating transitions is a theme continued in Erica Wimbush's chapter (Ch.5) about the social life of mothers with young children. She emphasizes the efforts which many mothers make to carve out space for themselves and the importance they attach to female support and the company of other mother-friends. The meanings attributed to leisure during this period of the life-course are constructed within the broader context of women's life-styles as carers of young children (and for many, male partners as well) which is characterized by diminished autonomy, social isolation and fragmented friendship networks. In order to maintain or establish regular, independent leisure, some mothers were prepared to negotiate with male partners over childcare and become drawn into ideological struggles with other women about the appropriate role of mothers.

Significant hallmarks of feminist analyses of individuals' progressions through the 'life-course' include the crucial relevance of gender in the shaping of transitions and the complexity of these in women's lives. This makes it imperative that studies of single strands (e.g. leisure) are located within the broader context of life-styles and communities. Furthermore, feminists have alerted us to the need to map trajectories which differ from the prescribed 'normal' sequential progression through the life-cycle stages. In this section we have also stressed the changing nature of women's responses to gendered social relations at different stages in their lives, demonstrating that leisure is an important sphere in which these struggles occur. In doing this, these chapters highlight the process of empowerment rather than passive acceptance.

References

Allat, Patricia; Keil, Teresa; Bryman, Alan and Bytheway, Bill (eds.) (1987) *Women and the Life-Cycle: Transitions and Turning Points*, London, Macmillan.

Deem, Rosemary (1986) *All Work and No Play: The Sociology of Women and Leisure*, Milton Keynes, Open University Press.

(1987) ' "My husband says I'm too old for dancing": women, leisure and life-cycles', in Pat Allat, Teresa Keil, Alan Bryman and Bill Bytheway (eds.) *Women and the Life-Cycle: Transitions and Turning Points*, London, Macmillan.

Graham, Hilary (1984) *Women, Health and the Family*, Brighton, Wheatsheaf Books.

Green, Eileen Hebron, Sandra and Woodward, Diana (1987) *Leisure and Gender: A Study of Sheffield Women's Experiences*, final report to the ESRC/Sports Council Joint Panel on Leisure Research, London, Sports Council.

Hakim, Catherine (1979) *Occupational Segregation*, Department of Employment Research Paper 9.

Martin, Jean and Roberts, Ceridwen (1984) *Women and Employment: A Lifetime Perspective*, London, HMSO.

Rapoport, Rhona and Rapoport, Robert (1975), *Leisure and the Family Life-Cycle*, London, Routledge & Kegan Paul.

Wimbush, Erica (1986) *Women, Leisure and Well-Being*, Edinburgh, Centre for Leisure Research.

3

Leisure and male partners

EILEEN GREEN AND SANDRA HEBRON

One of the most important ideological constructions for leisure is the representation of romanticized versions of coupledom and family life. Jerry Rodnitzky (1987) contends that the impact of mainstream feminism on American popular culture has led to overtly sexist representations of women being replaced by a particularly rosy representation of heterosexuality. We might take issue with just how 'new' these representations are, but happy couples are indeed presented as the norm, with or without children to complete the family unit. What is rarely visible is the extent to which joint leisure often relies upon the female partner providing the domestic labour and/or childcare necessary to sustain family- or couple-based activities. Servicing of this imposes restraints on women's opportunities to experience leisure of their own choosing (see Ch. 12). Another crucial omission from these pictures of family leisure is the more negative aspects of such togetherness.

This chapter focuses upon the extent to which the presence or absence of a significant male partner influences women's free time and the implications this has for both the nature and extent of their involvement in leisure. Given that the concern of this section is with periods of transition and change, we are restricting our discussion to three particular stages: courtship and becoming a couple; marriage or cohabitation; splitting up and becoming single again. Whilst we are aware of the fact that other major changes in the area of partnerships, such as bereavement, may have equally as dramatic an effect on women's leisure as the process we refer to as 'splitting up', an examination of their effects is beyond the scope of our data and this chapter.

An analysis of male partners' impact on women's leisure necessarily draws upon individual case studies and experiences – not just those of the women we interviewed as part of our research but also those of our families, friends and ourselves. However, individuals are of course situated within and actively reproduce the broader social context. Our own work indicates the problems inherent in trying to explain women's access to leisure in terms of separate variables or constraints. We are rarely constrained by one 'independent variable'; rather, it is the relationship between a number of determining and often themselves interrelated factors which either facilitate, or more usually circumscribe, women's leisure. The influence of male partners will obviously vary depending upon a host of other considerations, not the least of which are social class, ethnicity, age and life-cycle stage. More individual (although none the less socially constructed) characteristics such as personality, attitudes and opinions will also intervene in the process. Whilst we appreciate these facts, we are confident that male partners do influence women's leisure in significant ways and that most women in heterosexual partnerships share some common experiences in this respect.

Our starting-point for discussing the impact of male partners takes as given that women and men are unequal, that Western society and its institutions are male dominated. We are not going to reiterate the arguments here as to why this is so. What we do want to stress is the importance of ideology in upholding and maintaining unequal relations in a society divided along lines of gender, race and class. Ideologies of gender and gender-appropriate behaviour permeate all areas of life, not least leisure. What is perhaps ironic is that leisure is itself a key site of ideological work, as defined by Stuart Hall (1977). Many of the ideological 'messages' are carried through texts which we read in our leisure time: television, magazines, films, newspapers. Women's lives (and men's) are presented in particular ways which generally obscure a whole range of women's experiences. The messages are clear, although how we interpret them depends upon our own social position, beliefs and value systems.

We hope to look at the relationship of dominant representations of coupledom and family life to women's own experiences. Many of the women we spoke to clearly make sense of their lives within a framework which posited heterosexual coupledom as an ideal, but an ideal which has to be worked at and negotiated. Some of the most illuminating comments were from women for whom the negotiations had broken down.

Courtship and becoming a couple

Our own Sheffield-based study (Green, Hebron and Woodward 1987b and forthcoming) contained over a hundred women defined as single. These were mainly young women, many of whom were living in their parent's home. We found that this group compared favourably with most other women in terms of their experiences of leisure. On the whole they had greater access to leisure, having more time and disposable income and fewer domestic commitments than other women. In common sense terms at least, youth and leisure are strongly associated, with youth being seen as a period of freedom and enjoyment which comes before the serious business of 'settling down'. But it would be wrong to assume that all young people have equal access to leisure opportunities. Young people are divided along the lines of gender, class and race, with employment status also becoming an increasingly important division.

Although not explicitly concerned with 'leisure', the literature around youth subcultures demonstrates the difference between male and female experiences of leisure during adolescence and early adulthood (Hall and Jefferson 1976; Brake 1980). Such studies typically, though not exclusively, focus upon working-class youth, but whilst there are differences in the precise nature of the imagery, the representation of one set of activities and interests as masculine, and another as feminine, is not restricted to one class. From an early age girls learn that finding a 'steady' man should be their main aim in life. In Western culture a heavy emphasis is placed on the importance of the 'love match'. Leisure is an important source of opportunities for meeting romantic partners, or alternatively it offers the time and space to spend time with potential or actual partners. All the research literature suggests that when women do 'pair off' and become part of a couple, their leisure changes considerably (Griffin 1986; Hobson 1979, 1981; Rapoport and Rapoport 1975).

Certainly by the time that women are in their later teens, the most common pattern is for women to spend time with boyfriends at the expense of time spent with alternative companions such as family or friends. This can cause some resentment on the part of those left behind. In our study a number of the single women suggested that whilst they themselves would like to keep up contact with their own friends, they saw the drift away as somehow inevitable: 'I suppose you don't mean to, but you sort of cut your friends off a bit, don't see them as much' (Green, Hebron and Woodward 1987b: 73). Given that many of their friends were also involved in steady relationships, any attempts to hang on to female friends would require considerable determination, energy and planning.

What was interesting was the way in which couple-based leisure quickly becomes the norm, with female friendships taking on a more subsidiary role. Although there are exceptions to this, for many young women female friends are put on the back burner at least temporarily and sometimes for good, although they may reappear as central during times of crisis. Keeping up relationships with female friends was often viewed as a kind of safety net. Women recognized that the couple might split up, in which case it was felt to be important to have female friends to fall back on. However, women's attempts to keep up their own friendships were not always successful, particularly where such intentions ran counter to the boyfriends' wishes.

In their work on leisure and the life-cycle, the Rapoports (1975) draw on Diana Leonard's study of courtship in Swansea (Leonard 1980) and note how, during courtship, young women's leisure interests are subsumed under the interests of the boyfriend. Couples tend to go out with 'his' friends, usually other couples. The young men are already mates and the young women are expected to get on. Whilst having a steady boyfriend can confer some status on young women in the eyes of their peers, the drawback is that it generally makes the women dependent on the men for their social life. A more recent study in Birmingham by Chris Griffin confirms that this pattern still holds: 'If a young woman started to go out with a fairly regular boyfriend she gradually lost touch with her girlfriends, often at the young man's insistence' (Griffin 1986: 61). She also points out that there was rarely an equivalent breakdown of male friendships if a young man began to 'go steady' with a girlfriend. Similarly, a woman in our study commented, 'It was only when he took me out that it was different. He used to go to football matches and everything as normal, whereas I'd lost my friends so it was just sitting in the house and washing my hair' (single parent, late twenties).[1]

We found a persistent tradition in Sheffield of Friday night being seen as 'lads' night out, with Saturday nights being reserved for going out as couples. Viv Griffiths (Ch.4) found a similar pattern in her West Yorkshire study. Given that many of the young Sheffield women saw joint leisure as an ideal, Friday nights could sometimes be a cause of conflict within couples. What seems to happen amongst younger women is a kind of bargaining or exchange system, whereby the women respond by arranging their own single-sex nights out when their boyfriends are not available. What is important is the extent to which it is the men's leisure which sets the tone, with the women making their own arrangements to fit around those of the men. The women's nights out are a response, a way of getting their own back. This is as much the case now as it was when the Rapoports wrote, 'Gradually the girl's social affiliations change from a group to a network in which *she associates with others according to the nature of her relations with boyfriends at the time*' (Rapoport and Rapoport 1975, emphasis added). Related to this is the way in which male partners exercise some degree of control over the possibilities for women to have separate, individual leisure activities. We have already seen how being part of a couple cuts down the amount of time available for spending with friends or family. This may be inevitable given the finite amount of time which is free for leisure, but what is not inevitable is the way in which boyfriends put pressure on young women to restrict their leisure activities and companions. We have discussed elsewhere the repertoire of controlling strategies which men can draw upon (see Ch.12; see also Green, Hebron and Woodward 1987a). It is clear from our study that even at quite early stages in a relationship it was not unusual for women to be experiencing forms of control or restriction which they were not altogether happy with. One woman cited her boyfriend as the major constraint on her leisure: 'I do feel a bit restricted sometimes, but that's because of my boyfriend not because of my parents' (single woman, aged 21). All the young women interviewed experienced the independence they did have as a necessarily temporary phenomenon, closely linked to being single. They expected things to change in relation to marriage: 'I think . . . it depends whether you're married or not. I could do what I want because I'm single, but if you're married you've got ties and you've got to be in at certain times and things' (quoted in Green, Hebron and Woodward 1987b: 72). For these young women marriage was a question of 'when' rather than 'if'.

The experiences of adolescence, courtship and eventual coupledom are obviously quite different for women from different ethnic backgrounds or cultures. Amrit Wilson's work (1978) provides some useful insights into the lives of Asian women in Britain. Because of the significance of reputation, young Asian women are actively discouraged from having boyfriends: 'Reputation is a tremendous conservative force, controlling to differing extents, everyone in Asian societies. It is related directly to male pride or *Izzat*. Disgracing your family means hurting the Izzat of your fathers or brothers, and Izzat can be easily hurt or even destroyed' (Wilson 1978: 104). She notes how women's friendships and social networks are just one area where young women are expected to exercise care, but as she points out, 'in spite of all these rules, or perhaps because of them, many girls do do that risky and wicked thing, they do go out with boys' (ibid.: 102). However, most of the girls she spoke to were planning to go through with arranged marriages, and more than this, they 'believed' in them. On marriage, Asian women move from the control of their family of origin to the control of their husband and his family. The kinds of negotiations with male partners over access to leisure which many of the white women in our study entered into would be untenable for many Asian women.

If anything, leisure is even less visible as a separate area in the lives of women from ethnic minority cultures, but there is often a strong emphasis upon the handing down of black culture through activities which are traditionally associated with leisure in the West: music, songs and storytelling. A group of Afro-Caribbean women cite their mothers as crucial in this process of cultural transmission:

> we feel that our informal culture centres around our mothers. In black families our mothers are always the lynch-pins. Our traditions around food, clothes and ways of working come from our mothers. They're the ones who really organise family life and we're always more conscious of their presence than our fathers (which isn't to deny the influence of our fathers of course).
> (from a discussion about the Black Women's Radio Workshop in Bryan,
> Dadzie and Scafe 1985: 196)

Young black women are therefore especially likely to be influenced by their mothers and other female relatives when it comes to courtship and living with men.

Living together

Because there is a growing feminist literature on family life, and to a lesser extent on coupledom, we plan to be brief in our discussion here, although we do need to restate the diversity of family forms which do exist in contemporary Britain (Gittins 1985). Perhaps the general point we can make is that living with a male partner, whether husband or cohabitee, means less independent leisure for women. In fact it often also means less time for leisure of any kind. Living together does not just entail a change of social status, it also means an increased domestic load. Amongst the couples we interviewed, regardless of social class, life-style, stage in the life cycle and so on, we did not find a single household with an equal division of domestic work and childcare. In all cases, to a greater or (more often) lesser degree, men 'helped'. Some women, for example those with paid employment, were likely to receive more help than others. The fact that the majority of both men and women interviewed felt that men have more free time than women is itself a recognition of this inequality. But the inequality was more often than not taken for granted.

It is not just the quantity of time for leisure which changes but also how the time is spent. Being part of a recognized couple or family is the point at which, for women at least, the full weight of the ideology of joint or family leisure is brought to bear. In our interviews the majority of the married women said that the greatest part of their leisure time is spent with their husband, or with husband and children. Whilst the same was also true of some men, they were far more likely than the women to have retained some regular leisure time spent away from home and family. For the men, this was regarded as natural and normal, related to some masculine need or entitlement. A minority of the women had regular nights out, either women-only nights out or else nights used to attend classes (such as badminton, flower arranging) or other activities. For most of the women such nights out tended to be more sporadic. Many of the men said that they would be surprised if their partners expressed a desire for independent leisure, saying this would be 'out of character' as their wives had never made a habit of going out without them. Some also felt that it would signal some kind of problem or breakdown in the relationship, again drawing on the notion that whilst it is normal for men to have interests away from the family, for women it involves a disruption to normality and established order. Linked to this is the way in which women's nights out without their partners were significantly more likely to cause conflict than the men's nights out. This was in spite of the fact that men's nights out were generally both more regular and more frequent (see Ch. 12).

Men and women we interviewed largely shared the opinion that men are entitled to some independent leisure in a way that women are not. This in part harks back to the assumption that leisure is earned through paid work, a notion which is remarkably persistent given the current changes in the labour market. Other research on family life, if not specifically on leisure, shows how these kinds of differences span across class boundaries. Pauline Hunt (1980) illustrates how working-class wives accommodate to husbands' work patterns. Andrew Tolson (1977), in his study of masculinity, compares working- and middle-class experience and has this to say about the working-class male: 'He goes out to work for the others (the wife and family) partly on condition that they re-affirm his patriarchal status' (Tolson 1977: 67). One area where this reaffirmation certainly takes place is leisure. Tolson's study assumed an employed male head of household. An interesting finding from our study is the way in which during times when the patriarchal status is threatened, for example through male unemployment, leisure may be the key area where it is bolstered. Thus even in low-income unemployed couples the male partner was far more likely to have at least one night out than the woman was. Where financial resources are tight, men's leisure is prioritized even if this means sacrifices elsewhere. This was seen as important in boosting men's morale and raising flagging spirits.

In moving on to think about masculinity and middle-class men, Tolson comments on the attitude of superiority of the middle-class husband: 'Ideally it is he who chooses the couple's social activities; he who selects acquaintances and friends' (Tolson 1977: 95). This is echoed by Edgell in his study of middle-class couples. He sums up a number of telling examples by saying, 'it is usually the husband who is most dominant in this as in other 'important' areas of family life' (Edgell 1980: 86). In a similar way one of our male interviewees explained, 'some of the friends we currently have were friends of mine from before we were married'. He and his wife have been married for over twenty years and the only contact she has with her friends from before the marriage is via Christmas cards. In terms of time and other resources, most of the middle-class women in the Sheffield study had more potential access to leisure. However, they were still dependent upon male approval of their activities, which we found was more forthcoming in relation to traditionally 'feminine' activities such as keep-fit or floral art. The effect of male approval in determining women's participation in leisure outside the home is also discussed in Erica Wimbush's Edinburgh study (Wimbush 1986).

Linking a theorization of masculinity to changes in the population structure, Jeff Hearn notes that:

> changes in family structure follow from the population ageing, in Western societies at least. More men survive into old age; more marriages include substantial non-fertile years; and more men need more caring, often in practice provided by women. [Again] the impact of these changes is likely to be mixed, with more visibility of older men and yet the perpetuation of pre-existing patterns, for example between wives and husbands.
>
> (Hearn 1987: 8)

The generation of women influenced by feminism and looking forward to independent leisure when their children are grown, may still be accommodating to the needs of male partners caught in the timewarp of traditional masculinity.

Much of the existing work on masculinity deals first and foremost with the experiences of white men (and women). However, masculinity is not only cut across by class but also by race. There are cultural differences in terms of how being male is defined, but it seems to us there are also considerable similarities. In her study of 'Needletown', Sallie Westwood (1984) looks at the strategies which Asian women use to gain some autonomy and independence and highlights the importance of the predominantly female culture of the workplace in this process. The factory provided a space where both black and white women could be temporarily free of some of the more constraining aspects of their domestic lives, albeit within the confines of paid employment. Westwood cites examples such as Asian women eating 'forbidden' foods in the canteen, or in some cases engaging in banter with male employees.

One point worth noting is the way in which having children breaks down the pattern of joint leisure which was common amongst the Sheffield women. Some of the financially better-off households were able to pay for a babysitter and so free both partners to go out. What was more common was that couples engaged in mainly separate activities, with one partner minding the child(ren) whilst the other went out. This did not mean that both partners went out the same amount. We have already commented on how men are assumed to be more automatically entitled to leisure outside the home than women. This is reinforced by ideologies of good mothering which make women feel guilty if they leave children, particularly young children, for reasons other than essential errands or the very occasional break. Even the opportunities for a break away from children, which most of the mothers in our study felt was desirable or necessary, were more likely to take place during the day, when children could be left with female friends or relatives. A common pattern then seems to be for women's leisure to pass from primarily joint leisure, through a period of individual and considerably restricted leisure, to more child- and family-centred leisure as children grow older.

Splitting up/becoming 'single' again

With more and more couples experiencing some kind of breakdown in their relationships, be it separation or divorce, the traditional progression through the life-cycle stages is becoming less common. Separation from a partner and the end of a relationship are often traumatic transitions from one status to another. However amicable the separation may be, the repercussions are likely to be felt in all areas of life. This might be especially so for women who learn to prioritize family and home in a way which many men do not. We found that leisure was one of the key areas affected by splitting up with a partner, whatever the reason for making the break. For all the women we interviewed, the separation from their husbands had meant being 'on their own'. Although some of them had themselves initiated the break, none of them had done so because they were involved with another man. Where couples had split up because of infidelity, it had been the husbands who had been involved in extra-marital relationships.

Most of us recognize the way in which women are accorded social status on the basis of their relationships with men: as wives, mothers, daughters and so on. Splitting up with a man may mean not only a loss of confidence but also loss of status and loss of identity. All the women spoke about the ways in which they needed to readjust to their new status, and how lengthy this readjustment had been. This was particularly so for the women whose husbands had left them after lengthy marriages. The women had been typical wives in the ways in which they had spent their leisure time. All of them had had some joint leisure, although this tended to grow less frequent as the relationship moved towards its end, especially if the husband was already seeing somebody else. None of the women had had any regular social activities independent of their husbands. As we might expect, the women's social lives and networks had been built around their roles as wives or mothers. To be no longer a part of a couple had drastic effects.

One of the main changes was in terms of the companions that women spent their time with. As one of the women we spoke to put it, 'You've got to start reshaping your life from the beginning, so then you have to start making enquiries about other people who are on their own and what they do and see if you can get out with them a bit' (single parent, early forties). Typically, family became more important during the period immediately following splitting up, with the women having a greater reliance on their relatives, particularly on their own parents where this was possible. For several of the women, relatives had stepped into the gap left when couple-based leisure had ceased. Female relatives in particular had easier access to women's homes when their partners had gone. They were aware of the situation and generally were reliable sources of support. However, in most though not all cases, relatives were more likely to babysit and free the women to go out rather than to become leisure companions themselves. The exception to this was women's own children, who were often a major source of comfort and companionship after the break up of a relationship. This was not always unproblematic, given that the women felt there were only very limited facilities provided for women on their own with children.

An even greater problem which all the women had experienced was the lack of opportunities for leisure outside the home available to women on their own. This, combined with the loss of friends and the restricted nature of their social networks, increased the loneliness and isolation felt by the women. The loss of personal and social confidence after the breakdown of their marriages made them very uneasy about going out on their own, but given the lack of companions, in some cases this was the only option open to them. It is significant that the majority of the single parents we interviewed had joined one or other of the local organizations which specifically offer leisure activities and social gatherings for the divorced or separated. Even so, the re-entry into social life can be traumatic as this woman found on her first visit to a singles club: 'I just sat outside in the car for twenty minutes, I just daren't go in, I was trembling from head to foot' (quoted in Green, Hebron and Woodward 1987b). It is indicative of the extent to which so much of social life is based around couples, around women having a male partner, that women who find themselves without one are regarded (or may regard themselves) as such anomalies that they are ghettoized into clubs where they mix exclusively with other people in the same position. To a limited extent the same is true for men, although we would argue that separated or divorced men do have more opportunities for leisure. They are less likely than women to have given up their own friends and interests during the relationship; they may be in paid employment which offers some scope for socialising; and most certainly it is more acceptable for them to go to public leisure venues on their own than it is for women to do so. One of the women we spoke to told us how it had taken her over four years to build up her social life and that she still finds it difficult to cope in a world which at least seems to be completely dominated by couples.

What was more positive about this group of women was the extent to which they had all managed to take advantage of their new status. All of them felt able to be more flexible in their domestic routines and were more able to arrange their time to suit themselves, although the needs of children did still have to be taken into account. We asked the women to comment on how far their leisure and social lives were different from when they had been wives. With one exception all the responses were positive. Some of the women mentioned leisure as a source of conflict with their previous partners, and saw this as contributing to the breakdown of the relationship:

Q. Has your leisure time changed a great deal since you've been separated?
A. Oh yes, yes.
Q. Do you think it's changed for the better?
A. Definitely, definitely (laughing).
Q. What was it like before?
A. Well I wasn't free. It was like filling a time sheet in, you had to account for every minute of your day. Even if I went shopping to town he'd be spying on me. I never went out at night then.

(single parent, early fifties)

This was an extreme version of the kind of regulation that other women had experienced. Another woman said, 'I've made a whole new life. It's like being a teenager again to be honest' (single parent, early forties). She went on to talk about how difficult it was for her to know what to do with her new-found freedom: 'When I was on my own, everybody started saying things like "Well, you do what you want to do" and I sat back and thought "I don't really know what I like doing, all I've done is look after a husband and four children, what do I like doing?" you know.' Perhaps therefore it is not so surprising that some of the women were involved in new relationships and were experiencing some of the same constraints as they had with their former husbands. In some cases the women have taken on responsibility for washing, cooking and generally looking after the men. This seems to reinforce male attitudes about the women being 'their' women, rather than autonomous individuals. A woman who had built up a busy social life for herself commented on her new partner's fear and jealousy: 'I would still probably enjoy a night out with my girlfriends, but he doesn't like that . . . He thinks that I might go and meet somebody else and that would be it, so he's not too happy about it' (single parent, late forties).

Although it seems that the women are entering into relationships which apparently have at least some of the inequalities that their earlier relationships had, there is a sense in which some of the women are aware of these as potential problems. The fact that they have gone through an often difficult period of transition and have gained some confidence and autonomy does make a difference, however small, to their expectations. For the women we interviewed it is too early to say whether this will have a long-term impact.

Only one of the women declared herself to be happily 'single' again, at least to the extent that she would be unwilling to give up her autonomy and personal space: 'I'm not biased about marriage really, but I've had my freedom for so long that I don't think I want a man in the house' (single parent, early forties).

Conclusion

In this chapter we have examined the nature and extent of male partners' influence on women's leisure. More specifically we have explored the ways in which men's attitudes towards women's lives in general and their leisure in particular, serve to restrict women's freedom of choice and movement. Whilst underlining the importance of transitions for women and the effect such processes have upon their social position and consequent contacts and opportunities, we find it significant that men's leisure patterns remain more consistent despite such transitions.

Dominant ideological constructions of leisure offer sexist, and often racist, images of coupledom and family life. Perhaps the clearest message for women emphasizes the importance of accommodating their own needs and desire, in leisure as in other areas, to those of male partners and children. With the support of feminism, women are challenging such stereotypes and exposing the inequalities concealed in the 'private' areas of home and family. But the time for men to make their contribution is long overdue. Men as well as women need to recognize the political significance of interactions in the so-called private sphere, and need to recast 'the multifarious experiences, talk, conversations, use of language, touch, chores, childcare, housework and so on, that are usually considered "trivial" ' (Hearn 1987: 13), recognizing them instead as a central part of their lives, with a potential force for change.

Note

1. Unless otherwise referenced, all quotations are from our ongoing work on leisure and gender, originally funded by The Sports Council/ESRC Joint Panel on Leisure and Recreation Research.

References

Brake, Mike (1980) *The Sociology of Youth Culture and Youth Sub-Cultures*, London, Routledge & Kegan Paul.

Bryan, Beverley, Dadzie, Stella and Scafe, Suzanne (1985) *The Heart Of the Race: Black Women's Lives in Britain*, London, Virago.

Curran, J., Gurevitch, M. and Woolacott, J. (eds.) (1977) *Mass Communication and Society*, London, Edward Arnold.

Edgell, Stephen (1980) *Middle Class Couples*, London, Allen & Unwin.

Gittins, Diana (1985) *The Family in Question: Changing Households and Familiar Ideologies*, London, Macmillan.

Green, Eileen, Hebron, Sandra and Woodward, Diana (1987a) 'Women, leisure and social control', in Jalna Hanmer and Mary Maynard (eds.) *Women, Violence and Social Control*, London, Macmillan.

  (1987b) *Leisure: A Study of Sheffield Women's Leisure and Gender Experiences*, Report to ESRC/Sports Council Joint Panel on Leisure Research, London, Sports Council.

  (forthcoming) *Women's Leisure, What Leisure?*, London, Macmillan.

Griffin, Christine (1985) *Typical Girls*, London, Routledge & Kegan Paul.

Hall, Stuart (1977) 'Culture, the media and the ideological effect', in J. Curran, M. Gurevitch and J. Woolacott (eds.) *Mass Communication and Society*, London, Edward Arnold.

Hall, Stuart and Jefferson, Tony (eds.) (1976) *Resistance through Rituals*, London, Hutchinson.

Hanmer, Jalna and Maynard, Mary (eds.) (1987) *Women, Violence and Social Control*, London, Macmillan.

Hearn, Jeff (1987) 'Theorizing men and masculinity: specific problems and diverse approaches', paper presented to the Third International Interdisciplinary Congress on Women, Trinity College, Dublin, Ireland, July.

Hobson, Dorothy (1979) 'Working class women, the family and leisure', in Ziona Strelitz (ed.) *Leisure and Family Diversity*, London, Leisure Studies Association.

  (1981) 'Now that I'm married . . .', in Angela McRobbie and Trisha McCabe (eds.) *Feminism for Girls*, London, Routledge & Kegan Paul.

Hunt, Pauline (1980) *Gender and Class Consciousness*, London, Macmillan.

Leonard, Diana (1980) *Sex and Generation*, London, Tavistock.

McRobbie, Angela and McCabe, Trisha (1981) *Feminism for Girls*, London, Routledge & Kegan Paul.

Rapoport, Rhona and Rapoport, Robert (1975) *Leisure and the Family Life-Cycle*, London, Routledge and Kegan Paul.

Rodnitzky, Jerry (1987) 'The cultural response to women's liberation in the United States', paper presented to the Third International Interdisciplinary Congress on Women, Trinity College, Dublin, Ireland, July.

Strelitz, Ziona (1979) *Leisure and Family Diversity*, London, Leisure Studies Association.

Tolson, Andrew (1977) *The Limits of Masculinity*, London, Tavistock.

Westwood, Sallie (1984) *All Day, Every Day*, London, Pluto.

Wilson, Amrit (1978) *Finding a Voice: Asian Women in Britain*, London, Virago.

4

From 'playing out' to 'dossing out': young women and leisure

VIVIENNE GRIFFITHS

For adolescent girls, the transition to adulthood is a time of major development and change: in physical appearance, sexuality, relationships with parents and friends, interests, attitudes and feelings. Drawing on a study of 12- to 16-year-old girls in West Yorkshire, I shall discuss the effects of these changes on young women's leisure patterns – examining, for example, the transition from 'playing out' to 'dossing out', the relative importance of the 'culture of the bedroom' for girls of different ages, and the transition from school to work or unemployment.

Whilst acknowledging that young women's leisure activities are located within and shaped by restrictions, such as where and when they can go out, I shall stress the positive strategies which young women use to overcome constraints on their leisure time and negotiate their own space. I shall also highlight the ways in which young women resist pressures to get boyfriends and drop their girlfriends.

Little girls and young women

I spent a year in a mixed-sex comprehensive school in an industrial town in West Yorkshire, working with fifty girls aged 12 to 16, all but one working class. Thirty-four of these were in the second and third year (twenty-seven white, four Afro-Caribbean, three Asian); the remaining sixteen were in the fifth year (fifteen white, one Asian), and left school during my research.

Within the second and third years, the transition between childhood and adolescence was evident both in terms of the girls' physical appearance and their interests. Some still looked very much like little girls: they were physically immature and were not interested in fashionable clothes or hairstyles. These girls, whom I shall refer to as the 'younger-seeming' girls, tended to spend breaktime playing ball games or hopscotch. In contrast, other girls of the same age already looked like young women. They were taller and fully developed physically. Most of them also tried to make themselves look even older by means of modern 'punk' style haircuts (spiky and dyed blond), and by wearing make-up, jewellery and the then-fashionable straight slit skirts, all strictly speaking against the school rules. These girls stood around at breaktimes talking in pairs or groups. I shall refer to them as the 'mature' girls, the term they applied to themselves.

The 'mature' girls saw themselves as poles apart from the others whom they dismissed as 'babyish'. In front of their peers they would not admit to an interest in anything which might be regarded as childish or old-fashioned. In many ways they were responding to media pressures to become involved in adolescent culture. However, in reality the division between the younger-seeming and mature girls was not always so clear-cut. As I got to know the girls, I realized that many of them were at an in-between stage, combining both childlike and adolescent interests.

By the fifth year, the girls were clearly young adults and regarded themselves as such. Most were looking forward to leaving school; two had already left unofficially and were only coming in for exams.

Young women and leisure: an unproblematic picture?

Whatever their age, the girls enjoyed themselves a great deal together out of school: 'having a laugh' and 'messing about' were frequently mentioned. Most went out every evening, at least in the summer months. Whether mature or younger-seeming, the second- and third-year girls followed a wide range of leisure activities. Some went to youth clubs or other organizations, such as dancing classes; many went to local discos (see Ch.9). Others filled their time without going to any formally arranged events; for example, June and her friends 'play records, go for a walk, go out, go to t'swimming baths, go to town, go to t'pictures – when I get money'. Leisure patterns for the fifth years and school-leavers were rather different. As well as some of the activities mentioned already, they went to pubs and clubs in town, and to parties at each others' houses.

Looking at the young women's patterns of leisure in isolation suggests a largely unproblematic picture of unrestricted leisure, based on individual choice and interest. However, to leave it at that would be totally misleading and obscure important factors which actually shaped the young women's leisure.

Feminist researchers (Griffin *et al.*1982; Deem 1986) have argued that leisure has usually been defined by sociologists implicitly, if not explicitly, with reference to *men*. They stress that leisure is a problematic concept for women, not least because of the unclear division between paid work and unpaid domestic responsibilities which can take up so much of women's supposedly 'free' time.

Similarly, what adolescent girls and young women do in the evenings and at weekends cannot be fully understood without knowing what restrictions they have on their leisure time, and it is to these which I now turn.

Restrictions on young women's leisure time

The girls' leisure activities were both constructed and restricted by their class, race and gender. In the industrial towns of West Yorkshire, young working-class men and women had very little money, and there were few places to go locally. Although bus fares were subsidized (30p maximum fare outside peak times), the girls' spending money was limited (£1.50 a week average) and few of them had bikes. This restricted the young women to their immediate area, as other studies have found (McRobbie 1978; Griffin 1985).

For the many young people who faced unemployment after leaving school, this situation was unlikely to change. Those lucky enough to find employment might experience a slightly higher degree of financial independence, but leisure provision was still restricted. However, young women faced further constraints on their leisure not experienced, and indeed in some cases caused, by men.

These gender-specific restrictions affected most of the girls to a greater or lesser extent, regardless of ethnic background. However, compared to white and Afro-Caribbean girls in general, Asian girls were virtually invisible in any out-of-school activities. Laxmi Jamdagni (1980) explains that, for Asian girls, leisure centres on the home and family, and suggests that activities such as youth clubs would be considered unsuitable because they take place in public and clash with an emphasis on modesty and traditional roles in the home. However, Pratibha Parmar and Nadira Mirza question explanations premised on Asian girls' 'supposedly innumerable problems at home' (Parmar and Mirza 1981: 9) and argue that institutional racism lies behind Asian girls' invisibility in youth culture.

As a white researcher, I am wary of making generalizations based on insufficient knowledge and thus perpetuating stereotypes. There are considerable variations within Asian culture which must not be overlooked (Amos and Parmar 1981), as I certainly found in my previous research between Moslem and Sikh communities (Griffiths 1986). I must also stress that there were many white and Afro-Caribbean girls whose leisure patterns were similar to the Asian girls', spending a lot of time at home either through choice or because of restrictions. In both this and my previous research I was struck by the degree to which young women's common experiences overrode divisions of either class or race.

Three main gender-specific factors gave rise to restrictions on the young women's leisure time: (1) domestic responsibilities, (2) parental fears about safety and (3) youth clubs dominated by boys.

Domestic responsibilities

Home responsibilities were commonplace among the girls, as other studies have found (McRobbie 1978; Griffiths 1986). Most of the girls had to help with everyday domestic chores such as washing-up, cooking and cleaning. Childcare also formed a common part of the girls' home commitments. The actual amount of time spent on these jobs varied considerably, from lending an occasional hand to running the household. In almost every case these domestic commitments impinged on the girls' leisure time and were regarded as a taken-for-granted aspect of their lives.

Domestic duties seemed to increase as the girls got older and were regarded as more responsible; they impinged on the girls' leisure activities at the very stage the young women wanted to go out more often. For example, Karen went to a local youth club quite frequently in the second year, but by the third year she had stopped going 'cos I have to go babysitting'. For girls like Karen, their experience was preparation for unpaid domestic work as well as maternal duties. They were already learning to sacrifice their own time and interests to others' needs. The sense of familial obligation was strong, and in only one case (unlike McRobbie 1978) did a girl receive regular payment for these domestic duties.

Parental fears about safety

Almost all the young women I worked with experienced some restrictions on where and when they went out at night, as many other studies have found (Griffin 1985; Griffiths 1986; Lees 1986). These restrictions were generally imposed by the girls' parents because of worries for their daughter's safety at night. There are very real dangers to women from male violence and sexual harassment, which the girls themselves recognized. They talked about the threat from gangs, and violent incidents which had happened locally (including one of the 'Ripper' murders).

Many places were considered too 'rough' for the girls to go, for example the youth club or parts of town. Few girls were allowed out alone, but most were allowed to go out with a girlfriend or group of girls. However, safety in numbers was not usually considered sufficient safeguard by the girls' parents when the evenings grew dark earlier. Far more restrictions were imposed in winter, and this brought about a radical seasonal difference in many of the young women's leisure patterns. The girls had to come in earlier in winter (anything from 6.30 onwards), and some places, such as the park, which had been considered safe in summer became no-go areas. Some of the girls were not allowed out in winter at all unless there were going to be boys in the group too. This struck me as somewhat ironic since it was dangers from 'gangs of lads' which gave rise to the restriction in the first place.

Lack of transport was a further problem. Apart from the financial constraints on using public transport, buses late at night were not considered safe. Most girls had to walk to and from local activities, but this in itself was often forbidden in winter. Having parents who were able to drive their daughters to and from clubs or discos was rare and is more likely to be a middle-class phenomenon (Griffin 1985).

Such constraints were perceived as most severe by the 'mature' 12 to 14 year olds, who wanted to go out a lot, in contrast to older girls, who tended to be allowed more freedom, especially after they had left school.

Youth clubs dominated by boys

One of the few places for young people to go locally was the youth club, but very few girls went there because it was considered 'mainly for t'lads'. Facilities provided were football, pool, space invaders and table tennis, all of which were dominated by the boys. One or two girls played table tennis (always girls against boys), but otherwise they tended to watch television or stand around talking and watching the boys.

The problem of youth clubs being geared to boys' interests is now widely recognized (Youth Work Unit 1981; Nava 1984), but this youth club provided very little which interested the girls, except for trampolining once a week, and girls' nights were non-existent. Some other youth clubs in the area held discos and encouraged disco-dancing, and this was one way in which young women could find their own space within the otherwise male-dominated atmosphere (see Ch.9).

BIRMINGHAM UNIVERSITY LIBRARY

Finding their own space

In the light of the restrictions described above, which in some cases limited the young women's leisure activities considerably, I want now to look at ways in which the girls negotiated their own space, either on their own or within mixed-sex situations.

Resisting pressures to drop girlfriends

The pressures on adolescent girls to get a boyfriend and drop girlfriends are enormous, as other studies have shown (McRobbie 1978; Griffin 1985). However, all but one of the young women I worked with continued to spend a considerable part of their leisure time with their girlfriends, even when they had regular boyfriends (Griffiths 1987). Patterns of interaction varied according to what age the girls were and to what extent they were interested in boys.

Amongst the younger-seeming girls in the second and third years there was little interest in boys, so they spent almost all their time with girls only. In particular, the Afro-Caribbean and Asian girls (who went round together at school) showed a positive attitude towards maintaining their all-female friendship groups, and were scathing about the so-called 'mature' girls who were 'always mooning around after boys.'

However, even the mature girls spent very little time on their own with boys at this stage. They went round with groups of girlfriends in the evenings or in mixed-sex groups. Although they might become nominally attached to a boy within the group for a while, these relationships were very brief and the girls rarely 'went out' with a boy on an individual basis. By the third year, some girls were going out in foursomes, 'so we still see schoolmates', and they also saw their girlfriends separately.

By the fifth year, many of the young women had regular boyfriends whom they often saw individually, but they still saw their girlfriends frequently in the evenings. One way in which the girls maintained their female friendships was by having girls' times and boys' times. Schooltime, some evenings and most of the weekend were for girlfriends. Saturday nights and one or two other evenings in the week were spent with their boyfriends (if they had one). However, the young women quite often saw each other on a 'boyfriends' evening', either at parties, or by means of what I called 'chaperoning', where a girl would accompany her friend to meet her boyfriend – 'When I'm going to meet him she walks me' – and then meet her again afterwards. For most of these young women, boys were fitted into a busy social life with their girlfriends rather than the other way round. When a girl started to spend what her friends regarded as too much time with a boyfriend, they would exert some pressure, usually by teasing (as in Leonard 1980), until the girls' times were restored.

After leaving school I found, unlike most previous studies, that female friendships still persisted alongside regular boyfriends, as Kris Beuret and Lynn Makings (1987) also found in their research. The young women would see their female friends in each others' homes or when they went out locally. Friday nights were 'lasses' nights', as some studies have reported (Westwood 1984; Beuret and

Makings 1987), when groups of girlfriends would go out 'on the town', whilst Saturday evenings tended to be spent with their boyfriends. Only one young woman, who was courting, saw her boyfriend to the exclusion of female friends. Unemployed young women also found it harder to see their girlfriends, either because they had no money to go out or, in one case, because a young woman's best friend was moving away from the area to find work.

The culture of the bedroom

Angela McRobbie and Jenny Garber (1976) coined this term to describe what they regarded as one way in which girls resisted boys' domination of the streets, that is using their own homes as the base from which to explore aspects of teenage culture. Activities like reading magazines, dancing or listening to records could all be easily accommodated in the girls' bedrooms, along with talking about boys, fashion and music.

In my research, the extent to which the culture of the bedroom was evident varied considerably among different groups of friends. I found no girls who stayed at home to the exclusion of going out, but staying in had different meanings and took different forms depending on what age they were and at what stage of adolescence. Race was another important factor.

Bedroom culture depends on having your own private space, but many of the girls I worked with did not have their own bedrooms. Even when a girl had her own room, privacy was not guaranteed. For example, Janette's sister and parents often came into her room, so she and her best friend did not feel free to discuss boys or family relationships, and had to go out if they wanted to talk without interruption.

Staying at home was seen as least satisfactory to the mature 12- to 14-year-olds who wanted to go out as much as they could. Those girls who were not allowed out during winter evenings described what they did at home rather negatively, like Pam: 'Not much really. Just watch telly or play some games, just do owt.' It was as if staying in forced these girls to resort to more childlike activities. One activity mentioned by the mature girls as a positive reason for staying in was playing records. Some of the girls also stayed in to do CB radio, an activity which fitted into the culture of the bedroom rather like talking to friends on the phone. With CB there was the added interest that the girls could make new friends, often boys, as Elaine explained, 'You shout 'Breaker' and then you get talking to 'em and if you ask them for an eye-ball and you go and meet 'em somewhere.' I thought this was particularly interesting because it gave the girls a legitimate means of taking the initiative in starting relationships with boys, which might have given the girls a bad name in other circumstances (Lees 1986). The girls were also able to size up boys over the radio without necessarily having to meet them. The girls obviously enjoyed the excitement involved, the fun of adopting a radio persona such as 'Queen Bee' or 'Prawn Cocktail', and using the CB language. Apart from playing records and CB, going to each others' houses was something these girls were more likely to do in *mixed*-sex groups.

A more positive attitude to staying in was shown by the younger-seeming girls, particularly those who were friends with younger girls in their neighbourhood.

They enjoyed the ritual of going to each others' houses to play games. Other activities mentioned were knitting and reading, very different from the interests of the mature girls. The Asian girls also spent much of their time at home, usually in extended family groups rather than with friends, although they did see Asian girlfriends at weekends at the gurdwara (Sikh temple). Their interests were similar to those of the younger-seeming girls and they talked about what they did positively. These girls were certainly not involved in adolescent culture.

At the other end of the age range I found that some of the older girls also enjoyed spending evenings in with girlfriends, perhaps because they experienced fewer restrictions on their leisure time and had plenty of nights out. For young women who had left school, these evenings together were a way of keeping in touch, catching up with news and sharing problems.

The Afro-Caribbean girls in some ways came closest to McRobbie and Garber's description of bedroom culture. Like the Asian girls, these girls did much more in extended family groups, so finding privacy at home was not such a priority. They did not seem to experience such pressures as the white girls to go out or have boyfriends (Griffin 1985; Griffiths 1987), so although they were generally free to go out, they were often happy to spend evenings at home. One activity which occupied a lot of the black girls' time at home was doing each others' hair. They often came to school with beaded braids, which could take a whole evening to complete. Although doing each others' hair was a favourite activity among all the girls, in the case of the Afro-Caribbean girls it was an important part of their black identity. The black girls also spent time at home playing records, reading, helping each other with homework and talking.

Sue Lees has argued that bedroom culture is not a form of resistance for girls as Angela McRobbie and Jenny Garber suggested, but 'if anything, an adjustment to their expected feminine role which, by and large, is anticipated to centre on the home' (Lees 1986: 60). I regard this as an oversimplification. In my research, for example, activities such as CB radio enabled girls to go against an 'expected feminine role' by taking more initiative and control in starting relationships with boys. For the older girls in particular, bedroom culture was a way of resisting pressures to spend all their time with boyfriends (Griffiths 1987). I think it is important to distinguish between time spent at home on domestic chores, which did represent an 'adjustment' to traditional female roles, and time spent at home engaged in other activities. Apart from those girls with extensive home responsibilities, most of the girls spent time going out as well as time at home, as I shall now describe.

Playing out, 'dossing' and going out

As feminist researchers have pointed out, from Angela McRobbie and Jenny Garber's critique onwards (McRobbie and Garber 1976), much previous research on young people and subcultures (usually done by men) suggested that girls were invisible on the streets except as 'appendages' to boys (e.g. as girlfriends to gang members), and did not hang around in groups of girls. However, studies of delinquent girls by Lesley Shacklady Smith (1978) and Deidre Wilson (1978) showed that girls could be full members of gangs or mixed-sex groups, and could also associate in groups of girls, suggesting that the differences in findings could be attributed to the perspective and gender of the researchers. More recent research by feminists (Griffin 1985; Lees 1986) has shown that girls in general, not just deviant girls, are often highly visible on the streets in groups together, and I certainly found this in my research.

What the girls did depended on their age and stage of adolescence. There was a gradual transition from 'playing out' at the younger end, to 'dossing' or hanging around as the girls got older. Dossing was gradually replaced by 'going out', which depended on having more money and consequent access to places to go, and was therefore most evident among those young women who had left school and were at college or in work. However, there was not always a clear demarcation between these stages. In particular, the self-styled mature 12 to 14 year olds often combined playing with more adolescent activities. Most of the girls 'went out' in the more formal sense at least occasionally, to the cinema or local disco, but opportunities were more limited for the younger girls still at school.

The younger-seeming girls still spent a lot of their time 'playing out' after school. For example, Annette told me, 'We just mess about and come up to school and play in t'sandpits'. However, even some girls who regarded themselves as mature referred occasionally to playing out, usually when talking to me on their own. For example, Karen told me that she and her friends 'just sit down and talk and play stuff – hide and seek and that'. This combination of playing and talking was typical of many of the girls.

At weekends the younger-seeming girls tended to stay at home playing out with friends, although they sometimes went swimming at the Sports Centre in town. During the holidays they might go to the river or nearby countryside with their friends. I was told about butterfly-catching, pear-picking and fishing expeditions, which the girls described with great enthusiasm. As with the games they played at home, these activities were similar to those pursued by younger children. The adventurous nature of some of these trips, an aspect which the girls obviously enjoyed, also provided a contrast to some of their home-based pursuits.

For the mature second and third years upwards, the most common activity after school was hanging about together or 'dossing', as other studies have also found (Griffin 1985; Lees 1986). Although apparently casual, dossing was quite a ritualized procedure. The girls would call for each other, as they did on their way to school:

Mandy: Well we meet at one person's house, say if Lorraine says, 'Come for me at half six', then we'd all t'lot of us'll go to her house and then we'll go somewhere else so that we can meet.

Once gathered together, the girls would 'just stay on the street' or 'just wander round'. The word 'just' which often prefaced comments about dossing sounded slightly self-denigrating, as though the girls felt they should have been doing more. It also seemed to indicate a certain dissatisfaction at the lack of things to do locally. There was a constant tension between this and the girls' determination to make the best out of limited circumstances, as the following comments indicate:

Sarah: There's nothing much to do any time really is there?
Jenny: (interrupting) But we always find summat good to do, cos we go
          down t'chippy and have a laugh don't we?

The chip shop was one of the popular places to gather. The local park was another
favourite 'dossing' ground. Jeanette described what the girls did: 'Sometimes we
just walk around and sit on the swings and talk', another example of the combination of playing and talking which characterized these girls' behaviour. In spite of
its limitations, dossing was generally seen by the girls as a positive occupation,
equated with 'having a laugh'. 'Just a right good doss' was the highest accolade.

However, dossing came to an abrupt end in winter. It was very noticeable how,
during the dark winter evenings, groups of boys still hung around the street
corners but the groups of girls had virtually disappeared. Nevertheless, this does
not undermine the fact that for part of the year at least, the streets were girls' space
as much as boys'. Many of the girls preferred hanging around the streets to going
to youth clubs, because they could enjoy themselves with their friends without
boys taking over. They might join together with a group of boys on occasions, but
they could choose not to do so. Dossing gave them this kind of freedom and
control, and a strong sense of independence.

Largely because of lack of money and because it was considered unsafe at night,
the girls rarely went into town on weekday evenings unless they belonged to a
club, such as St John's Ambulance Cadets, which met in town. Dossing around
the streets in town would have had a very different connotation from hanging
about the estates where they lived (Lees 1986). However, Saturdays were usually
spent in town. Many of the fifth-year girls had Saturday jobs such as shop work or
waitressing, which restricted when they could meet their girlfriends. For those
who did not have jobs, and more particularly for the mature 13 to 14 year olds,
most of the time in town on Saturdays was spent dossing, hanging around the
shops.

What little spending money the girls had, which averaged £1.50 a week, they
would use to buy records or magazines. Fashionable clothes were extremely
important to the mature girls. As Pam said, 'I wouldn't want owt that was out of
fashion'. However, clothes were generally too expensive for the girls, and were
usually bought by or with their mothers, which was often a cause of conflict as
other studies have found (Griffin 1985; Griffiths 1986). Whilst with their friends,
the girls were therefore restricted to window shopping. For some of the girls, going
to town was also an opportunity to meet groups of boys, as Carol explained: 'We
meet them in town every Saturday and go round in a big gang. About ten of us.'
By and large, however, Saturdays and Sundays during the day were times to see
girlfriends.

In contrast to these girls, young women who had left school were less likely to
spend time dossing either in the evenings or at weekends. Those who had gone to
college (sixth form, art or tech.) had access to far more social activities such as
discos organized by the college or parties held by other students. Although they
were all still living at home – 'keeping close and spoiling' (Leonard 1980) was
very much the norm here – these young women had greater freedom than when
they had been at school. They were allowed to stay out later, and sometimes

stayed overnight with girlfriends. Those in work had greater financial independence and could go into town to pubs and clubs, or shopping for clothes at the weekends. Going out became the norm rather than the exception.

However, for unemployed young women the picture was very different. With no spending power, they were cut off from the goods and services to which their money-earning peers now had access. The wider social activities of the students were not available to them either, so they remained trapped as it were in the previous stage. Some could be seen dossing around the streets or gathered outside the Job Centre. Others became isolated in their homes, depressed and filling their time with domestic duties.

Clubs

The girls went to various different clubs and societies and I shall give two contrasting examples: the all-female Girls Friendly Society and the predominantly male Air Cadets. Dancing was an important activity for many of the young women, and this will be described separately in Chapter 9.

Some girls got over the problem of boys dominating youth clubs by going to all-girl groups. For example, four of the mature white third years went to the Girls Friendly Society (GFS), a Church of England organization for girls between the ages of 7 and 16. They had a somewhat ambivalent attitude towards the group. Sometimes they talked about it in lukewarm terms: 'it's just a bit boring at times'; 'it's summat to do'. However, at other times they described what they did enthusiastically. For instance, Penny told me, 'We do games and have parties and things like that and we go on trips and camping'. A clue to the girls' ambivalence was provided by Penny, who called GFS 'a bit babyish'. As part of the mature group, these girls were keen to appear grown up. Going to a club which included 7 year olds, where you played games and did model-making, could easily have been regarded as childish. Because the girls were at a transitional stage in adolescence, they did still enjoy these younger-type activities, but they could only bring themselves to admit it when talking to me on their own.

What tipped the balance in favour of GFS was that these girls were encouraged by the women running the group to create a dance for the local disco-dancing competition (see Ch. 9). This was an acceptable activity in the eyes of the other mature girls so they could talk about it more openly. For a while at least it put GFS in the spotlight and made it seem like an exciting place to go.

In contrast to this supportive all-female environment, three of the mature white third-year girls were pioneers because they were among the first girl members of the local Air Cadets. This was certainly a non-traditional interest, and a somewhat surprising choice for these girls who were among the most fashionable of the mature group. However, they were extremely enthusiastic about the activities, as Elaine described: 'You can go at rifle range, you can do engines, radar and radio. Airmanship . . . You do all sorts of stuff. It's a good laugh really.' The girls were keen to learn flying; Elaine herself wanted to become an air-traffic controller. Meeting boys seemed to be an added bonus rather than a major reason for joining. The girls had to go through arduous training exercises and needed to be genuinely dedicated to continue, and to overcome the initial opposition they faced from the men who ran the cadets.

However, the girls were still fighting a battle to become 'official': girls were not yet able nationally to be full members of the Air Cadets. Until that rule was changed they would not be allowed to fly or wear a uniform. So although the girls were allowed unofficially to go to Air Cadets, take part in the classes and move up the ranks – a big step in itself as they had at first been classified as canteen ladies – their membership was still only partial, was on different terms from the boys and barred them from one of the main purposes of joining, learning to fly. Their situation was unsatisfactory, but it nevertheless represented a considerable achievement, and the girls were determined to continue.

Conclusion

The picture which emerges of young working-class women and leisure is a complex one. I have outlined some of the different ways that the young women in my research negotiated their own space within the context of restrictions, and according to the stage in the transition to womanhood they had reached.

There was no single pattern of leisure, even among girls of the same age. Many preferred places where they could meet together and enjoy themselves without interference from boys, whether at home, 'dossing' or at groups like the Girls Friendly Society. Others preferred the challenge of creating space in mixed-sex or predominantly male environments, such as the local youth club or Air Cadets.

In spite of cultural and ideological pressures, there was by no means a simple transition from childlike to adolescent interests or from girlfriends to boyfriends. The girls often combined home-based and outside interests, or traditionally feminine with non-traditional activities. Female friendships were largely maintained alongside relationships with boys, even when the young women had regular boyfriends.

Girls with extensive home responsibilities and unemployed young women experienced most pressure to conform to traditional female roles. This was true regardless of ethnic background. These young women suffered from isolation and a contracting rather than widening of opportunities as they got older.

However, the young women generally retained a positive approach in spite of often considerable restrictions on their leisure time. Most held traditional views about the future: marriage and motherhood were taken for granted. They saw adolescence as a period of relative freedom, a time to enjoy themselves and 'have fun' before they settled down. As Vicky said, 'I don't want to get tied down at 16. I fully intend to enjoy my life to the limit before that happens.'

References

Amos, Valerie and Parmar, Pratibha (1981) 'Resistances and responses: the experiences of black girls in Britain', in Angela McRobbie and Trisha McCabe (eds.) *Feminism for Girls: an adventure story*, London, Routledge & Kegan Paul.

Beuret, Kris and Makings, Lynn (1987) 'Love in a cold climate: women, class and courtship in a recession', in Teresa Keil, Pat Allatt, Bill Bytheway and Alan Bryman (eds.) *Women and the Life Cycle: Transitions and Turning Points*, London, Macmillan.

Deem, Rosemary (1986) *All Work and No Play? The Sociology of Women and Leisure*, Milton Keynes, Open University Press.

Griffin, Christine (1985) *Typical Girls? Young Women from School to the Job Market* London, Routledge & Kegan Paul.

Griffin, Christine, Hobson, Dorothy, McIntosh, Sue and McCabe, Trisha (1982) 'Women and Leisure', in Jennifer Hargreaves (ed.) *Sport, Culture and Ideology*, London, Routledge & Kegan Paul.

Griffiths, Vivienne (1986) *Using Drama to Get at Gender*, Studies in Sexual Politics No.9, Sociology Department, University of Manchester.

   (1987) 'Adolescent girls: transition from girlfriends to boyfriends?' in Teresa Keil, Pat Allat, Bill Bytheway and Alan Bryman (eds.) *Women and the Life-Cycle: Transitions and Turning Points*, London, Macmillan.

Jamdagni, Laxmi (1980) *Hamari Rangily Zindagi: Our Colourful Lives*, Leicester, National Association of Youth Clubs.

Lees, Sue (1986) *Losing Out: Sexuality and Adolescent Girls*, London, Hutchinson.

Leonard, Diana (1980) *Sex and Generation: A Study of Courtship and Weddings*, London, Tavistock.

McRobbie, Angela (1978) 'Working class girls and the culture of femininity', in Women's Studies Group CCCS (eds). *Women Take Issue: Aspects of Women's Subordination*, London, Hutchinson.

McRobbie, Angela and Garber, Jenny (1976), 'Girls and subcultures: an exploration', in Stuart Hall and Tony Jefferson (eds.) *Resistance through rituals: Youth Subcultures in Post-war Britain*, London, Hutchinson.

Nava, Mica (1984) 'Youth service provision, social order and the question of girls', in Angela McRobbie and Mica Nava (eds.) *Gender and Generation*, London, Macmillan.

Parmar, Pratibha and Mirza, Nadira (1981) 'Youth work with Asian girls', *Working With Girls Newsletter*, Issue 2 March/April, pp. 8–9.

Smith, Lesley S. (1978) 'Sexist assumptions and female delinquency: an empirical investigation', in Carol Smart and Barry Smart (eds.) *Women, Sexuality and Social Control*, London, Routledge & Kegan Paul.

Westwood, Sallie (1984) *All Day Every Day*, London, Pluto.

Wilson, Deidre (1978) 'Sexual codes and conduct', in Carol Smart and Barry Smart (eds.) *Women, Sexuality and Social Control*, London, Routledge & Kegan Paul.

Youth Work Unit (1981) *Working With Girls: A Reader's Route Map*, Leicester, National Youth Bureau.

5

Mothers meeting

ERICA WIMBUSH

The theme of this chapter is women with young children and the significance of leisure in their everyday working lives as mothers. I am drawing on research carried out in Edinburgh in which we examined the role and meaning of leisure in the general health and well-being of mothers with pre-school age children (Wimbush 1986).[1] The location of the study and the structure of the samples [2] has meant that the findings are culturally specific to white Scottish women and may say little about the experiences of mothers from other ethnic groups.

The study produced rich material about different aspects of these mothers' lives which were important to their well-being. The significance of 'leisure' in their well-being was understood mainly in terms of having time and space for themselves to relax away from the pressures of children and home. Since social isolation is a common experience for women as carers of young children, the company and friendships developed through social and recreational outlets were an important aspect of leisure and also contributed to the mothers' support systems.

In this chapter I will look at the opportunities which mothers have for meeting people, and what these contacts bring in terms of company, friendships and support. Equally important, however, is to understand the differences and divisions between the support networks and leisure opportunities that various women have and why, for example, some women shy away from groups of mothers' meeting. But before discussing the social networks and recreational outlets of mothers, I will locate this within the context of the dramatic changes most women experience in their lives once they have children.

Becoming a mother

Across all ethnic groups, perhaps one of the most resonant consequences of becoming a parent is that it is the mother rather than the father for whom extensive change is heralded. This is not just due to the physical effects of pregnancy and childbirth, but more importantly because of the social allocation of childcare as 'women's work'. Without adequate state childcare provision, having responsibility for the care and welfare of children brings with it an unremittent sense of responsibility, an increased domestic workload and, having left the job market to have children, even more limited employment prospects when trying to re-enter the labour force.

Combining employment with motherhood is a necessity in many households, and for the woman it is a complex business: it involves the demands of making childcare arrangements, the tiredness brought with a double workload and the conflicts of assuming a 'double identity' (Sharpe 1984). Although the financial gain may be small (after childcare is paid for), employment is sometimes seen by mothers as worth going to considerable lengths to secure for the sake of what it means as a small measure of autonomy. This has many parallels in the difficulties and rewards which mothers experience in keeping up regular outside recreational activities.

In becoming the children's mother, the man's wife and a housewife, women give up a great deal of autonomy. Part of this feeling is losing a sense of 'self', of being a separate, individual person. The ideology of motherhood centres on the tenet of self-denial – putting the needs of the family first (and yourself last):

> When you have a child you tend to put yourself last. There's not so much money around so you can't dress as you'd like to or buy things for yourself. It may be better once I'm selling more jerseys and I can keep some money for myself sometimes, but most of it will go towards the family.

Liz Heron (1986) suggests that underlying this notion of women existing to serve and soothe others – whether with food, clean laundry, or kind words and a well made-up face – is the idea that women do not wholly belong to themselves. In order to resist, or escape from, the pervasive demand to be on call to others day and night, the need to create a space for themselves – 'a room of one's own' – is an essential aspect of personal leisure for mothers.

But for the majority of mothers we interviewed, looking after the welfare of children, husband and home took priority over creating time and space for themselves. Furthermore, the realities of coping with the near constant demands of pre-school children and their care imposed many practical limitations on the amount of time, energy and money which mothers had at their disposal. This woman also recalled how having a child curtailed her control and choice over how she spent her time and with whom:

> It takes a lot of getting used to in that you've no time to yourself. Just because you want to do something doesn't necessarily mean that she [child] will want to do something so you have to think twice before you make any plans . . . I mean before you have a baby you never ever believe that it would be the way it is, whereby *every* minute of the day you have to think about them. Not that I mind, it's just that it's so different from the way I used to live – go to work and be able to suit myself all the time. I can no longer do that and I don't know whether that's a good thing or a bad thing.

Related to their diminished control over time, since having children the women had also experienced a decline in the nature and frequency of their socializing and recreations away from the home and family. These now had to be reconciled with the day-to-day routines which revolved around the essentials of managing the children and home. Since most of the mothers complained of tiredness and lack of energy after a busy working-day, staying at home in the evening often became a preferred option to going out:

> The very thought of going out at night, you think 'och, I'll sit down and do nothing and go to bed. I'm using any free time to relax rather than to pursue hobbies I suppose, just because I don't have as much energy, and probably too once you do get them off to bed it's nice just to sit down, to knit, to think, because you don't have much thinking time during the day.

The women could not 'just go out' spontaneously as they had before having children. As mothers, going out now incurred an extra workload of getting organized and making arrangements for babysitters, a hurdle that was often too daunting for those already exhausted by the end of the day.

For many of the mothers, these changes in life-style were accepted as a feature of the 'natural' process of growing up and taking on adult responsibilities: 'I used to go for a drink, but since the children I've really quietened down. I realize I've got responsibilities for the kids – the bairns are important to me.' Meeting the needs of children and the paucity of acceptable, alternative childcare were seen as the most immediate factors circumscribing women's outside interests, recreations and friendships. But this only exacerbated the impact of earlier changes associated with becoming a couple (see Ch.3). Looking back to the more active social life they had enjoyed in their school days and when employed full time, many of the women pinpointed the onset of married life as the time when their pattern of friendships and socializing underwent a major refocus:

> *Q.* Did you find your pattern of activities changed when you got married?
> *A.* Yes, very much so. I suppose we did more things together. I would maybe go out with my friends from work before I was married, then it changed to going out with my husband rather than a group of girls from work.

Leisure within marriage consisted primarily of going out as a couple, with or without other couples, or supporting the husband's recreations. The women's own female friendship networks had become fragmented in the process:

> I used to go out with my girlfriends, but now they're all away, all married and can't get out. It's a big change.
> *Q.* Do you see many of them now?
> *A.* No, not now – it changes when you get married and have your kids.

> I think when you get married you lose your pals – you do 'cos I've got a lot of friends and they all said when I got married 'oh, I'll come and visit' but I never see them. Once you're a married woman you're not so interested in going out with single people . . . you want to be with your husband.

Moving to another area and having limited mobility and personal money were other factors which disrupted women's earlier social networks. As mothers, their networks were now shaped by their children and consisted primarily of other mothers; this contrasted with their earlier social lives as girlfriends and wives when company was mixed. Losing touch with girlfriends to go out with in the evening and knowing mostly other women with children were important factors contributing to the 'choice' of many mothers to stay at home in the evenings.

Needless to say, the man's social networks and friendships seemed largely unaffected by parenthood, while the woman again made the adjustments. In the majority of households, the man had not only kept on his job and thus contact with workmates, but kept up his own regular nights out, his sports activities or hobbies, and sometimes his own weekends and holidays away. Thus, having children often marked a point where the leisure and social outlets of couples became more unequal and separate. This reflects the tendency for two-parent households to work a shift system for babysitting so that if one went out, the other parent stayed at home. However, in practice these shifts were seldom shared equitably between partners – women do far more babysitting. For the most part, this growing leisure inequality between partners was accepted on the grounds that a man needed time away from home (as well as private time/space at home). This mother, now separated from her husband, regarded this acceptance as a possible mistake:

> Basically recreation used to be a mixed crowd. Then Lisa was born and Jim started going out on his own and I stayed in. I never minded Jim going out on his own for a drink in the evenings. Right from before we got married, before too, there was always a boys' night out – that was a Thursday evening. That carried right on through to when Nicole was born and then Jim was made manager and he was introduced to a wider circle of friends. Another thing Jim used to be quite fond of doing was he liked a holiday on his own once a year. You see, I've gone wrong right from the start! But it never bothered me. I quite accepted he was that kind of person and he needed time away on his own. I've never had a holiday for God knows how long! He used to go off on golfing holidays.

From the woman's standpoint, acceptance of the man's continuing pattern of evenings out was not without some benefits. It gave the mother a chance to have some time and space to herself at home – whether this was used to catch up with household chores undisturbed, to relax in peace, to watch what she wanted on television or to read a book.

The common feeling of being more isolated and trapped at home with the children meant that getting out of the house and having contact with other adults was something that had become increasingly important to women since having children. In going on to explore women's social worlds as mothers, I will distinguish between the female domestic circles in which women were involved in the course of their working lives as mothers, and the more limited exit routes from domestic life through which women sought independent social lives. The former were more accessible because they incorporated the children and their needs. Furthermore, they did not go against the grain of being a 'good mother' as often did the activities which some mothers managed to maintain independent of the home and children. However, common to both these social arenas was the common context of female company, a theme I will consider in the final section.

Mothers' circles

Although going out less and losing touch with earlier friends is part of the general pattern of change in motherhood, it does not necessarily mean that women do not develop new friends and networks. The vast majority of the women we interviewed had day-to-day social contact with other people through their children and their neighbourhood, although this was more regular for some than others.

The structuring of the mothers' timetables, and often their interests, by the needs and activities of children both facilitated social contacts with other mothers as well as constrained the development of social networks beyond these perimeters. Everyday sociability was also restricted geographically to their local neighbourhood since with young children and pushchairs to manoeuvre, walking was the easiest form of transport, unless a car was available. For these reasons, the streets, local schools and nurseries, playgroups, mothers and toddlers groups, and local social amenities like shops, health clinics and community centres, played an important role in daily life as meeting places:

> I meet other people through nursery, mothers and toddlers – just even around here, neighbours. Mostly because you've got children, you meet other people with children . . . they're the ones you've got most in common with I think . . . If you know other people with children, it's a lot easier to get together with them rather than with people who don't have children because people who don't have children their homes aren't usually geared for children at all.

The homes of neighbouring mother-friends and relatives featured strongly in women's everyday social lives. Visiting friends and family at the weekend, dropping in to visit a friend for coffee on a weekday and the more formalized gatherings like coffee mornings or Pippadee/Basketware parties were popular home-based activities when women got together to talk. Activities organized by mothers during the day, like coffee mornings and mothers and toddlers groups, gave their children a chance to play together, but at the same time allowed the mothers an opportunity to meet other women, sit down, relax and have a coffee, a chat and a good moan:

> I have a couple of coffee mornings during the week. My daughter isn't involved 'cos she's at playgroup but my son is. But it's a case of the children disappearing upstairs or in other rooms and, you know, let them create havoc as long as you get your chance of a natter and a bit of peace. Also at the mothers and toddlers group you can sit and talk to somebody and have your coffee and generally have a moan about the children or your husband or whatever you're going to moan about – the children can run around and play.

The importance attributed to meeting other mothers and the outlets sought for this showed marked class cultural differences. The middle-class mothers recounted twice as many opportunities in their daily lives for meeting other mothers as the working-class women. Three-quarters of these outlets were centred on the children, such as their playgroups, nurseries, mothers and toddlers groups, and taking children to their recreational activities or on daytime outings with other mother-friends and their children. Away from the children, classes in local community centres and schools (especially if a crèche was available) and groups like the National Childbirth Trust provided valued opportunities to meet other like-minded women. Due to their greater mobility, some of the middle-class mothers included in their regular social networks old friends who were also mothers but who lived outside their locality.

Only half the working-class mothers regarded nurseries and playgroups as outlets for meeting other women like themselves. Nor did the more formalized interest-based groups, classes and activities feature to the same extent as meeting places. Partly for financial reasons, but also because they more often had their own families living nearby, they laid greater emphasis on visiting the homes of neighbouring mother-friends and female relatives for company. As one mother said:

> Most of the people I know are in the same situation as I am – they're sorta broke. So you can't really afford to have nights out. The next best thing is sitting in each others homes, friends come up. And sometimes my sister will babysit and I go to other people's houses – I enjoy that.

In this study Pippadee and Basketware parties held in people's homes were one of the few local evening events where working-class mothers met away from their children. The local and domestic setting, the female company and the congruence with their domestic roles made these social gatherings an accessible and acceptable outlet for some mothers. The attraction of these parties was less the chance to purchase goods or get a bargain, but more the opportunity to have a space away from home to meet up with other women friends for a chat:

> Night before last I went out to a friend's house. They were having a sort of clothes party, selling things. Well that part of it was pretty dreadful – I don't really like that sort of party and I didn't buy anything – but it's nice just to see a lot of girlfriends and have a chat and some food. It's nice.

But for the hostess at home gatherings – whether Pippadee party, coffee morning or a casual visit – having friends round involved the work of hospitality. Thus most mothers found it more relaxing to go out to visit other women's homes.

In addition to financial constraints, some mothers kept away from the local mothers' circles (e.g. mothers and toddlers, coffee mornings) because they felt themselves to be outsiders to the 'happy family' stereotype which prevails in these groups. They were often wary of the controlling aspects of gossip within these networks. What are often regarded as private family matters – such as marital relationships, childrearing practices, children's clothing and appearance – were more vulnerable to critical scrutiny in these groups. Thus women who preferred to keep away from mothers groups included those without male partners, those with marital or domestic problems, an older mother in her forties and women from low-income households (including unemployed families). For example, this separated woman told how she had become wary of the grapevine within local women's circles:

> I did trust a friend, but then I felt that some things that were being said were being given away. So that kinda put a stop, although now I've still got

friends I don't tell them too much. It's only my family I really talk to now. I feel a lot better telling them because I feel that they'll keep it to themselves.

Withdrawal from the talk of mothers' circles exacerbated social isolation. In daily life these women tended to be more dependent on the company and support of their relatives (if they were living nearby) and perhaps one or two close women friends who shared and understood their position. For example, these two mothers who lived in the midst of an affluent area became friends on the basis of their common position as 'underdogs':

I just met Joan walking down the street one day. She was taking her wee one to nursery and she actually met me by complaining about her oldest daughter being victimized at school because she had bought her child wellies that were slightly more old-fashioned than the other children's. And that's how it started. We realized there wasn't too much difference in the way we thought about things, so we kept together at nursery. And then Joan was having trouble with her husband and she had to call the police out, and she's going 'Oh Moira, all the neighbours will be talking about me – we'll be the underdogs of Barnton!' So we have something in common that way. We find it quite amusing.

For the middle-class mothers who shied away from local mothers' groups, it was more often because they rejected their propensity for domestic chat and 'baby-talk'. They sought the company of like-minded friends to get away from this:

I have the one friend – she's a real tonic. She's in the same boat as me. We can sit for hours and not mention the kids or the house. Whereas I've got a neighbour next door and all she talks about is the house, her daughter, what she wants for the house, what she's getting for the house. She drives me mad really – yet she's got a heart of gold. I think she must be bored.

Others looked to adult education classes for a space away from domestic life and to extend their horizons. However, apart from keep-fit, the classes provided for women with young children (i.e. with crèches and at convenient times of the day) were often subjects like cookery, upholstery and dressmaking.

The local forms of socializing centred around children were seldom regarded as personal leisure by mothers because these were so much part of their everyday routine. Moreover, friendships made via these circles were often transitory because they were based around the children's friends and activities, rather than their own, and these changed as the children grew up. For example, this woman described how her intricate network of mother-friends had developed through introductions by neighbours, coffee mornings and waiting around at the nursery, the school and at her daughters' swimming and dancing lessons. But she concluded by saying:

It's nothing lasting, as soon as the lessons finish that contact will be dropped again. Since the children were born, you sorta move in groups, circles of friends. You move from circle to circle as the children get older or as different things happen in your life.

What was more often regarded by mothers as their own leisure were those rarer occasions that did not involve their children and provided an exit route from the home, albeit temporarily. These independent social outlets provided a greater sense of autonomy and often a greater continuity in friendships. They relied strongly on the company and support of female relatives (especially mothers and sisters) and on female friends and neighbours who shared a common position.

Exit routes

For some mothers, having a sphere of involvement independent from the home and children was an important aspect of their well-being. Getting out of the house and having a break from the children and domestic routines, together with the desire to meet up with friends and enjoy the company of adults, fuelled their impetus for seeking or maintaining outside activities of their own. While social class influenced the nature and range of available exit routes from the domestic sphere, it affected less the motivation to seek forms of independence.

The occasional night out with girlfriends or workmates or a day off to go shopping in town with a friend were commonly cited examples of special occasions when women had space and time free for themselves. But the frequency of these kinds of personal leisure was restricted by both finances (especially for lone mothers) and the availability of others (but particularly husbands) to look after the children:

> There's a lot of people offer to babysit, it's been really great. They say 'anytime I'll babysit', but I just don't really have the money. So when I do go out, I like to really go out – go out early and stay out late – maybe go for a few drinks, then to a dance or the pictures and then for a pizza.
>
> (single mother)

> I get a day off now and again. I've got to apply for it in advance. I say to him [husband] 'can I have a day off?' and the day's mine. That's lovely – sort of go up town, meet a friend for lunch, do a bit of shopping. I love that. It doesn't happen very often.
>
> (married mother)

Regular exit routes often took the form of having part-time jobs (particularly for the working-class mothers) since the wages earned meant that this outlet could more easily be justified in terms of its contribution to family welfare. Going out to work was also seen as a legitimate reason to seek regular support with childcare. For mothers, like others, jobs provided a space away from the pressures of the home and children:

> I must admit some days I'm glad to get there [work], you know, just to get away. Last Wednesday I had one of those days I was that glad to get to my work – just to have a seat and think about other things. So I look to that as a form of relaxation I suppose.

Jobs were also an important source of regular social contact with other people beyond their own families, a theme often talked about in terms of having a good laugh or moan with women workmates:

and you do get plenty of time to chat and have a laugh about things. You know, the usual – going on diets and moaning about this, that and the next thing.

It's a group of women I work with. We tell each other our wee stories, even things that crop up at work – hilarious things that happen! It's just being in a group of women.

For those who had changed occupation since having children, their workmates were again mainly other women, since their jobs were largely those part-time occupations dominated by female labour (e.g. shop assistants, office workers, cleaners, caterers). Among the small minority of employed mothers who had returned to their previous occupation (mostly professional), there was often a greater continuity in their social networks. Not only did they retain daily contact with old workmates, but they were also better able to keep up former friendships (energy and time permitting) because they had the advantage of greater personal income with which to pay for childcare and had often established a wider support network to facilitate their independent activity outside the family.

But for the majority of mothers, securing regular time away from the children and home for personal leisure was difficult to reconcile and organize. It was mothers who did manage to achieve this who made up one of the samples in the research. This sample of 115 recreationally active mothers was distinctive in terms of the predominance of middle-class women (72 per cent) and those living in two parent households (90 per cent). These social advantages were underpinned by the material benefits of higher levels of household income and access to private transport compared to other mothers interviewed in the study. These are important factors facilitating mothers' access to independent leisure.

The middle-class mothers were subject to the same constraints as working-class mothers with regard to the gendered division of caring responsibilities and the social construction of motherhood. However, within middle-class culture participation in social and recreational groups in the community is a more accepted aspect of women's lives, although the form which participation takes is closely circumscribed by gender. Their greater mobility also allowed them to maintain contacts within a wider geographical area.[3] Having wider social networks of mother-friends and more social outlets accessible meant they had a larger pool of people and situations from which to seek support. Their greater financial resources allowed them more scope to buy time off from childcare and domestic work. For those women whose previous occupations were of professional or managerial status, the 'identity crisis' experienced in becoming a full-time housewife and mother was often a factor which fuelled their motivation to establish other spheres of independent activity and seek support from other women in similar situations.

Among the married, middle-class mothers who managed to secure some form of regular independent leisure, it was evident that this was facilitated by negotiations with husbands over the division of domestic labour. The vast majority of husbands were said to provide moral support and encouragement as well as practical help (most commonly babysitting) to enable their wives to go out on a regular basis. The man's approval of the woman's activities and company was often a necessary precondition of his co-operation and support.)

While the recruitment of help and support from husbands was of undoubted benefit to these women, the partner's co-operation became more difficult to secure the greater the woman's outside commitments and thus the greater the demands made upon him. Even when help was on hand from husbands, responsibilities for children and their care were not renegotiated and remained with the mothers. The strain on women of having to organize and co-ordinate their outside activities with domestic commitments was evident. For example, poorer health was shown among those women with the most extensive commitments outside the home.

Ideological divisions between mothers cut across the class differences in the exit routes available to women. On the one hand, there were mothers whose life-style was almost exclusively centred around domestic concerns, and on the other hand, there were those whose life-style also included investments in spheres beyond the domestic, whether these were paid employment, voluntary work in the community and/or recreational activities. Those mothers with the most extensive commitments outside the family (i.e. full-time employees and those whose recreational participation went beyond seven hours a week) were the ones who most frequently encountered disapproval from others (e.g. from their own mother, other mothers, husbands). In this sense, disapproval was most keenly felt when the mothers' time and resources for the family were most stretched. Opposition and resentment from other women was as much about the 'unfair' extra demands made on husbands as they were about the detrimental consequences that the children might suffer from having 'selfish' mothers. For example, both these women had full-time jobs and regular recreational commitments:

> Other mothers [disapprove] who are quite happy to stay at home and not do anything. They think its awful that I'm out 'gallivanting' and James [husband] has to cope on his own. I've come across this quite a lot, especially when I can't make domestic chat with other mothers. I don't have much in common with them.

> You find resentment from other women who haven't been able to keep up a separate life – they tend to be the most critical of my irresponsible childcare [using childminder] and think I must have a hen-pecked husband.

But it would be misleading to equate mothers' participation in outside activities with a challenge to family ideology. For the vast majority of mothers interviewed who had independent recreations, their first priority remained with meeting the needs of their children, husbands and homes, and their own activities had to fit in around this. There were some, however, who questioned the prevailing belief that mothers should give up their personal recreations when the children are young. They believed that by recognizing and meeting their own need to have spheres of independent involvement, this brought benefits to the family:

> I feel strongly that if it's valuable to you then the rest of the family will benefit from your involvement. You have more energy and can do more for them because you are involved.

> It's good for the children to see me doing other things and having other roles. I'm not just a mother and they appreciate me more.

Its beneficial for the kids because I'm not so frustrated and I'm more interesting and they get to meet more people.

In this way, personal leisure could be reconciled within family ideology and the internalized guilt and conflicts that many mothers experienced were minimized.

Women's company and support

Whether in local mothers' circles or in spheres of independent leisure activity, having the company and support of other women who have common experiences, problems and outlooks was an important element in adjusting to the many changes brought about by motherhood.

Talking about worries and problems in family life and consulting each other about children's ailments and developments was what brought these women together – for 'a good moan' or 'a good laugh'. The company of other mothers was often regarded as more supportive and relaxing because they were felt to understand the everyday trials and tribulations inherent in the job of bringing up children and, for example, problems with babysitting, time and money management, getting jobs and coping with a double workload. Times of crisis in women's lives, such as separating from a husband or the death of a child or close relative, were also periods when the support and help of female friends and relatives were highly valued. The changed significance of women's company was explained by this mother:

> I feel more at home in some ways being with all women. I think it has changed. It's because I feel they understand, I think. Particularly as most of them are in the same situation as me, I feel they're not criticizing me. I sometimes feel that other people think you're incompetent if they're looking at you and think, 'I could do much better than her. If it was my child it wouldn't throw a tantrum.' I used to be the same before I had children, I think you look at these people in supermarkets and you think, 'If I have children they won't be like that.' Other mothers understand on the whole. It's quite restful being with other people who understand.

Although it was husbands from whom the married mothers sought and wanted positive feedback concerning their toils over managing the home and children, it was more often good friends and female relatives from whom this was obtained. Husbands were not always the most sympathetic or understanding audiences when it came to listening to their wives' worries and concerns:

> You know what it's like with a husband and wife – we can discuss everything, but you know there are some things that men think 'Oh, here she goes again' or 'I don't know why you're worrying about that'. And again I can go to my sister and say, 'Oh, this is getting me down'.
>
> *Q.* What sort of things don't you expect him to understand?
> *A.* You know, when you feel tired – some weeks you feel 'Gosh, I've never been over the door, I've never been away from the children and he's been out working and I'm stuck'. Things like that you don't say to them, but I'd say to my sister . . . You don't want them [husband] to think

things are getting on top of you and that they're getting the better of you 'cos they tend to sally through.

Grandmothers often provided a mainstay of support, more often in the practical sense of helping out with babysitting than in terms of verbal encouragement and moral support for their daughter (in-law)'s outside recreations. Intergenerational differences in approaches to motherhood meant that the support received from grandmothers could be difficult to manage and equivocal in its consequences. While they would never expect any payment for their babysitting services since this is part of their customary obligations as grandmothers, they would on the other hand expect to have more of a say in their daughters' life-style. As a tacit acknowledgement of this form of control, women whose mothers(in-law) were not encouraging of their outside activities, were less likely to ask for their help.

Not asking others for help, 'keeping to themselves' and 'coping alone' can be seen as a strategy that some women adopted to enhance their personal autonomy as mothers; it helped to minimize the controls that others could impose on their life-style by 'helping them out' or 'doing them a favour'. Paradoxically, this strategy put limits on the mothers' independence as much as enhanced it: it exacerbated isolation and meant that reciprocal relationships and negotiations over the division of labour were avoided. For the most part, these mothers were dependent on the provision of crèches or other forms of public childcare to facilitate any independent leisure.

The most characteristic form of practical mutual support between mother-friends with outside involvements (job or recreation) was reciprocal childcare. This had the advantage of being free and because the service was exchanged did not mean feeling in debt to someone else. For this reason, it was a form of help that was often acceptable to those women who would otherwise not delegate their responsibilities for children to others:

> I've been brought up not to ask for help with my children so I won't. But I will accept offers of help or invitations. I have an exchange arrangement with another mother who does voluntary work like me and we do swaps with taking each other's children at lunchtimes.

However, such exchanges required that the women involved were in similar circumstances (e.g. number and ages of children, employment commitments, marital status, access to transport) and had similar approaches to childcare and mothering. Exchange arrangements with mother-friends was less common among the working-class mothers. Asking for help with childcare and needing support outside their own family tended to signal being either an irresponsible or inadequate mother. In a class culture where women have fewer social outlets, and therefore know fewer mother-friends who go out regularly (except to work), there were less opportunities available for exchanging childcare:

> My neighbour Sandra's always saying, 'if you need a babysitter . . .', but she never goes out so I can't return the favour. She goes out once a year sorta thing . . . I feel I could ask her now and again and I know she would do it, but I feel guilty because I can't return it.

It was regarded as unfair to impose, or 'palm off', their responsibilities onto other mother-friends and difficult to justify increasing another woman's workload in order to facilitate their own leisure:

> But many a time I say something to her [neighbour] and she says, 'God, you could've asked me, I would have done it [babysat]'. But you feel she's got a wee one his age and feel well . . . I'm not the type of person who likes to dump them on somebody. Plus if he's sleeping it's OK, but you canna really say 'can you come down?'. She's maybe got to get on with something . . . I never asked anybody apart from my mother and mother-in-law. I don't like intruding.

The more restricted and localized social networks of the working-class mothers helps to explain their more solitary approach to coping with their domestic work-load and the fewer occasions when they could seek, or obtain, support.

For most women recreational activities were only accessible if they had another woman-friend to go with. Female friends and co-participants were also an important source of initial encouragement and motivation to continue:

> I don't know if its encouragement, but the fact that a few of us in this area go is probably a help. If I don't go one week, someone would call to find out if anything was wrong.

> I think the fact that my neighbour and I go together is a great help. I might be tempted to stay in if it was wet.

Some described the support received from their female friends in terms of boosting their morale and sense of individual worth, something which had ebbed in motherhood:

> She regards me a me . . .

> They make me feel like I have a contribution to make . . .

> She tells me how great I am and that I'm doing fine and gives my confidence a boost . . .

> They support me when I'm down and laugh with me when I'm up.

Although not all the mothers with independent leisure took part in women-only groups, even those in mixed-sex activities often gravitated towards other women's company and support.

Many of the mothers regarded groups organized by and for women as more welcoming, relaxing and enjoyable. Self-organized groups were also said to be more flexible in their arrangements, and would organize activities to accommodate the needs and timetables of mothers. For example:

> There's others there who have children and do jobs and so provide moral support. I get a lot out of the women's meetings because they're not a duty and the discussions are more relaxed and open. I don't feel I would be hounded for saying something that was 'uncool' . . . they meet at a later time because they realize the problems that mothers have in getting there for 7.30.

We try to arrange times to suit everyone for rehearsals. Often this means pretty elaborate arrangements because the others are women with children as well.

Together we can support each other and make sure that each manages to make time, adapt our arrangements to suit and include each other as far as possible. We can also share childcare or bring the children along if we have to, without feeling bad.

In this way, the shared recreational interest was often coupled with a sense of solidarity with other female participants who understood the problems and benefits for mothers in seeking involvements independent of the domestic.

Conclusions

Even within the framework of constraints which shape and fragment women's social networks and leisure opportunities, many women do carve out spaces for themselves amidst the routines and busy timetables of their working days as mothers. But because of the restrictions on mothers' time, money and mobility and the paucity of places which cater for, welcome or are geared towards children, the social outlets accessible to carers of young children are few and far between.

Those which do exist are largely ones organized by and for women within their own homes or local communities; these activities and groups often have the ostensible purpose of fund-raising, domestic business or providing recreational opportunities for children. More pertinent perhaps is that these groups give women a legitimate opportunity to get out of the house and provide a space where they can get together – to talk, to have a laugh or to have a good moan. Jane Szurek's (1985) anthropological study of 'Seaham' in the north-east of England captures this in her ethnography of women's organizations in a mining community. She describes the way in which the formal business of the meetings usually had to proceed against 'the background of a low din of continuing voices' as women talked among themselves and discussed their own business. In this way, women's voluntary organizations like the Womens Institute and the Co-operative Women's Guild have long been playing a rare and valuable role in leisure provision for women. This was something that Virginia Woolf came to appreciate: 'It gave them in the first place the rarest of all possessions – a room where they could sit down and think remote from boiling saucepans and crying children' (Llewelyn Davies [1902] 1977, Introduction). For mothers, the question of leisure has no simple answer. It raises issues concerning women's right to time off and to 'a room of one's own' away from the demands of others, a privilege that many men take for granted and are not always willing to relinquish in order to support women's leisure. For mothers, time off from work goes hand in hand with the perennial struggle for improved childcare provisions and renegotiating the division of this labour. Furthermore, leisure is relevant to the issue of women's health, not least in helping to develop the supportive social networks which Brown and Harris (1978) confirmed as an important factor protecting against depression among women who are lonely and isolated as carers of young children.

Notes

1. This chapter is based on research undertaken by the Centre for Leisure Research among mothers with pre-school children in Edinburgh. The aim of this study was to explore the nature and meaning of leisure in the context of mothers' everyday lives and the role this played in their general health and well-being (Wimbush 1986). The project was sponsored by the Health Promotion Research Trust. Unless otherwise stated, all quotes are from women interviewed in this research.

2. In the first phase of the project, seventy mothers were interviewed in depth about the things important to their well-being in daily life; the sample was selected to include one- and two-parent households, employed and non-employed mothers and women from working- and middle-class backgrounds. In the second phase of the study, a further 115 mothers were interviewed in a questionnaire-based survey. This sample only included mothers who had managed to keep up some form of recreational involvement away from the home and family on a regular basis.

3. Those middle-class mothers whose mobility was restricted to public transport and walking (which included most of the lone mothers) were often more isolated than those working-class mothers who tended to have relatives and friends living in the locality.

References

Brown, George and Harris, T. (1978) *The Social Origins of Depression*, London, Tavistock.

Llewelyn Davies, Margaret (ed.)[1904](1977) *Life as We Have Known It – Cooperative Working Women*, London, Virago.

Heron, Liz (1986) *Changes of Heart: Reflections on Women's Independence*, London, Pandora Press.

Sharpe, Sue (1984) *Double Identity: The Lives of Working Mothers*, Harmondsworth, Penguin.

Szurek, Jane (1985) 'I'll have a collier for my sweetheart': work and gender in a British coal-mining town, PhD thesis, Dept of Anthropology, Brown University, Providence, Rhode Island, USA.

Wimbush, Erica (1986) *Women, Leisure and Well-Being*, final report to Health Promotion Research Trust, Centre for Leisure Research, Moray House College of Education, Edinburgh.

6

No peace for the wicked:
older married women and leisure

JENNIFER MASON

In this chapter I will consider some aspects of older married women's leisure. Although there is a growing body of research about women's leisure, relatively little attention has been directed to the situation of older women. Yet as well as telling us something descriptively about leisure in later life, an analysis of the leisure of older women is important if we are to begin to understand more about the construction of gender divisions across life-courses.

Michael Anderson (1985) argues that in recent years a 'modern life-cycle' has emerged, characterized among other things by periods in people's later lives which are historically as well as biographically new. For example, unlike in the nineteenth century, most people are now likely to survive a long period of middle to old age without childcare responsibilities or paid employment. During that time, they are likely to live to see not only the adulthood of their own children but also the marriage of at least some of their grandchildren. On the face of it, it might be construed that this means the opening up of a new 'slot' in the life-cycle primarily for leisure. Certainly this is the kind of reasoning behind the Rapoports' charting of a family leisure life-cycle (Rapoport and Rapoport 1975). They suggest that by their mid-fifties, married couples will find work decreasing in importance, and their children will have left home. Leisure then becomes the route to meaning in life, and the problem to be solved at that stage of the family cycle.

Yet it is not that simple. Transitions occurring in later life do not necessarily appear in uniform sequences or constellations as the notion of a leisure life-cycle stage implies. For example, at least 30 per cent of women in Britain fail to pass through sequential stages of marriage – childbearing – and still being married after children leave home (Murphy 1983: 55). Even for those who become and remain married with children, those children do not necessarily leave home sequentially, or at all, and retirement may come 'early' through redundancy, sickness and so on, or 'late' through prolonged full-time or part-time paid working (Mason 1987a; Parker 1982). More importantly, to assume that retirement from paid work inevitably heralds a period of leisure is generally to misunderstand the meaning of the concepts of work and leisure, and more specifically to ignore the salience of various kinds of unpaid work – particularly domestic labour and caring. This means that it is misleading to extrapolate from analyses of historical and social changes such as Anderson's the opening up of a new leisure life-cycle phase in any simple sense. However, even though it may not be accurate to identify a uniform post-employment, post-parental leisure stage, it is clear that life-course *transitions* currently occurring in the lives of people aged, say, over 50, have implications for leisure, not least because they involve a shifting of work and non-work boundaries.

My discussion is based upon findings from a study of eighteen long-married couples all aged between 50 and 70 and living in Kent. Eleven of the couples were working class and seven were middle class. All but one couple had children. The research involved in-depth interviews with wives and husbands both jointly and individually, and was designed to investigate the ways in which they were negotiating changes in their married lives (Mason 1987a). I discovered that much of their negotiation centred on access to and control of time and space, particularly in the home but also outside it. Therefore, in broad terms, leisure emerged as a major issue in both the construction of married life and of gender inequality.

The shaping of leisure choices

When considering the leisure of older married women undergoing life-course transitions it is misleading simply to look at activity patterns or lists of hobbies, since in isolation these tell us little or nothing about the conditions of choice, constraint and inequality from which they are constructed. It is important also to assess what factors shape the choices older women make about how to use time and space in their lives. This means analysing changing frameworks of constraint and opportunity which make possible certain patterns of leisure for both married women, and their husbands, in relation to each other.

Perhaps the most obvious factor which we might suppose will affect leisure choices in later life is retirement. The statutory retirement age is 65 for men and 60 for women, but economic activity rates show that the ending of employment for an increasing minority of the population comes earlier. At around the age of 50, economic activity rates for both men and women show a decline, and by 65–9 only 17 per cent of men and 8 per cent of women are officially economically active (OPCS 1981).

But formal retirement, or the ending of economic activity, does not necessarily mean that work is finished. Not only may people continue to be involved in informal paid work, but also the way in which economic activity is measured takes no account of unpaid work, which may or may not continue past retirement. Yet public concern about retirement as a leisure problem has tended to reinforce the view that only formal, paid employment counts as work, and consequently only formal retirement counts as work ending. This is in part because the very concept of retirement has been constructed in relation to most men's experience of employment – ideally as full-time and continuous over the life-course – and its ending, often without considering the possibility that this may not translate easily into women's experience. Sociological studies of men's retirement have tended to be used to make generalizations about retirement *per se*, qualified sometimes only by a footnote about the respective retirement ages of men and women as though that were the only difference. This means that most women's (and some men's) experience has become either invisible within discussions of the retirement of *people* who are in reality *men*, or considered to be unrelated to the issue of retirement (Szinovacz 1982).

Consequently, not only has the role of transitions or continuities in unpaid work around retirement age been neglected in both sociological and popular wisdom, but retirement is seen publicly as an issue and a problem for men and not for women. For example, there is concern about how far men become 'disengaged' or socially isolated, what kind of damage the loss of wage-earner status does to their self-esteem, and how they can occupy themselves and manage their time on a reduced income (Parker 1982; Phillipson 1987). There is much less evidence of public concern for the ways in which women are able to manage the transition to retirement, reflecting a popular view that employment is less central to their identity and experience, despite increasing sociological evidence to the contrary (Coyle 1984; Martin and Roberts 1984).

Employment had been important to the women in my study, both for their identities and the economic maintenance of their households: all but one of them had been in paid work for most of their married lives. Nevertheless, their jobs had been seen by them and their husbands as secondary and supplementary in a way that their husband's had not. They had negotiated absence from employment for childrearing and/or family crises, returning mainly on a part-time basis: meanwhile their husbands had generally been employed in full-time, continuous and more highly paid work.

An extension of this in later years was that, without exception, it was taken for granted by both the women and the men that the wives should either retire before their husbands or at the same time, even though they might not officially be required to do so: retired men should not be left at home while their wives went out to work. Retirement, as a stage of married life, was defined by the husband's departure from the labour force and in thirteen of the cases practice was in accordance with this normative prescription. In the remaining five cases, the husbands had left the labour force early and, more problematically, before their wives. Yet in these cases, justification was spontaneously given in the interviews for dissonance, where in the other cases no explanation was deemed necessary.

This is significant for the shaping of leisure choices because men's needs for leisure and relaxation – symbolized through retirement as a reward for a lifetime's labour – were taking precedence over those of their wives. There was no corresponding *rite de passage* for the women; that is, at no point in time were they symbolically rewarded for having finished their lifetime's labour. The fact that all the husbands received or expected better pensions than their wives reinforced both the validity and finality of men's labour, and the gendered nature of this particular transition.

Indeed, certain aspects of women's work not only continued but in some cases intensified. If married women's paid-work histories are intermittent this is largely attributable to other work responsibilities, particularly for family care and domestic labour. Out of the seventeen couples with children in my study, twelve now lived alone, their children having grown up and left the parental home. However, the other five had adult and/or dependent children, either still at home or returned, for example following divorces, and it seemed that 'going home to mum' was a potential resource which parents would not deny their children. None of these adult children however did much housework, and although their presence no longer created a need for *child*care, it did produce extra domestic work for their mothers at a time when the normative expectation was that this kind of work would decrease. As one woman put it: 'Just when I thought I'd have time to put my feet up because the last one had gone . . . the first one comes back. No peace for the wicked is what I call it [laughs]. But no, they know they've always got a home here if they need it.' Most of the women were also involved in inter-household domestic work, generally babysitting grandchildren for those of their children who lived nearby. Furthermore, eleven of the women – but none of the men – had been involved in later years in caring for sick and/or elderly relatives. This means that the departure of children from the parental home is not inevitable and predictable, their return is always a possibility, and that the associated domestic labour does not necessarily cease, albeit it may take a different form.

Clearly, whether or not children remain at home, there is still domestic work to be done, although there might be less of it than in the past. Over their lifetimes all the couples in my study had followed a traditional division of domestic labour, but in ten of the cases husbands had recently begun to do more to help their wives. For these couples the retirement of the husband and/or the ill health of the wife were prerequisites of this changing division of labour, although equally men could retire, and women could be ill, with no change occurring. Yet in none of the cases was the division of domestic *responsibility* modified: all the women continued to carry overall responsibility for seeing that housework got done and remained liable to be called to account for it. In more general terms they remained responsible for ensuring the well-being of their families and now particularly husbands.

The tendency for this domestic responsibility to be obscured behind a façade of couple retirement, ties in closely with another factor shaping the leisure context for women in later life: control of money. Many activities associated with leisure or hobbies require money. For example, membership of clubs and societies generally involve subscriptions, and even going out to the pub or into town requires money for drinks, petrol, bus fare and so on. What is more, having access to one's own money can bestow legitimacy on certain activities. Conversely, and more importantly, having to use someone else's money, or simply not having access to money for an activity can put its legitimacy into question. At the very least, the person providing the money is likely to exercise a degree of control over what activities the recipient uses it for.

Most of the couples talked about the increasing need to 'tighten our belts' with the ending of employment income and, for some at least, continuing financial support to adult children meant that the monetary benefits of their leaving home were negligible. In fact, financial inequalities between the couples appeared to be fairly wide as one might expect in this age group. But what is also important is the extent to which husbands and wives had unequal access to household income to spend on their own leisure or on themselves.

The husbands were clearly generally viewed as the owners and ultimate controllers of money whatever the system of income or money management in the household (Mason 1987b). Thus even in the more affluent households, or the minority where the women had a personal income somewhere near comparable to that of her husband, the men were the ones who 'treated' their wives to an evening out occasionally or who bought the drinks for example. In some of the households this was sometimes translated into a tendency for the husbands legitimately to be able to decide whether or not the couple would be 'frivolous' with the family money, by having a meal out for example.

The point is that it was easier for the men to spend money – on themselves or on their wives – without censure, and spending money on leisure activities was a part of this. Women's freedom of choice in leisure activity was without exception consequently circumscribed in a way that men's was not. There were of course differences between couples in the exact way this was played out, based not only on class differences but also on personalities, but the structure and inequality of the relationship was constant.

Personal ill health is likely to some extent to be another constraint on activity in later life. However, although nearly all of my interviewees had some kind of limiting condition – most commonly arthritis, rheumatism, angina – the connection between that and leisure activity was rarely made explicit other than in the form of comments like 'I don't do as much now you know, I'm not as young as I used to be'. For women, though, the health and well-being of husbands, as well as themselves, was a constraint, as we shall see shortly.

The interviewees were more clearly aware of normative and social controls on their behaviour, however. Many of the women spoke of feeling uncomfortable or frightened going out alone, particularly at night. This could be either simply to walk down the road or to go for a drink in a pub without their husbands. Most of the women never did the latter. These factors militated against women's extensive leisure activity with other women. One woman, who did go to a pub about once a year with an informal 'ladies group' said, 'I don't really like it. A gaggle of women, you know, I feel uncomfortable. And going to the bar . . . I'd prefer to go with the husbands really.' These kinds of findings are paralleled in studies of younger women where informal male social control over women in public places, for example through teasing and covert or overt violence, is a major contributor to women's feeling ill at ease (Green, Hebron and Woodward 1987; Imray and Middleton 1983; Whitehead 1976). But it is likely that older women feel increasingly physically vulnerable as well, suffering the double burden of ageism plus sexism (MacDonald with Rich 1984; Hemmings 1985). Certainly, older married women are unlikely to begin to gain a new independence from husbands at this time in their lives.

Added to this is another kind of dependence on husbands for women over 50: men of that age are three times as likely to have driving licences as their female contemporaries (Allan 1985). In my study, only two of the women, as compared to seventeen of the men, were both able to drive and had personal access to a car. As one of them, Ivy, explained, the inability to drive is a severe restriction on many out-of-home leisure activities:

Ivy: I used to play that game called bat and trap, used to play for a pub just down the road.
Jennifer: Don't you play anymore?
Ivy: No, well it's not . . . when I played, it just used to be round

Canterbury. Now you've got so much travelling to do you see you've got to go to Ramsgate, you've got to go to Nonington. I can't get there.

Being able to drive allows and legitimates a certain spontaneity in the use of time and space; for example, being able to pop out of the house for a drive, or to go to town and so on, without having to rely on public transport, on others, or on fine weather and one's own feet.

Leisure activity patterns

In principle, then, the ending of employment together with the departure of children from the parental home might allow more time for leisure activities both inside and outside the home. But in practice, few of the interviewees who had permanently left the labour force and/or whose children had all left home, reported either taking up new out-of-home activities or spending a great deal more time in ones previously established. However, the latter was more common. This finding accords with those of other researchers who have investigated leisure after *men's* retirement (Long 1986; Long and Wimbush 1979). Nevertheless, a minority of the men and one of the women regularly engaged in sporting activities outside the home. Other outdoor or hobby-type activities were sometimes mentioned by both women and men, such as painting, riding, swimming, birdwatching, but it turned out that these were generally performed infrequently, or had simply been done once or twice in the past.

There was evidence amongst the couples of membership of clubs and societies, and of participation in voluntary organizations. In the working-class couples the women tended not to do these things, but several of the husbands were in work- or ex-work-associated clubs, or in organizations such as the Territorial Army or the Naval Association, where membership usually dated back to the war. In the middle-class couples the situation was a bit more varied, so that a minority of the men were extremely active in, for example, the Freemasons, the local council, the church, sailing clubs, cricket clubs and so on, but most were relatively inactive in these sorts of areas and, with one exception, did not belong to work-associated clubs as the working-class men did.

On the whole the middle-class women were much more active than the working-class women in these ways; it was common for the former to be engaged in fund-raising activities for local charities or the church (e.g. jumble sales, whist drives) and one was a Freemason. A minority belonged to formal or informal women's associations such as the WI or local housewives' groups. Only one woman belonged to a women's group which had no charity focus, but was solely a social and support group for the ten women involved. She was also a member of a sailing club, along with her husband.

One middle-class woman gave a rare account of an increase in this type of out-of-home activity due to life transitions. She explained that she had been 'charged with a new vitality' when her children left home and after her menopause. She told me that 'I felt I could do anything. I was me and not mum anymore'. At that point in her life she had taken up bird-watching and theatre-going with a group of female friends. Her part-time employment as a secretary had financed her new activities and, unlike the other women, she reported having no qualms about spending her wages on her own interests because her husband had 'spent a lifetime being mean with money'. Although he was in employment at that time, he was made redundant shortly afterwards, and then she began to curtail her activities: at the time of interview she explained that she now rarely finds the time or money for bird-watching or visits to the theatre. Since her husband's redundancy it is more difficult for her to spend her part-time earnings on her own leisure.

The other women, and the majority of the men in the study, were doing the same or indeed rather less in the way of out-of-home leisure activity than they had in the past. Indeed, by far the most commonly reported leisure activities for both the women and the men were home based, and generally a great deal of time was spent at home – reading, watching television, gardening, and for women also knitting and sewing. With the exception of watching television, these home-based activities were generally undertaken separately by wives and husbands, although the territory in which they took place was on the whole a 'shared' one. I will discuss the issue of sharing and contesting space shortly.

It was in their at-home activities that people reported or anticipated the most change in the light of transitions. Most people said that the departure of children made an enormous difference to the home environment, or they anticipated that it would. Both the men and the women noticed a changing sense of time and of time norms at home. Although most of the women felt they were still busy, they acknowledged a change of pace and a slowing down. The men on the whole were grateful for, or looking forward to, relaxation. However, a majority of them, yet none of the women, regretted a loss of cohesiveness of time structure and described a kind of normlessness, that is a general feeling of purposelessness and of somehow, and regrettably, no longer having good routines such as those imposed by the working-day and the presence of children. The men were particularly concerned about becoming physically inactive, and of 'stagnating' in retirement and in some cases it was clearly problematic for them to reconcile this with a desire for relaxation.

However, the most important change concerning at-home activity was simply that people were spending (or anticipating spending) more time there – whether or not this was defined as work or play. Not only that, but husbands and wives would be spending more time in each other's company than before. Indeed, this was a stated pleasure of many of the men in the research, for whom a 'lifetime's slog' in employment, as one of them put it, was to be rewarded by a comfortable retirement spent at home with his wife. The overwhelming pattern was for the men to look forward to this period of more sedate togetherness, in the comfort of their own homes.

Negotiations between wives and husbands

One effect of the husbands' tendency to begin focusing their values and their presence on the home was to compromise the wives' previously autonomous time and, to a degree, space. Although most of the women had, at least until recently, been employed outside the home, they had over the years spent more time at home than their husbands. Their identities as wives and mothers were bound up with the work of domestic servicing and 'homemaking'. Most importantly, through their own domestic organization and household routines the women had practised a certain autonomy. This led them to be ambivalent about the relative benefits of the increasingly full-time company of their husbands at home.

First of all, simply by their physical presence during the day, husbands could contribute to a problem of finding separate or private space in the household. This is clearly a problem in small houses, but it is also a problem even where there is potentially a lot of space if the parties are not sensitive to it. For women who had become accustomed to being in charge of the domestic domain and having autonomy there for at least some of the day, this could mean an encroachment on what they felt to be 'personal' time and/or space. As well as complaining of husbands 'getting under their feet', some women felt threatened by the potential for surveillance of their established work and leisure practices that the presence of husbands presented. Although the women had laboured in and out of the home all their lives, amongst most of them was prevalent a 'guilty' view that their lot had been rather better than their husbands' – they had taken breaks from employment, 'chosen' to go back to work, had 'time-off' during the day, and so on. Not only would 'personal' time and space no longer be private and be taken to suit one's own timetable, but husbands would be able to observe just how much of it they had. What this really meant was potentially having to account for what one woman called 'the silly little things that I do', and for one's private moments. This is a particular problem *for women* because they are more constrained, as we have seen, in out-of-home activity than their husbands.

As well as presenting a problem simply by 'being there', husbands also were beginning to create different forms of domestic work for the women. Partly this was accounted for by the same kinds of domestic labour which women had always undertaken for their husbands, but now they were being called upon to do certain things 'to order' during the day, when before they had some freedom in constructing their own daytime domestic timetables (within the spaces created by the husband's working-day). For example, where women had often previously got a snack for themselves at lunchtime, some were finding themselves cooking, in Anne Murcott's terms, a more substantial 'proper' meal for the two of them (Murcott 1983).

However, more importantly, the women had responsibility not just for domestic servicing but for caring for their husbands' health and happiness in a much broader sense, and the husbands' home-centredness in some ways intensified this (Mason 1987a, 1987b). This was particularly pertinent because this time of life is seen as problematic for men, and like never before, family status and public approval centres on their successful use of 'leisure time', because retirement is seen largely as a problem of leisure – that is engagement, adjustment, assimilation and so on.

Therefore, as well as losing some control of the domestic timetable, the women were spending large amounts of the day worrying about whether their husbands would stagnate in retirement, and in trying to ensure that they did not by preventing them from being bored, lonely, inactive or lazy, and generally in helping to structure their time and facilitate their leisure.

What is more, the women on the whole tried to make sure that their husbands were only rarely at home on their own. We have already seen that the women tended to retire with their husbands, and for those who had not, this was seen as problematic. Whilst they had been in full-time employment the men had been used to spending their at-home time in the company of their wives. It is perhaps not surprising therefore that many of them viewed retirement as a time for togetherness, since home was likely to be associated with this in their experience. For those men who had retired, the majority of their time at home continued to be spent jointly with wives, although for some of them, especially where wives were still in paid work, there was an increase in the amount of time spent alone at home. Conversely, the women had been used to having more time at home without their husbands, although this varied according to factors like the number of hours spent in employment. It seemed that for all of them, this time had been interspersed with out-of-home time, generally associated with domestic labour, for example spent on going to the shops, the post office, the bank, the dry cleaners, and for some of them to meet children or grandchildren from school and so on. In a sense this accords with findings of other researchers who argue that younger women occupy 'communal spaces' during the daytime to a greater extent than do men (Cornwell 1984; Finch 1984; Allan 1983). Although privileged in having few constraints on their out-of-home activity, husbands, by their own accounts, did not appear so readily to strike up conversations in grocers' shops or with neighbours met in the street, as their wives, whose accounts were often interspersed with this kind of detail. However, once retired, the women spent much more time in their husbands' company at home even where the men were involved in casual employment.

Yet the women with housebound husbands had modified their own activities because they were reluctant to go out and leave husbands alone at home. As one woman put it, 'You can't just go and do things like you used to. You're not free. You have a conscience'. What this means is that the men potentially could seem rather helpless, 'like a fish out of water' as one woman put it and the women felt responsible and guilty for their husbands' dependence. Another woman, who had been a keen tennis and badminton player, had given up her sporting activities when her husband had a coronary thrombosis because she felt it would have been unfair for her to carry on. As she explained:

> I got rid of my racket and things when I realized he couldn't play. Well so did he. So I got rid of mine, which was quite heart-rending at the time. I had to give it up you know, which was quite sad, but I don't think I ever showed that I was miserable about it. I just thought 'I've got to. It's not fair if I do it and he can't'. So that was the end of that.

This meant that the situation was a rather contradictory one for many of the women: glad to see more of their husbands, resentful that husbands were encroaching on their own domain, space and behaviour, worried about husbands health and happiness around the difficult time of retirement and about whether they were seeing enough friends now the social contacts of employment had been cut, and about public opinion as to husbands' adjustment. It was against this context that the women were negotiating their own 'personal' time and space.

Some of the women were in better negotiating positions than others. Obviously, factors like the degree of 'dependency' of husbands; previously established patterns of 'personal' time and space within the marriage; the availability of legitimate reasons or excuses for 'escape' from the household and of resources to enable such escape, and so on, are vital in enabling or constraining.

But it is important to appreciate that the increasing home-centredness of husbands, and prevalent norms of togetherness in retirement, actually make the initiation of overt negotiation for their own leisure spaces rather difficult for women because it looks like a confrontation, and is likely to seem rather unfair. In fact, only one of the couples had such negotiations. Generally, however, women achieved 'personal' time and space, not always unambiguously for leisure (and to varying degrees of success): by default, for example where their husbands spent a lot of time in a garden shed or allotment; by moments of conflict, for example one woman told me the spare bedroom was her own personal space 'when I have my airs'; and most importantly, by *strategy*. For example, although popping out to the shops spontaneously was becoming more difficult, one woman who liked 'mooching' round the shops told me that 'I'm going to start going when he's up the ladder. I'll wait until he's at the top, get my coat and bag and shout "bye dear", and be off like a dose of salts before he can get down and come with me.'

For those, mainly working-class, women whose adult children all lived nearby, visiting daughters during the daytime provided a legitimate way out of the household, although this was not always discernible from kin support in the form of babyminding. But overall the women were extremely innovative and ingenious in their strategies. Others ranged from providing husbands with a list of pressing home-improvement and repair needs or generally hinting about work that needed doing, to 'nagging' about husband's domestic performance and 'getting under my feet in the kitchen'. It is likely, also, that my research only touched the tip of the iceberg here, as the line between conscious strategies and subconscious practices becomes fuzzy and unreportable.

Conclusion

It is important, in conclusion, to emphasize a cautionary note about interpretation running through this chapter. That is that we cannot generalize activity *patterns* from a small sample, and that even within the sample there are important divisions. One is always pushed to generalize findings in short articles based on qualitative research, when the data are constantly speaking against crude generalizations and classifications. Of course, not all the men were frantically home centred, and not all the women felt an urgent need for 'personal' space which they could not get. Factors such as the pattern of children leaving home, of employment ending, clearly also make a difference.

However, qualitative research is able more adequately to provide *valid* observations, and we have seen the reality of various constraints on women's at-home and out-of-home leisure. Women are divided, for example, along class lines or in terms of their own relationship with their husband, but the reality of potential constraint is in evidence for all the women in the study. Similarly the process, and the overt and covert negotiations surrounding women's leisure, are issues which unite them, as also, and perhaps most importantly, are the methods and strategies by which they manage to carve out at least some time and space from a framework of constraint.

References

Allan, Graham (1983) 'Informal networks of care: issues raised by Barclay', *British Journal of Social Work* 13: 417–33.
  (1985) *Family Life*, Oxford, Blackwell.
Anderson, Michael (1985) 'The emergence of the modern life cycle', *Social History* 10: 69–87.
Cornwell, Jocelyn (1984) *Hard Earned Lives*, London, Tavistock.
Coyle, Angela (1984) *Redundant Women*, London, The Women's Press.
Finch, Janet (1984) 'Community care: developing non-sexist alternatives', *Critical Social Policy* 9: 6–18.
Green, Eileen, Hebron, Sandra and Woodward Diana (1987) 'Women, leisure and social control', in Jalna Hanmer and Mary Maynard (eds.) *Women, Violence and Social Control*, London, Macmillan.
Hemmings, Sue (1985) *A Wealth of Experience: The Lives of Older Women*, London, Pandora Press.
Imray, Linda and Middleton, Audrey (1983) 'Public and private: marking the boundaries', in E. Gamarnikow, David Morgan, June Purvis, Daphne Taylorson (eds.) *The Public and the Private*, London, Heinemann.
Long, Jonathan (1986) 'Continuity as a basis for change; leisure around male retirement', paper presented to Annual Conference of the British Sociological Association, 'The Sociology of the Life Cycle', University of Loughborough, March.
Long, Jonathan and Wimbush, Erica (1979) *Leisure and the Over 50s*, London, Sports Council/SSRC.
MacDonald, Barbara and Rich, Cynthia (1984) *Look Me in the Eye: Old Women, Aging and Ageism*, London, The Women's Press.
Martin, Jean and Roberts, Ceridwen (1984) *Women and Employment: A Lifetime Perspective*, London, Department of Employment/OPCS, HMSO.
Mason, Jennifer (1987a) Gender inequality in long-term marriages' unpublished PhD thesis, University of Kent.
  (1987b) 'A bed of roses?: women, marriage and inequality in later life', in Pat Allatt, Bill Bytheway, Alan Bryman and Teresa Keil (eds.) *Women and the Life Cycle: Transitions and Turning Points*, London, Macmillan.
Murcott, Anne (1983) ' "It's a pleasure to cook for him": food, mealtimes and gender in some South Wales households', in E. Gamarnikow, David Morgan, June Purvis and Daphne Taylorson (eds.) *The Public and the Private*, London, Heinemann.
Murphy, M. (1983) 'The life course of individuals in the family: describing static and dynamic aspects of the contemporary family', in OPCS/British Society for Population Studies, *Occasional Paper 31, The Family*.
OPCS (1981) *Census*, London, HMSO.
Parker, Stanley (1982) *Work and Retirement*, London, Allen & Unwin.
Phillipson, Chris (1987) 'The transition to retirement', in G. Cohen (ed.) *Social Change and the Life Course*, London, Tavistock.
Rapoport, Rhona and Rapoport, Robert (1975) *Leisure and the Family Life Cycle*, London, Routledge & Kegan Paul.
Szinovacz, M. (ed.) (1982) *Women's Retirement*, Beverly Hills, Sage.
Whitehead, Ann (1976) 'Sexual antagonism in Herefordshire', in Diana Leonard, Diana Barker and Sheila Allen (eds.) *Dependence and Exploitation in Work and Marriage*, London, Longman.

PART 3

Exploring the myths

INTRODUCTION

Because leisure is integral to our social lives, its analysis and description are inevitably coloured by social assumptions about gender roles. This is often not a process of conscious misperception, but a process which allows descriptions which merely reproduce what is already taken for granted. Myths are the product of this process and help to perpetuate its cycle. Myths embody sets of assumptions and beliefs which, while being based on particular ideologies, legitimate and maintain the prevailing social system as 'good' and 'necessary' in its present form.

In such a process, forms and strategies alternative to what is perceived as 'natural' and 'normal' tend to become stigmatized as inferior, irrelevant, marginal or deviant. Women who take part in the leisure activities described in this part have all suffered from having their participation derided or undervalued, simply because their activities take place in all-female groups or are associated with particular views of femininity, sexuality or female capacity. Their own perceptions of their activities and participation have tended to be private, invisible and lacking in legitimation. One of the important functions of this part is to allow women who have enthusiasm for their leisure activities to present them in positive ways, in terms of their benefit to them as women and of the way success within them contributes to their self-image and confidence as human beings.

Disco dancing, bingo and sport are the three activities under scrutiny in this part. Women's participation in them is embedded in gender inequalities, yet at the same time women are able to demonstrate some control over their involvement and even over the form and nature of the activity. The concept of 'agency', used predominantly in cultural studies, corresponds with women's effects on the activities in which they participate.

Myths serve mainly to perpetuate the dominant values and beliefs integral to the cultures which have created them. By reinterpreting leisure activities, and imbuing them with alternative values, women (consciously or unconsciously) generate competing ideologies. By rejecting or adapting the rules and mores of these activities to suit themselves, women are also challenging the structural determinism inherent in the expectation that social life should continue in its present form.

The study of popular culture has been defined as a site of *positive* political engagement by both socialists and feminists in their concern to identify both those aspects of popular culture which serve to secure consent to existing social arrangements as well as those which, in embodying alternative values, supply a source of opposition to those arrangements.

(Bennett 1986: xii)

Bingo, dancing and sport serve as illustrative case studies which debunk assumptions about popular culture and women's activities. However, in that they provide largely separate and segregated leisure experience for women, it may also be argued that these activities perpetuate women's marginal place in the male culture.

Rachael Dixey's study of bingo (Ch. 7) demonstrates the importance of the function of myth within one activity: part of the unique attraction of bingo lies in its ritual and expected form. 'Being safe' and comfortable in a public space is unusual for women, and bingo is one context which provides it. What is more, women as the consumer group control and regulate the social interactions within the bingo club – 'bingo is an opportunity which women have seized' – and bingo players have reconstructed a leisure activity which subverts the complex of constraints which operate on working-class women. This has not prevented it from being viewed in negative ways, both by the media (until newspaper bingo!) and by people who do not play. The moral panics and derision prompted by bingo have constantly been resented by its players, who see it as part of everyday life and as a major source of community and social contact.

Similarly, the girls observed by Vivienne Griffiths (Ch. 9) used dancing, often in an all-female group, as a focus for social activity, and 'having a laugh together'. Disco's provided opportunities for the girls to express style and to control access to their groups while enjoying the ability to display sexuality in a relatively safe context. Griffiths describes disco dance competitions as avenues for achievement 'in a girls-only arena'. Ironically they also reify the stereotyped images of femininity which binds girls' behaviour and expectations. A few girls combined fantasy with a commitment in their pursuit of dancing as a career. At all three levels, girls showed their enjoyment of physical movement – dispelling the myth that females dislike physical activity.

Margaret Talbot's analysis of sportwomen (Ch. 8) also challenges this myth: all the women mentioned the joy of vigorous movement as a major benefit of their involvement in sport. Sport is traditionally seen as male, and women who play sport are helping to redefine both sport and femininity.

All three studies serve to illustrate the notion of 'empowerment', the ability and capacity of women to speak for themselves, to control their own activities, to be taken seriously, and to redefine elements of their world according to their own terms and values. Lack of space has prevented coverage of work on other activities which act as a focus for women's attempts to interpret and define their lives in their own way: their use of television, radio, books, magazines and home video; their involvement in religious and local community groups. These are all areas which would repay further study. Neither has it been possible to discuss women's perceptions and imagery of other leisure activities – ones which women see as theirs, belonging to others, irrelevant, offensive or impossible. There is still much to learn about the ways in which women manage to appropriate and transcend certain activities for their own purposes.

References

Bennett, Tony (1986) 'Introduction: popular culture and "the turn to Gramsci" ', in Tony Bennett, Colin Mercer, Janet Woollacott (eds.) *Popular Culture and Social Relations*, Milton Keynes, Open University Press.

7

'Eyes down': A study of bingo

RACHAEL DIXEY

The data on which this chapter is based was collected during 1981 and 1982. The author had a brief to carry out research into bingo specifically, why it was so popular with women. The resulting research was in two parts. First a community study was carried out in an area of Leeds, Armley. This is a largely working-class area, stretching from near to the city centre towards the suburbs. Its economy today is based on textiles and light engineering. It has a number of industrial estates and new housing estates interspersed among the nineteenth-century back-to-back housing and brick factories. Levels of unemployment have risen in recent years, and the area faces not inconsiderable poverty. There is a large amount of community activity and sense of both history (Armley was mentioned in the Domesday Book) and of 'community'. Over a period of a year, the author spent time in Armley getting to know people, and administered (to women only) a lengthy questionnaire on leisure activities and also interviewed a number of women in depth. At this stage respondents did not know of my interest in bingo. Leisure for women in Armley revolved around the 'big five' of being with people, television, reading, drinking and playing bingo. The second part of the research was more extensive and concentrated only on bingo. Eighty bingo sessions were attended in a range of cities, towns and villages from Edinburgh, Glasgow, through the North East, Manchester, West Yorkshire, the Midlands, South Wales, London, and down to Brighton. A questionnaire containing twenty-six questions on such matters as frequency of playing, which venues, amount spent and so on was filled in by 7,166 players. Together, the two parts of the research generated a large amount of data not only about bingo but also about other ways in which women spend their time. Figures and quotations used in this paper refer to data collected in the research, unless it is stated otherwise (see Dixey with Talbot 1982).

There is no single reason which explains the popularity of bingo; what is of interest is its complexity. It is an activity undertaken by a section of the population (largely working-class women), at a specific historical point, to meet the particular needs of that group at that time. Each of the ingredients of the game is necessary to create the combination which has proved so successful. These ingredients will be explored here.

Before embarking on this exercise, we can ask why a study of bingo is important. First, it is important because bingo is an activity which is important to
women; if we are concerned with understanding women's leisure, it is necessary
to understand why large numbers of women are attracted to a particular activity.
Second, it is possible to see bingo as an opportunity which women have seized.
Working-class women have adopted this activity which was offered by commercial concerns, and fashioned it in order to make something useful and meaningful
for themselves. In other words, within the contrived nature of bingo, women have
restructured some of the essential parts of working-class life. Of course, this
reconstruction has taken place within the constraints (political and economic)
imposed on the working class, but that reconstruction symbolizes women's ability to create their own space, within a tradition of 'making the best of
things'.

If a constraints model of women's leisure is adopted – in other words, that
women's leisure takes place within the constraints of time, finance, resources,
mobility and social expectations, and that it is necessary to understand, first, the
factors (such as the role of housewife) which have resulted in particular leisure
outcomes – then it is relatively easy to put forward a superficial (but valid),
account of bingo's popularity. Bingo clubs are local, handy, cheap, acceptable to
menfolk, offer the excitement of winning: bingo is flexible in terms of commitment and does not require the acquisition of complicated skills. At a less superficial level, there are other characteristics of bingo which help to explain why it 'took
off' in the early 1960s. Through discussing their involvement in bingo, the
women in the study were given a chance to explain 'the actor's point of view'. We
are used to hearing the opinions of bingo's critics and opponents (some of which
are outlined below); the research exercise thus served to explore and perhaps
debunk some of the myths surrounding bingo.

Whilst it is easy to recognize that bingo overcomes the constraints faced by a
group in society with limited economic and political power, those in positions of
power find it difficult to comprehend why people should play bingo. The group
with cultural hegemony use bingo to deride the working class. Commenting on a
radio programme about it, a reviewer wrote, ' "God knows what we'd do if we
didn't go to bingo" said one hooked lady. And that's surely a sad comment on our
education system' (*Radio Times*, 11–17 September 1982).

When commercial bingo emerged in the early 1960s, players were presented as
decadent or socially inadequate. According to Downes *et al.*, bingo has 'come to
epitomise the "dead-end" use of leisure to which a newly "affluent" working
class has resorted in the absence of anything better to do with their time' (1976:
174). One newspaper reported in the 1960s, 'To the uninitiated, bingo seems
utterly dull and pointless, yet people still flock to it in thousands, in many ways the
only way of filling a huge vacuum in their lives' (*South Wales Argus*, 26 May 1965).
Earlier, *The Times* had been particularly scathing: 'Those who hopefully scan the
social scene for growing evidence of the "creative use of leisure", one of the
promised fruits of universal education, are bound to be depressed by the success of
this cretinous pastime' (*The Times*, 14 September 1961).

Women are portrayed as irresponsible in the newspaper articles which still
appear:

As cinemas and dance halls close, bingo palaces take over. More and more women are being drawn into the world of gambling. It is a world of deceit and ruin . . . where the prayed-for 'big win' is worshipped with all the anticipation of the second coming. And where nothing is sacred if it can be sold for betting money.

(*Glasgow Evening Times*, 25 March 1980)

Another response is to patronize, which can be illustrated by the Home Office and Gaming Board, which have been concerned to protect women from themselves:

Bingo is a very popular game, especially amongst housewives, and it soon became apparent to the Board that the half a million or so women who play each day should not be exposed to the temptations of hard gaming

(Gaming Board 1969: 9)

Players, of course, are conscious of this attack. For some it tinges their favoured activity with guilt and for others it adds to the idea of a 'ritual of resistance'. What is of interest is why there should be a sustained attack on bingo. The root of it is, perhaps, because bingo is associated with what is female, working class and middle aged. In an ageist, sexist and élitist society, and also one which has fixed ideas about what constitutes 'worthwhile' leisure pursuits, this reaction is not surprising.

The available data on bingo playing does bear out the picture of a female, working-class, middle-aged activity, but this does not give a fully accurate description. The data which is available is not standardized; that is, some figures include only bingo played in commercial clubs and others include bingo played at other venues. Gaming Board figures suggest that 14 per cent of the adult population played bingo in 1980 and that 83 per cent of the players were women. Figures collected by the Target Group Index show that 86 per cent of male and 82 per cent of female players are drawn from social classes C2, D, E; further, 72 per cent of male and 82 per cent of female players are aged more than 35 (see Dixey with Talbot 1982: 2–6). The area where most bingo is played is the north east of England and in the north of Britain generally, it is more popular, mirroring the distribution of social classes. (With 35 per cent of the national population, the north has 45 per cent of the commercial bingo clubs.)

The historical juncture

Commercial bingo was made possible by the 1960 Betting and Gaming Act which enabled members of private clubs to gamble. Designed to clear up the anomalies surrounding existing laws and to sweep away the large amount of illegal gambling activity, the Act in fact catapulted Britain into a new gambling age, leading to the 'greatest gambling boom outside the state of Nevada' (Booker 1969: 19). This coincided with a time of relative affluence and of increasing participation of married women in the paid workforce, giving many women their 'own' money to spend for the first time. The early 1960s was also a time, of course, of rapid social change. There was the beginning of the emphasis on 'youth', of looking young, of being young. There were changes too in the way in which people spent their leisure time:

The steady spread of affluence and the increasing tempo of change was creating a rising appetite for excitement throughout England. . . . The bright lights were indeed reaching the provinces – and not just the bingo palaces and striptease clubs and steak houses, but the Chinese restaurants and French films and the taste for Spanish holidays.

(Booker 1969: 49)

With the new came the passing of the old. The slum clearances, the ideology of classlessness and affluence, and the shift of emphasis away from work, craftsmanship and production to non-work, new technologies and consumption, brought profound changes to working-class life. Whilst it is easy to romanticize the gregarious conviviality of the 'traditional working-class neighbourhood', there were important changes in the physical structure of communities which affected social networks. Extended families faced increased distance between members due to rehousing, and the new housing estates and tower blocks destroyed the sense of community based on the communal street, pub and corner shops. The loss of semi-public space in which interaction could take place was lost; perhaps this speeded up the move to home-based leisure which had already begun. Whilst the working men's club and pub still provided opportunities for male companionship, these were not available to women in their own right; their activity became increasingly centred on the private sphere of the home if young children were present, or if not working outside the home. In the early 1960s, then, the commercial bingo club simply provided one place for unaccompanied women to enjoy the non-intimate, public, type of companionship traditionally present in the working-class neighbourhood. (To a large extent this is still the case; few women in the Armley community study said that they would go to pubs unaccompanied by husbands.) Also, the bingo clubs, opening in former cinemas benefited from an established tradition of women socializing at 'the pictures'. In the 1950s:

It is not at all unusual for women to attend the cinema unaccompanied. For many women with young children the cinema is the sole relaxation outside the home and they often come alone while the husband looks after the children.

(Kuper 1953: 119)

The cinema was used in ways which echo the use of bingo a decade later:

The main recreational activity for women is the cinema. Gong to a show is an occasion for active neighbouring; it expresses an established relationship . . . As for the men, the cinema has little effect on neighbouring. They attend less often than the women; 'the fathers have to stay at home with the children'.

(Kuper 1953: 120)

In other ways, too, there were continuities with the past. Whilst many players do not regard bingo as 'a gamble', it is a form of gambling and there is a history of working-class female involvement in betting and lotteries (McKibbin 1979; Bell 1911). This mainly took the form of small-scale, systematic betting, often in a deliberate attempt to add to the household income, spending amounts which would not have made a great difference to the standard of living if saved. (Bingo is seen in a similar way). Second, there is a history, particularly this century, of the working class buying commercially provided leisure. From the 1880s companies such as Mecca have provided leisure activities, changing them as tastes changed (e.g. from dance halls to cinema to bingo clubs). In a dialectical way, Helen Meller comments that by 1905, 'popular taste was being formed by commercial entertainment' (Meller 1976: 222).

By the early 1960s, then, there were established traditions into which bingo fitted, together with some fundamental changes occurring within working-class life. Several of these changes afforded women new opportunities but in other ways, as in any time of rapid social change, attempts can be seen to reassert the older values and social patterns which were under threat. Bingo, likewise, can be seen to offer women new opportunities and at the same time to celebrate central features of the 'traditional' culture which was under threat.

By the early 1980s, commercial bingo had been part of British life for twenty years. It is beyond the remit of this paper to discuss how British life has changed during that time, but we can bring the account of bingo up to date, and see the ways in which women use it in the 1980s.

The game

Bingo as a game requires the minimum of initiation. The game is relatively simple. Each card has fifteen numbers on it and the object is to cross them off as they are called out in random order. If six cards are played, each number from 1 to 90 is present and the player crosses off a number at each call. Each game lasts several minutes with a pause while the winning card is checked. The atmosphere is serious; there is none of the caricatured 'legs eleven, number eleven' and so on. There is complete silence apart from the voice of the caller whilst the game is in motion. It is essential that mistakes are not made when large amounts are at stake.

It can be suggested that an essential ingredient of bingo's success is that it is a game of pure chance. As it requires no special skills, there can be no criticism for failing to win and neither can one's confidence be undermined, as the result had nothing to do with one's own efforts. The absence of competition or the opportunity to show skill minimizes the possibility of conflict and the game can proceed (usually) in an amiable manner. As it is important that individuals get along with each other, it is important that everyone is equal before fate: no one can use skill to get ahead of anyone else.

Sociability

When asked why they play bingo, players' answers centred on sociability and winning. Of the national survey, 44 per cent gave their reasons for playing as 'winning some money' and the rest gave other reasons mostly to do with being with people. In practice, players found it difficult to disentangle these motives. Bingo might be used for regular organized contact, to meet sisters, mothers, friends, but also simply to find female companionship: 'The reason I come in the afternoon is to get women to talk to. I've got a house full of men . . . and well, men don't talk as much as women do'. It is also used simply to be among other people, without necessarily interacting with them:

> If you're not a person who does mix easily, you can sit down and you don't *have* to mix.

> There are certain times that I do just totally ignore anybody; well, say hello and that, but don't encourage them to chat. And other times it's handy to have somebody to talk to.

This flexibility is valued, as is the fact that 'bingo is one of the easiest places to start to be sociable', and 'you don't notice one person coming in on her own to bingo'.

For many elderly women the club was their main source of social contact in an otherwise lonely existence. Of the national sample, 55 per cent of the 76 years and older age-group played three times a week or more, compared with 18 per cent of the 18–25 age range. It is possible to argue that in an age where caring networks have failed, the bingo club provides the focus for a 'moral community'. In many clubs the management takes its welfare role very seriously, sending flowers to members when widowed or ill, asking after members' health and so on. More than one club reported opening on Christmas Day for those with nowhere else to go. Many of the elderly women would arrive up to two hours before the afternoon session started, to eat, talk, knit, read or play cards with others in a warm place.

Whilst 69 per cent of players are aged over 46 years, there are considerable numbers of younger players. Some younger women enjoyed playing on their own, sitting, not having to talk to anyone, getting a break from home and children: 'I usually go for a bit of sanity', and, 'It's just more or less – a need to get out of the house'. In whatever ways the club is used for social interaction, players need to create 'space' for themselves, either to ensure that all the group find seats together, or to create distance from others:

> The table's more comfortable, but you can't occupy a whole table to yourself. If you want to be on your own, you can sit in those [cinema] seats and put your bags down and such, so that no one will come and sit with you, but at a table you'd always get somebody pestering you.

One reason for arriving early is to enable more control over social interaction, because 'if you go a bit late you have to squash in with somebody', that is somebody you might not know.

Remarks made by women during the course of fieldwork suggest that the club is seen as a 'home-from-home'. 'At-homeness' refers to a state of being comfortable in and cosily familiar with a physical place. In 1959 Richard Hoggart made the point that in English working-class life the living-room kitchen constitutes a deeply private place, where the family is truly 'at home'. It was only men who experienced a similar feeling in other places; thus Dennis, Henriques and Slaughter (1956) suggested that miners felt more 'at home' in the pub than in their actual homes. For some women the bingo club may provide a similar place, helped by the fact that the club may have been physically present in the community for many years, as a cinema.

The notion of 'at-homeness' has a reverse side, that of feelings of territoriality which may involve aggression. Territoriality involves the organization of space into 'clearly demarcated territories which are made distinctive and considered at least partially exclusive by their occupants' (Soja 1971: 19). Thus inside the club 76 per cent of the national sample said that they always like to sit in the same seat. This can cause arguments: 'people do moan if you happen to sit in their seats. It's the older generation who do that.' In effect, players were referring to the defence of space, and to the fact that this allows greater control over neighbours. It also provides a logical reason for arriving early, when perhaps the real reason is to extend the period outside the home.

Ritual

The concern over seating is partly to do with spatial expression of social networks, but it also adds to the ritual of the game. Any participant observer is struck by the ritual of bingo. It can be called ritual if 'ritual' is defined as a 'striking or incongruous rigidity . . . some conscious regularity' (Goody 1961: 156). Bingo is a public ritual engaged in by many players. Its repetitiveness and the fact that it is always known what will happen is seen as an asset. As explained by a player, ritual has an important function:

I think people feel safe. I think people get frightened at too much change. . . . People tend to just want to stay as they are. Everybody wants more money and to live a bit better, but they don't want to see things change too much. You get all these computers and things like that and it frightens people because they are losing control . . .

Earlier, in 1953, the writer Doris Rich remarked, of repetitive leisure activities:

Through this constant repetition of the same kinds of activity it seems that people find satisfaction in consolidating the world they know rather than expanding it, in making secure their old roles rather than seeking new ones. It is thus, by keeping 'still' . . . that the individual can avoid the impact of the powerful and unknown forces of 'society'.

(Rich 1953: 361)

'Safety' and feeling 'safe' were mentioned many times; 'It's a pleasant evening, you have a chat, you have a laugh, and you're sort of safe with people'. This has to do with feeling comfortable, but importantly for women, with feeling safe from unwanted contact with men, which could not be guaranteed in a pub. Another feature of the rigidity of the game which is important for women, is that the session always starts and finishes at the same time, enabling women who need to, to plan their time and public transport.

Finally, another reason for repeating actions is concerned with luck. Some players would wear the same clothes, use the same pen, sit in the same seat as it was 'lucky'. Others would always buy their cards as soon as they arrive, or just before the game started and so on; within the ritual, individuals also develop their own routines.

Winning

The chance of a win, that is of the unexpected happening, disguises the extent to which the event is always the same. Undoubtedly the possibility of a win is an essential ingredient:

> People will go to bingo and if they won a big house, say they won £1,000 on a Wednesday, right, they'll go back next Wednesday and say 'Maybe I'll get it again' – well that's human nature.

It is also exciting, as one 20 year old describes 'nearly' winning £1,000:

> I was shaking . . . And he started to say 'On its own . . .' and I got ready to shout and he said 'Number 5' and the lady next to me shouted it, and I couldn't stop shaking. My heart was going 'boom boom' with getting all excited and that . . . I said [to my mother] 'I nearly won a thousand pounds' and she says, 'calm down, you haven't won it'. It would have been lovely if I'd have had, you know.

However, players do not expect to win and do not see it as the main rationale for playing: 'I'm not here to win really. If I win, good enough, but I'm here for the company and relaxation.' Winnings tend to be used to cement existing social relationships; friends will sometimes agree to share prizes, and relations may gain too:

> If it's bigger I share it [with my mother]. I'm right good to my mam but she's right good to me. I don't know when I get a bit older when I'll be needing her, if I get married and that, but I've always looked after my mam.

Although 73 per cent of the national sample described bingo as gambling, it is not seen in the same way as other gambling forms. Outlay is known and players usually spend the same among each session. As one woman said, 'They can turn around and say they've lost £12 [playing on one-armed bandits]. Well there's no way I can lose £12 sitting here.' The cost is not offset against winnings but against the cost of other activities, such as going to the cinema or pub. There was a feeling from women that they had a right to spend money as they wished if they had earned it: 'I work all week so I feel I'm entitled to that £10.' In 1982 the usual amount spent per session was £3, with a range between 85 pence and £20. Of the national sample, 2.6 per cent spent more than £10. Those spending more than the average tended to be in the 36–45 age-group, and to spend money at the bar, one-armed bandits and party bingo (in the interval). For the majority, however, bingo is a cheap night out.

Players are conscious that others benefit from their expenditure. They acknowledge the symbiotic relationship between club owners, managers and players: 'Well, they say he's [the club owner] just been to Israel on our money, when he comes back with his lovely tan . . . [but] it's just a joke . . . we know we spend our money here of our own free will'. In a situation where women were conscious of their lack of political and economic power and felt their powerlessness acutely, the bingo club provided a venue where they could exercise choice; even if some of the players did recognize that others benefited at their expense, they could still say that this was so because they chose it. The consensus from the players was that the outlay was worth the returns, in terms of companionship and the creation of a largely female space to share with friends and family, where the humour (and sexual innuendo), pace and ambience were determined by themselves.

Players and non-players

Whilst 47 per cent of the women interviewed or questioned in Armley played bingo, the rest did not, although most had tried it at some point. The younger age-group saw bingo as a 'game for old biddies' and they felt that they had 'much more interesting and rewarding things to do'. Most comments were short and to the point – 'hate it', 'dull', 'boring' were typical. However, one woman wrote, 'Find it makes my blood pressure go up – too exciting!'

Non-players tended to see bingo as an instrumental activity for which they expected larger returns for their expenditure than the prize money on offer. One woman described the experience of her grandmother:

> I don't think she's won in the past four or five years anything, and she goes religiously every week, and yet she won £20 and she was over the moon about it. She could have a hell of a lot more than that just on money she spends going to bingo.

Many shared the myth of bingo players as irresponsible women who gambled away their housekeeping money. Comments were made about 'addiction', ('it's a fever with some people'), and also about the cost ('to me it's all wrong'). The myths can be used by non-players to justify their non-involvement and to distance themselves. One woman commented:

> If you had a good wage you'd never find better class people going into the bingo hall, only the ordinary lower types, low wages and working-class people and they're always chasing money. The attraction is the money, but if you were better off, you wouldn't think that way. . . . I've got friends who've got their own businesses and worked their way up from nothing . . . you wouldn't get them going in there. . . . They would be thinking what they could do with that £5 note . . .

Thus, where people perceived themselves as upwardly mobile, they saw this as incompatible with the image of the bingo player. To some extent, playing bingo at the church could relieve any cognitive dissonance, as this was for a 'good cause'. Others, however, had nothing against players or bingo itself; they simply said that they did not like it and were involved in other things. In general, the players in the sample were older (by an average of twelve years) than the non-players, and many of the differences between the two groups are attributable to this fact. Players were more likely to be widowed, live alone, to live in council housing, and not to have a car. Considering only those aged 40 or less there was a significant difference in levels of educational attainment; 35 per cent of the non-players had continued beyond the age of 16 at school compared with 6 per cent of the players. Players were more likely to prefer ITV to BBC, to do the football pools, not to take an annual holiday, and not to be regular church-goers, compared with non-players.

Final comments

It is not surprising that bingo was launched and had (perhaps) its heyday in the turbulent decade of the 1960s. The market for bingo did not continue to rise much after 1970, the year that the Gaming Board commented, 'It seems clear that bingo has come to stay in Britain' (Gaming Board 1970: 12). The need for a place in which women could meet was mentioned as early as 1939 by Margery Spring-Rice:

> Both young and middle-aged women need some form of recreation; they need opportunities to use the leisure they may have, and to indulge in activities outside the home. They need to meet their fellows, to form social ties, to laugh . . . in short they need a club to which they can go at any time on any day for a few hours' rest and recreation.
>
> (Spring-Rice [1939] 1981: 201)

Such a place was provided by bingo clubs, against a background of loss of semi-public space. In keeping with a capitalist society, such clubs were provided by commercial concerns using a game which had a long history but which was restructured to produce profit. The fact that commercial bingo is facing a period of relative decline may indicate that women now have other opportunities; it may however be an indication of increased poverty. The national survey of course did not include those who have stopped playing, but of the existing players, one-quarter played less at the time of the survey than they had one year previously. Eighty per cent gave a financial reason for the change. Bingo clubs still attract between a third and half a million people every day, but despite its obvious popularity, there is some evidence to suggest that some women would prefer to engage in other activities if they had the opportunity, and that bingo is not played as a positive choice but due to a lack of alternatives. Thus, of the retired people interviewed by Ian Dobbin, 4 per cent of the men and 19 per cent of the women played bingo, but when asked which activities they would like to do more of, none of the men and 1.7 per cent of the women mentioned bingo (Dobbin 1980). As Cornish points out:

> The presence of institutionalized expressive activities in a culture does not necessarily imply that they owe their existence to their superior ability at meeting special expressive needs . . . for each new generation the satisfactoriness of these contingent arrangements is once more on trial.
>
> (Cornish 1978: 361)

The significance of bingo lies not in the game itself – a simple game of calling out numbers and ticking them off, with a prize to the first person to do so. To members of the middle and upper class, it may be pernicious, symbolic of the decadence and apocalyptic powers of popular culture. To the government, bingo represents a substantial source of revenue. Further, it can be argued that bingo saves the government expenditure on community care. Bingo provides a living for large numbers of people, not only for the businessmen who own Britain's 1,500 clubs but also for the staff employed.

To the player, bingo is an unremarkable fact of life, a home-from-home, an invaluable source of companionship, a refuge which offers excitement. It is not surprising that 84 per cent of players are women, given the options bestowed on them by virtue of their gender and class. The future of bingo is dependent not only on changes in the leisure market and in the state of the economy but also on changes in the allocation of gender roles. For the present, bingo is an activity adopted and fashioned by those not in a dominant position within the limitations of an imposed structure. Bingo is used to give expression and meaning to that position; it is also a most important means of coming to terms with that position and making it more attractive.

References

Bell, Lady Florence (1911) *At the Works: A Study of A Manufacturing Town*, London.

Booker, Chris (1969) *The Neophiliacs: A Study of the Revolution in English Life in the Fifties and Sixties*, London, Collins.

Cornish, D. B (1978) *Gambling: A Review of the Literature*, London, HMSO.

Dennis, Norman, Henriques, Fernando and Slaughter, Clifford (1956) *Coal Is Our Life*, London, Tavistock.

Dixey, Rachael with Talbot, Margaret (1982) *Women, Leisure and Bingo*, Leeds, Trinity & All Saints' College.

Dobbin, Ian (1980) *Retirement and Leisure: A Preliminary Research Report*, Centre for Leisure Studies, University of Salford.

Downes, D.M. *et al.* (1976) *Gambling, Work and Leisure: A Study Across Three Areas*, London, Routledge & Kegan Paul.

Gaming Board (1969) *Report of the Gaming Board for Great Britain*, London, HMSO.
  (1970) *Report of the Gaming Board for Great Britain*, London, HMSO.

Goody, Jack (1961) 'Religion and ritual' *British Journal of Sociology* 12: 142–64.

Hoggart, Richard (1959) *The Uses of Literacy*, London, Chatto & Windus.

Kuper, Leo (ed.) (1953) *Living in Towns*, London, Cresset Press.

McKibbin, Ross (1979) 'Working-class gambling in Britain 1880–1939', *Past and Present* 82 (Feb.): 147–78.

Meller, Helen (1976) *Leisure and the Changing City, 1870–1914*, London, Routledge & Kegan Paul.

Rich, Doris (1953) 'Spare time in the Black Country', in Leo Kuper (ed.) *Living in Towns*, London, Cresset Press.

Soja, Edward (1971) 'The political organization of space', *Commission of College Geography Resource Paper* 8, Washington, DC, Assoc. of American Geographers.

Spring-Rice, Marjery [1939] (1981) *Working Class Wives*, London, Virago.

8

Beating them at our own game?
Women's sports involvement

MARGARET TALBOT

It might be easy, in studying the evidence of the number and nature of the constraints which militate against women's participation in sport, to be surprised that some women actually *do* manage to take part, having overcome or circumvented the constraints which have been so well documented, and which can make such depressing reading. It is therefore all the more important that the experiences of women who play sport are presented as positive and visible examples of the ways in which women succeed in controlling aspects of their own lives, and of the potentially rich and varied rewards which sport can bring.

Women who play sports have shown, to themselves and to others, that there is no inevitable conflict between sports participation and femininity, indeed that the peak experiences of sport can be expression at the same time of both their femininity and their humanity – for their sports experiences transcend issues of gender role, in helping them to realize their own human potential. Viewing women's sports experiences from a positive rather than a positivist perspective shows us that these experiences have the capacity for further enriching and widening ideas of what sport is, and what sport should be – a range of opportunities for extending physical limitations, developing a positive sense of physical self, enjoying the satisfactions of learning new skills, and of co-operating with and competing against others:

> In no way can the male gain more achievement, joys or sorrows through sport than the female.

> (Harris 1980)

It has been important to identify and analyse the sources of inequality in sports participation for women, both as an element of leisure studies, and as a component of feminist analyses of patriarchal society. However, establishing that there are inequalities does not necessarily bring about the political or policy changes which would redress the balance. There has been a tendency, especially from within the institutions of sport, to see gender differences in sports participation as functions of sex differences, an attitude reinforced rather than challenged by the statistical data, instead of reappraising the current restrictively narrow conceptions of sport. Many people are excluded from the joys of sport, simply because sport is itself constituted in a distinctively masculinist way which prevents it from serving more of humanity.

While acknowledging the importance of the framework of structural and social constraints within which women live, feminist perspectives take, first and foremost, the experience of women as their perspective and their evidence. It is the purpose of this chapter, not to argue the case for equal opportunities in sport, but to assume it, and to examine women's sports experiences in a positive way:

> a drive to self-knowledge is more than the dilatory self-interested pastime of the so-called liberated woman. It is a serious human enterprise. It is a protest against the dehumanization of society made by women on behalf of everyone.
>
> (Oakley 1984: 2)

This section will therefore emphasize women's own perceptions of their experiences and the contributions which women have made to extending the notion of sport, by challenging prevailing expectations of behaviour for men and women, and the restrictions which stereotypical notions of masculinity place upon it. Women who play sport, whether in spite of, in defiance of, in ignorance of, or with apologies to social preconceptions of the female role, are making a statement which can help to redefine both femininity and sport, and in Iris Young's (1979) terms, to push sport towards 'exhibiting its potential humanity'.

Much of the evidence to be used comes from ongoing research (Talbot 1987) with forty Yorkshire women who were, at the time of interview, participating in sport – a group of top-level hockey players, and a group of self-programming, non-club member badminton players. In general, the hockey players had professional or clerical jobs, and in fact several were physical education teachers in local schools. The occupations of the badminton players were more varied, including a shop worker and a school catering assistant and several full-time mothers at home with young children. While the women's ages ranged from 18 to 47, the average age of hockey players was younger than the badminton players, and the hockey players had participated more or less continuously since learning the game at school, while the badminton players tended to have taken up the game later. All played on Thursday evenings at the same sports centre in Kirklees, where the women were approached to take part in the research interviews. All the women were white; there were no black women, neither Asian nor Afro-Carribean, at the centre on these evenings, even though the school which also used the centre during the day had around 20 per cent black pupils. While this can be explained partly by the fact that many of the black children were bussed to the school and therefore did not see the sports centre as their local community centre, it is clear that the decision to interview players from this context led to unintentional ethnocentrism.

One of the intentions of the research was to allow women themselves to describe how their sports participation related to the rest of their lives, and what their participation meant to them. Each woman was encouraged to give a retrospective description of her work, family and leisure life since leaving school; and these biographies were followed up by a series of questions designed to verify, amplify and complement the information derived from the women's descriptions.

Some illustrations, however, will be taken from international sportswomen's interpretations of their own experiences as women and sportsplayers. These are used, not to imply that their experiences are more important than those of the other women, but in order to reflect the potential of sport for women's self-development.

> I think the simplest explanation of why tennis has dominated a huge slice of my life is the extreme pleasure I get from playing it . . . tennis is the ultimate form of self-expression for me . . . tennis gives you a chance to produce something for yourself . . . you never really stop learning. Without you [tennis] I would never have been able to travel, never been able to excel at something, never been able to experience those fleeting moments of joy.
>
> (King 1981: 13)

Sportswomen who have not aspired to or achieved the heights of Billie Jean King still acknowledge, like her, their debt to their chosen physical activities. One of the Yorkshire women cited the importance of her hockey as a unique arena where she could express herself and be confident through her superior skill: 'scoring goals is something I *can* do – I'm good at it – I have a great deal of difficulty in expressing myself otherwise.' Other women referred to the significance, to them, of 'playing well':

> in games I don't care as long as it's been a nice clean, skilful game. I couldn't care what the result is . . . if the ball's doing reasonably well what you want it to, and if you're meeting the crosses and sending decent crosses yourself . . . there's an intent in it.

For most of the women interviewed, the result was less important than the experiences of 'having a good game' – an attitude which, according to the research evidence on sports motivation (see, for example, review in Talbot, 1979), sports-*men* learn rather later in life. Another crucial and distinctive factor for the women was the concept of duty, and not letting people down:

> I think women are trained like that, you know, always to be there if you say you will. I've been nearly on my deathbed but I've still gone to play – or taken my sandwiches anyway! I can't see a man doing that, unless he sent his wife with them!

Claims commonly made for the general benefits of sports participation were reinforced by many of the women, but it was noticeable that they commented on their experience relative to other women's. Women who did not play sport were perceived to be missing a great deal, especially the feeling of well-being and the positive aspects of fitness, much valued by the participants: 'I think if you feel physically on top, then your personality comes out a lot better, you can cope with life much more easily if you're feeling good.' It was also clear from some of the older women that, once experienced, physical fitness was much missed if lost, for example after childbearing. For several reasons, their hockey careers seemed to legitimate and assist a return to physical fitness after the birth of their children: 'as soon as she was born and I got fit I went back . . . I think once you've been used to being active you miss it. I felt like a cabbage.' The badminton players were generally less committed to that particular activity, and had begun to play more recently than had the hockey players, who could all be described as long term 'career players'. (The hockey players not only travelled further to play than the badminton players, but also commonly played several times every week, as well as going to sessions of coaching or physical training for their sport; in general, the badminton players used the nearest or most convenient sports centre to their home, and all but two played only once a week.) However, the badminton players, too, had recognized the potential of engaging in the game as a legitimate reason for getting out of the house, increasing their physical fitness and for 'getting into shape' or losing weight: 'badminton was physical and it was exercise I needed, . . . doing something for myself, in my own time'.

Sheila had grown up in the United States and had been influenced to run by the exercise boom and especially by Ken Cooper's books:

> I read this book and I thought, yeah, I'm going to try this . . . you feel better and more relaxed . . . it doesn't make you slim, but it helps in that direction, and it is certainly good for your heart, prolongs your life . . . that's changed my life.

The need for, and value of, general physical action was another factor frequently mentioned, as was the capacity for sport to provide opportunities for achievement and success. These women certainly challenged the popular wisdom that women avoid success. Indeed, for one hockey player the achievement of being selected for junior territorial trials meant more to her than her degree – 'no-one's failed ophthalmic optics in years!' An older hockey player still remembered with pride the honour of being selected to carry a banner for the school in the Bradford Schools tournament, while a badminton player reflected on her pleasure at her improvement at the game – 'that feeling of pushing back frontiers'. Another, novice badminton player's most treasured achievement was beating first her son, and then her husband, at the game which they had taught her. All the women, whether club hockey players or casual badminton players, could give criteria by which they judged their performances, and those of others: some did not conform to the traditional criteria of winning and losing, and demonstrated that they had made decisions about the type of experience which they wanted from their sport, and how as females they related to their sport. Reassessment of the function of school sport for girls had been undertaken in a very conscious way by one of the hockey players who was also a physical education teacher:

> We've got the best sort of philosophies of what we're trying to do. We aren't bothered about pot-hunting and things like that, but I've got six hundred girls who I could take anywhere, and they all try to be feminine and respectful to each other.

Sheila Scraton (1986) has described the ways in which female physical education teachers, and the girls whom they teach, grapple with the problems of coming to terms with the ideology of femininity within physical education. Another kind of reappraisal is described in Marge Piercy's (1980) novel, in which the central character, Leslie, attempts to avoid for her students the pressure to adopt male defined means of achievement and motivation:

It moved her, watching the women begin trying to use their bodies in a different way. . . . They had put themselves in her hands to learn something new about how to be in the world, a new relationship to their bodies, new possibilities. . . . 'We won't stay with the karate ritual that men have developed', she said suddenly.

'At the beginning of the class instead of bowing we'll hold hands in a circle. Would you like that?'

(Piercy 1980: 263)

Another struggle to demonstrate belief in feminist principles during an all-female expedition to Annapurna is beautifully described by Arlene Blum:

Fortunately we had not simply buried our hurt feelings and gone marching stoically up the mountain. It had been worth it to take the time to face up to each other and expose our vulnerability, hurt, and anger, and then our fears. We realized again how much we cared about each other, and our shared laughter had been the final healing touch.

(Blum 1980: 119)

While the Yorkshire women had not made explicitly feminist decisions, they had made their participation conditional upon their being able to have an influence, a degree of control, upon it – sports playing on their own terms:

the more leisurely, recreational, social side has become more important.

you like to think that you're well presented when your visitors arrive, you know, you like to think that there's a nice table laid for their refreshments, nice clean, freshly painted balls, and have we got an umpire . . . wonder if they'll remember the table covers?

For this woman, her training and experience as a family manager carried over into her hockey: it was as important to her that the visiting team should be properly received by the home side, as the game itself. The ways in which the sports experience can be an extension of existing friendship or kinship systems were illustrated especially by the badminton players, who were less committed to the activity *per se* than to the relationships which framed it during their badminton evenings. Pat, for example, had consciously chosen badminton as a family activity which she and her husband, along with their two teenage children, could play *together*. Linda, similarly, saw it as a means by which the family and friendship ties could be strengthened:

Well, it's all altogether, isn't it? I enjoy going for a shower afterwards, getting all hot and sticky and then relaxing upstairs with a pie and a drink – so it's part of a whole evening really – because the children can enjoy it, and we get together with the other couple we play with, and also, John's brother and his wife come, not to play the sport, but just to come up to the bar afterwards and have a drink; so we sort of make an evening of it, really.

Her description embodies so much of the ideology of that rare occurrence, family sports participation, and yet at the same time illustrates that for it to succeed, it should happen as an extension of established relationships rather than as a sudden and radical change of behaviour imposed from without. There is another message, from which providers might learn much about extending the franchise of participation – that is, 'the game is *not* necessarily the thing', a finding which has been long known to providers of evening classes. Some of the staff of Action Sport did seem to have arrived at the same conclusion:

> Although the sport element is there, many women use the classes, sessions, etc. as a more social factor, making new friends etc. I think if kept on this level of involvement I don't see any reason for Action Sport not to succeed
> (Glyptis, Kay and Murray 1984: 47)

There is, however, a danger that such findings may lead to a determinism based on the notion that women *only* want social contact from sport, and not the variety of experiences which are possible. Angela's choice of badminton as an activity which could help her sister to exercise progressively after an accident which had injured her leg, demonstrates that women's range of uses for activities is much wider, even within the confines of the family, than some providers appreciate. Similarly, the use of their sport to meet people, to adjust to moving to a new area, and to be part of a group, were all mentioned as reasons for taking part, or as outcomes of taking part:

> The integration of the lives of those based at home means that activities outside the home are often not seen as separate experiences. They are a continuation of the process of developing relationships embracing other experiences and social networks.
> (Gregory 1982: 50)

The influence of the family was paramount in all but a few of the badminton players, and most of the hockey players, especially where there were children. But their commitment to their sport had allowed them to assert their needs within, and even through, the family. In some cases the family itself was managed around the sport experience, especially where the women had had a long term 'career' in sport. Several women spoke of the need to choose a partner who understood their desire to play sport, and of their appreciation of the support they received from their partners. Where couples were fortunate enough to share their sporting interests, there was evidence of rich and rewarding mutual experience:

> I think we mix. I'll do football jerseys to help him out; he'll go round his business associates for prizes for raffles for me, you know, we work that way. I tend to answer the telephone, with people phoning up on a Saturday morning asking about his football, but I don't object because he's out doing my shopping – *our* shopping.

Many of the women had demonstrated that, even within family constraints and obligations, they were able to assume that at times *their* activities had priority. Their common observation that there is a need to 'find a balance' illustrated the negotiations between partners and within households, which were necessary for partners to arrive at the stage where, as Andrea put it, 'he respects my freedom time'. For her, this state of affairs in their marriage was a revelation after a somewhat repressive childhood with very strict parents. All of the women were very conscious of their privilege, relative to other women, in having partners or families supportive of their participation, and there was frequent admission that, 'well, you just couldn't do it otherwise, could you?' Husbands who were prepared to get their own meals or eat in the canteen at lunchtime to compensate for not having a cooked meal in the evening, or feed the children, were much appreciated, although it was also clear that 'normally' these responsibilities were largely or wholly the responsibility of the women. It is relevant perhaps to speculate whether these women's sports participation actually gave them stronger bargaining power in the family negotiating process – resulting in (or possibly beginning with) a tacit agreement that, by virtue of their personal investment and achievements in their sport, they had earned a 'right' to leisure.

It would also be interesting to discover what they might have been forced to trade for this established leisure space in their lives; it is possible that, in accepting the traditional notions of the division of labour, some women lost some of their bargaining power because they felt obliged to their partners for 'helping them out'. There was some evidence of role strain and role conflict. Some women referred to their decisions to give up certain of their activities because of pressure at home, either directly from partners or indirectly because partners refused to help them with the total load, and a few of the women had been forced to trade one activity against another – 'playing badminton's enough – I mean, I couldn't cope with the keep fit as well'. The women who had continued to meet heavy commitments in and around their sport – mostly young professionals – tended either to have husbands who did the same ('we're ships that pass in the night'), or to have successfully asserted their right to continue their participation before marriage; none had young children. More research is needed to investigate the reasons why women feel they need to give up sports participation, and the processes of negotiation which surround continued participation.

However, the Yorkshire women frequently referred to the way they organized their lives around their sport, using their commitment as a kind of benchmark for organizing their other obligations and activities. For Pauline, her hockey helped her to 'keep the housework in proportion'. Christine arranged her weekly routine around her hockey and her husband's football: 'everything seems to fit in easier than it did when I first left school, because when you get married, you seem to organize your life around the sports that you do'. Sheila felt that her early morning running helped her to face the day at home with her young children: 'I'm back and showered and dressed and ready to meet the day by about 7.45 a.m. I like that – it's a good feeling.'

Sylvia, a hockey player for over thirty years, referred to the way that she felt able to combine motherhood with her hockey playing, because it was expected by the hockey club – an example of the potential for a female subculture to challenge the traditional expectations held for women to take responsibility for childcare and therefore to disengage from other activities. Her reference to her first son as a 'touchline baby in the pram' illustrates at the same time her ability to be both a mother and a player, the support of the female subgroup for that combined role, and the fact that she still was responsible for the care of her baby while her husband was at work in the shop. On the other hand, she had been led, by her previous enjoyment, to adapt her role as mother to encompass hockey: 'I thought , I'm a mother now, and I can't possibly play hockey any more [laughs], but I got bitten by the bug again, so I continued.'

Beryl had identified as a real achievement her being able to continue to play long enough for her daughters to play alongside her in the team:

> It was something I'd always wanted, I didn't always think I'd do it at the time, but I always said I'd like to play when they play, so that we could play together, and I didn't think I'd manage it, but it's quite nice really. Not so much now, because they're telling *me* what to do [laughs].

Through her own involvement in sport, too, Beryl was able to be supportive in an informed way for her children's participation. She felt that this was a positive expression of parental interest and concern, and valued it as a means of keeping in contact with her children and sharing their achievements: 'I mean, some of them don't seem to be able to talk to their children about anything.' Her family had responded to her hockey playing also with practical help with chores and house-work. Again, it was as if her hockey, in her family's eyes, entitled her to help which they may not have perceived her as needing had she not had this established commitment.

Children's activities, for several women, had extended their own horizons. Iris, a badminton player who had recently begun playing badminton with five of her fellow school dinner ladies, had never been closer to a horse than donkeys at the seaside previously, but was encouraged (in typical style) to 'have a go' by her pony-mad daughter: 'She says, "go on, Mum, if you do, I won't tell them it's my mother, I'll tell them it's an old woman who wants to go". I says don't be cheeky.' Iris clearly had enjoyed this foray into an activity which she had never seen as possible, or even relevant, for her; and she was appreciative of the fact that her daughter could enjoy opportunities which had been denied her. It was a sign to her that all her and her husband's hard work had been worthwhile.

The opportunities to rediscover sport through children were frequently high-lighted, along with the determination that their children should have better experiences than they themselves had. This is supported by evidence from another Yorkshire study of women in Armley:

> Children help you discover all sorts of things. You wouldn't dream of going out and putting a pair of ice skates on but when you've got children you don't think twice about it.

> I was 12 or 13 when I learnt to swim and I always hated it. . . . I'm deter-mined she's going to at least get used to the water . . . and it will be a pleasant experience for her rather than something she hates doing.

(Dixey with Talbot 1982: 60)

The challenges set by sport to the traditionally restrictive expectations for older women's behaviour were seen by the women to have extended and enlarged their opportunities for personal fulfilment. They were conscious and proud of redirecting their own lives, by taking advantage of publicly provided facilities which had not existed in their youth – 'I do more now I'm over 40 than I ever did before'. This awareness is also supported by the findings of the study of Armley women (Dixey with Talbot 1982) that, in leisure terms, 'life begins at 40': more women than in any other age-group described their forties as being their best period for leisure. To what extent is this reflected in public recreational policy and provision?

Sue, one of the badminton players, had used sport in a particularly crucial way, to re-establish her identity and confidence after a long and acrimonious divorce:

> That's when I actually decided, right, my life is my life, this is when I start living again . . . this is when I decided to play badminton and come out a bit – and it's helped me considerably, it really has. Yes, it's sort of made me feel alive again. It maybe sounds stupid, but I feel as though I've got something to look forward to, as I say, it's that outlet, and you know, you can forget about upsets and things whilst you're playing, it's the pleasure, the enjoyment of it. I really, really enjoy it.

Recovery was a recurrent theme in the women's reminiscences: recovery from work, from childbearing, from loneliness, from disastrous relationships. There was a shared perception of the capacity for sport to help women to return to physical, emotional or mental balance after crises or during periods of stress. Conversely, there were also opportunities to re-evaluate the place of sport in their lives after or during periods of adjustment in their lives, most often bereavement or pregnancy. For women who had been top-level competitors, the restrictions applied by getting older or facing increased or different sets of obligations, could result in their seeing sport from a fresh angle and occasionally valuing its new form even more highly than before. Irene's hockey, after her conversion, became more than an enjoyable pastime or a competitive activity which she had played at county level. It became a context through which she could live and demonstrate her Christian life: 'I'm doing more good amongst hockey players in the pub than being in the Church'.

There is still much to be learnt from the ways in which the meanings of activities change over time, and how those meanings are constructed dynamically. For these women, it was obvious that neither 'hockey' nor 'badminton' remained the same throughout their lives, and many of the women commented after the interview that they had appreciated the opportunity to articulate and discuss this. Gwen Moffat captured eloquently her moment of revelation about her climbing and her body, caused by her pregnancy and increased awareness of what she was doing:

> I told them I was having a baby in July. Consternation! Most of the club were on the cliff (including several doctors) and messages were relayed from climb to climb, and up and down the ropes, to the effect that Moffat was having a baby and what was the quickest way to get her off the cliff? One would have thought I was about to be confined on the Great Terrace. . . .
>
> I refused to be stampeded. I had come to the meet to join the club if possible and I was going to lead my climb to qualify. Besides, since we were on the Great Terrace, I pointed out that the easiest way off was to climb. So I led Red Wall and Longland's Continuation – barefooted of course – while

a frieze of Pinnaclers sat on the top and watched critically. I felt like a cripple who rediscovers his body while swimming. Here on the airy slabs of those two delightful climbs, where the holds are one-toe holds in places and the run-outs are long, I could forget for a while my pear-shape and feel the old elegance. And, not illogically, there flashed through my mind the hope that the baby would be a girl.

(Moffat 1961: 120–1)

The opportunities for personal identity development in and through sports participation, including recreational sports, is also borne out by the women who claimed that sport had given them, especially in later adolescence, an active sense of identity, unlike what they saw as the passive fulfilment of expected roles of other girls. Pride in long-term engagement, especially among the hockey players, was very apparent. Commitment over time was also demonstrated in answers to one of the verifying questions: if you had to give up playing for any reason, what would you do? A majority of the younger women maintained that *nothing* would make them cease to play – some even referred to withdrawal symptoms during the summer close season! Older women, who had obviously considered the matter, gave in their answers, clues to the salience of the sport for them:

Yes, I'd have to replace it with something now, I think. It's got my adrenalin flowing now, you see [laughs]. You really look forward to it, thrashing that shuttlecock, I think that's it, getting rid of that emotion.

Sue's age had caused her to re-examine her previously unquestioned assumptions about her level of playing hockey:

I thought maybe I'd have gone off on different channels, but I have never lost my interest in playing hockey over all the years. And I think loyalty to the club . . . I admit I'll have to go into second team hockey, which if you'd said that to me five or six years ago, I would have been horrified . . . but one accepts these things as one gets older, and I don't think I mind at all.

Some of the older women had already identified badminton as an activity they could 'manage' as they got older; this was a perception of the game shared also by younger women who had never previously played sport since leaving school – in both technical and physical output terms, badminton was seen as possible, 'less hectic than squash':

you don't have to run after it [like tennis], the shuttlecock just falls, doesn't it?

You can play it without getting a sweat on, you know, it's a sociable thing. Squash isn't because you are just two people just locked in a corner and all you can do is play, you can't sort of sit out and talk to people

While these perceptions of badminton would certainly be violently refuted by top-level badminton players, they do help to inform knowledge of how these less competitive participants 'see' different sports, and to widen narrow concepts of what constitute sports.

Even at world-class level, Nadia Comaneci was also driven to question the kinds of behaviour expected of female performers in gymnastics, an activity dominated by pre-pubertal girls, when her body changed after puberty and she no longer felt comfortable acting in a way she saw as staged and inappropriate for her as an adult.

> Bela could not accept that I was now grown up. . . . 'This is ridiculous, I'm not making those stupid little gestures in my floor exercise – they might look very cute on a child of ten, but they look foolish and phoney on me. Do I look like a child? . . . I'm damned if I'm going to make a spectacle of myself'.
>
> (Comaneci and Buxton Smither 1981: 95–6)

This reluctance to expose themselves to ridicule is a very common feature in reasons given by women for their non-participation in sport, and perhaps constitutes the other side of the coin of women's pride and satisfaction at being skilful in their sport. Some women had experienced both: Anne, a county hockey trialist, remembered her feelings during netball lectures at physical education college:

> I hated every minute of it, because they were all flying here there and everywhere, and there I was sort of trolling along, not knowing what the hell to do, not knowing where I could go, why I'd been stopped.

For her, this had been a salutary experience, allowing her to feel what it was like to be inadequate in a game situation; she maintained that it had made her a better and more sympathetic teacher.

Sports experience had also led some women to question the way they perceived that they had been brought up as females never to excel, not to achieve. Pat recollected with some bitterness that she had never had any encouragement over anything at school: although she was told that she was clever, nothing was expected of her – and that is what she achieved. Anne regretted never being encouraged to concentrate on one activity in order to develop one to a higher level; instead, she was a 'jack of all trades, master of none'. The same type of rueful self-assessment after an outdoor development course was given by Kathy Damouni:

> I learnt a lot about myself during the outdoor development course – mainly how far I could cope with mental and, essentially, physical strain. I also learnt that I lack the urge to lead, but am a good follower and that I need to improve my communication skills.
>
> (quoted in Bank 1985: 72)

Similarly, the late Jackie Gillott as an adolescent was alerted by school sport to the awareness of the restrictions of being female: 'What gave me particular pleasure were cricket pads. . . . Once strapped up, it was impossible to walk like a girl. Legs stoutly apart, one *strode* (Gillott 1981: 67). Likewise, the badminton and hockey players affirmed their pleasure in simply moving freely in a large space, wearing suitable clothes and footwear: the hockey players also clearly valued being in the fresh air, and movement at speed – all sensations denied to many women for much of their time because of the restrictions imposed upon them by their work, clothing and social expectations. Andrea's experience illustrates the change between expected behaviour at school and at work:

I like to lose a lot of energy in hockey . . . I mean, I've got an office job, where I'm sat down all day, sometimes I must admit I'd like to stand up and scream, you know. And I'd always been really active at school, and when I started work, it was just so different, to be sat down all day

Beryl used hockey to defy the march of time: 'Once I get on that pitch and I start playing I forget everything else: . . . I don't think, oh no, I'm getting too old now . . . I go for it.'

The variety of the sports experience of these women, and of their reasons for continuing their participation, could mislead one into concluding that there are no generalizations which can be made. But there is a number of observations which can show that sport for women is not only an activity from which they can derive as much benefit as can men, or that they participate because they are fortunate enough to be able to overcome constraints. It can be much more than that: it can be a primary boundary of women's lives, and a motive force which helps them structure their own experience and control their own activities, on their own terms and in their own ways. Three of the women articulated their pride in their achievement of setting up a new hockey club with their own aims and intention: their success in overcoming problems – identifying their dissatisfactions with their existing club, articulating them, finding a pitch, attracting other like-minded club members, organizing fixtures, convincing other agencies they were 'serious' and engaging in the leadership roles so new to them – was cited as their greatest achievement, both collective and individual.

Being taken seriously, at whatever level they played, was another recurrent theme. Some women had made reasoned choices to play at a less competitive level, and resented the way their participation was consequently trivialized or ridiculed by partners or facility providers. The fallacy that sport for people who play at the 'lower' levels of competition somehow matters less, can lead to a kind of determinism of provision, in which the 'best' clubs or groups are allocated the most generous share of resources. Women who had experienced this, particularly when men's groups had received what they saw as an unfair allocation, spoke of their frustration at the apparent lack of valuation of their activities and achieve-ments. Liz Leather has argued the case for groups based more in the community than in institutionalized sport:

My account is asking providers of planned leisure to listen and not to impose; it is asking planners not to see disadvantaged groups as having problems which with help can be overcome, but to be sensitive to the per-ceptions of other groups and to meet their needs accordingly.

(Leather 1984: 2)

For these badminton and hockey players, needs had at least been partially met, and the women themselves had been prime movers (in many senses!) in this process. A woman who had changed jobs so that she could return to Saturday afternoon hockey; one who had identified badminton as an activity which fitted in to the parameters of her established evening-class routine; and the woman who spoke about arranging her diary around her fixtures – each had demonstrated ability to organize her life and defend her free time for something which she valued. It is not possible to deduce whether this ability was a precondition of, or a result of, her sports participation. How *do* women acquire these skills, and the ability to structure their use of time to play sports? And how does this compare with men's experiences?

This chapter has attempted to show how women can invest their sports experience with their own values. This not only clears the way for them to enjoy sport on their own terms; it may also improve sport itself:

> the traditional stereotype . . . is breaking down . . . the idea that the role of female and the role of athlete is incompatible. You do need qualities like determination, aggression, physical robustness, but that doesn't mean such qualities aren't feminine. Nevertheless, I do think it's a pity that in some sports women are just emulating the male stereotype . . . some of them frighten me, the way they behave. . . . I think it's essential to create a unique set of values for women's sports, not a copy. Sport can be very crude but it can be very beautiful, so don't imitate. If you try to imitate, you won't achieve the potential that women's sport possesses.
>
> (Brackenridge 1982)

References

Bank, J. (1985) *Outdoor Development for Managers*, Aldershot, Gower.

Blum, Arlene (1980) *Annapurna: A Woman's Place*, London, Granada.

Brackenridge, Celia (1982) 'Celia's girls will be girls', *Observer*, 26 September.

Comaneci, Nadia and Buxton Smither, G. (1981) *Nadia*, London, Proteus.

Dixey, Rachael with Talbot, Margaret (1982) *Women, Leisure and Bingo*, Leeds, Trinity and All Saints' College.

Gillott, Jackie (1981) 'Twelfth Man', in M. Meyer (ed.) *Summer Days: Writers on Cricket* London, Eyre Methuen.

Glyptis, Sue Kay, Teresa and Murray, Michele (1984) *Action Sport West Midlands: The Involvement of Women and Girls*, a report to the Sports Council and Project Directorate, Birmingham.

Gregory, Sarah (1982) 'Women among others: another view', *Leisure Studies* 1(1): 47–52.

Harris, Dorothy (1980) 'Personality Research: implications for women in sport', *International Congress on Women and Sport*, Rome, ICSPE.

King, Billie Jean (1981) 'A Queen and her court', *Yorkshire Post Colour Magazine* 8, 4 April, pp. 6–7, 11–15.

Leather, Liz (1984) 'Women stepping out to play', unpublished paper.

Moffat, Gwen (1961) *Space below My Feet*, London, Hodder & Stoughton.

Oakley, Ann (1984) *Taking It Like a Woman*, London, Jonathan Cape.

Piercy, Marge (1980) *The High Cost of Living*, London, The Women's Press.

Scraton, Sheila (1986) 'Images of femininity and the teaching of girls' physical education', in John Evans (ed.) *Physical Education, Sport and Schooling*, Brighton, Falmer Press.

Talbot, Margaret (1979) *Women and Leisure*, London Sports Council/Social Science Research Council.

(1987) 'Women's leisure behaviour, with particular reference to physical activity', PhD research, University of Birmingham.

Young, Iris (1979) 'The exclusion of women from sport: conceptual and existential dimensions', *Philosophy in Context* 9: 44–53.

9

Stepping out: the importance of dancing for young women

VIVIENNE GRIFFITHS

One of my most treasured possessions as an adolescent girl was a black velvet dress which my mother had worn to go dancing in the 1930s. To me at 13 it seemed the epitome of glamour, sensuality and freedom, a source of fantasy and a symbol of the life my mother gave up when she became a housewife.

Dancing and its trappings – the clothes, the music, the places – exert a power-ful attraction; but whilst the influence of other media on young people, particu-larly television and pop music, have been widely researched, the role which dance plays in young women's lives has been underexplored.

In this chapter I shall analyse some of the often contradictory meanings dance has for young women, drawing both on the experience of the 12- to 16-year-old girls I worked with in West Yorkshire and, because of the lack of much previous research, on personal recollections.

In one of the few accounts of dance from a feminist perspective, Angela McRobbie (1984) suggests three main ways in which the importance of dance for young women can be understood: dance as image, as fantasy and as social activ-ity. As well as examining these, I shall also stress the liberating aspects of dance as sensual pleasure and the importance of dance as a source of self-esteem for young women.

From ballet to disco-dancing

Dancing was a favourite activity among the young women in my research. Many of them had been to dancing classes – ballroom, tap or ballet – when younger, but by the age of 13 most had transferred their interest to dancing at discos or at youth clubs. This was just one of the ways in which childhood interests were being transformed into aspects of female youth culture (see Ch. 4).

I shall describe three different types of dance: dancing at discos; disco-dancing routines usually prepared for competitions; and dancing classes with an emphasis on dancing as a career.

The first kind of dancing was the most popular and widespread, and usually involved groups of girls and their girlfriends 'having a laugh' together. It was enjoyed by young women as a form of self-expression both for its own sake, without reference to men, and in certain contexts as a form of sexual display to young men.

In contrast, the other kinds of dance were more disciplined and competitive, and tended to reinforce particular kinds of feminine stereotypes. I shall discuss these with particular reference to a group of three friends who entered a local disco-dancing competition, and a 13-year-old girl who wanted to become a professional dancer. Although these forms of dancing demanded dedication and often involved disappointment, they could also provide the girls concerned with a sense of positive achievement in a girls-only arena. Dancing as a potential career, whilst in many ways being an acceptable feminine choice, also offered a more glamorous alternative to a future based on marriage and motherhood, and held out the promise of status and fame to those who succeeded.

Before turning to these, I must mention those young women who did not have the opportunity to go dancing. For girls who experienced particular restrictions on their leisure time (see Ch. 4), their only access to dancing was in the (relative) privacy of their own homes or in dance lessons held at school. This was true for some girls of all ethnic backgrounds. However, whilst many white and Afro-Caribbean girls *did* take part in dancing at discos or youth clubs, I never saw or heard about any Asian girls dancing outside school, even in single-sex situations. This reflected their relative exclusion, as a group, from leisure activities in general outside the home (see Ch. 4). For these girls, school provided possibly the only opportunity they had for dancing. In my earlier research (Griffiths 1986), dance lessons formed part of PE and took place in single-sex groups. In this research, a dance club was run by a woman PE teacher and to my knowledge was a girls-only group. For the Asian girls, who would not have been allowed to take part in physical activities alongside boys, such single-sex provision was particularly important.

Dancing the night away: discos

Discos were one of the most popular leisure activities among the young women. Given the lack of other places to go locally, it was hardly surprising that they were always 'packed out'. Angela McRobbie (1984) draws a contrast between the 'respectable' city discos and subcultural or punk discos. In my research, a similar contrast existed between the school discos and those held at the local working-men's club. Discos were also held at some of the local youth clubs.

Because school discos were organized and supervised by teachers, they were regarded as 'safe' places for girls; even girls who hardly ever went out were allowed to go. However, because of their respectable image they were considered 'boring' by most young people, and were eventually cancelled because of poor attendance. In contrast, 'thousands' went to the discos at Barnsdale Club every other Friday night for young people between 13 and 18 years old. The popularity of these discos actually made dancing difficult; this was both a cause of some complaint from the girls and the reason for the good atmosphere which attracted them in the first place.

One of the main attractions of the Barnsdale Club disco was that it provided young women with a 'real night out', as one of them described it, rather than another evening hanging around the streets with nowhere to go. The girls could get dressed up in their most fashionable clothes, which they normally had few opportunities of wearing. A mixture of styles was accommodated, from mainstream to subcultural, and the discos were popular with both Afro-Caribbean and white girls. Some girls were into punk; whilst their appearance had to be toned down at school, they could appear at their most outrageous at the disco. Others adopted styles of dress linked to popular film and television series about dance, ranging from *Saturday Night Fever* to *Fame* and *Flashdance.* What links these diverse styles, as Angela McRobbie argues (1984), is that they provide non-traditional images for girls as active and independent rather than passively feminine, whilst at the same time maintaining elements of romance and fantasy. The girls were given a sense of confidence by their appearance which carried over into their behaviour.

Groups of girls went together to the disco rather than with their boyfriends. For example, Marilyn and five other Afro-Caribbean girls aged 13 to 14 all went to the disco in a big group. Unlike many of the white girls of the same age, Marilyn and her friends were not interested in boys; they went to the discos because they enjoyed dancing. Although some girls did meet boyfriends at the Barnsdale Club, it was primarily a place where young women went to dance with their friends. In fact, a fundamental reason for the popularity of these discos among the girls was that, unlike the formal dances of my early adolescence, which were a 'convention of courtship, dating, and sexual bargaining' (Mungham 1976:85), girls did not have to go with a boy or depend on a boy asking them to dance to enjoy themselves. This meant that, like the punk girls in Angela McRobbie's study (1984), the girls went out with the active intention of enjoying themselves, rather than with the more passive aim of being 'picked up' that Simon Frith describes (Frith 1978: 67).

Interaction between the sexes did take place, but in a way that gave the girls far more freedom and control than in their everyday relationships with boys at school. I would argue that this was due to the present-day conventions of dance culture, evident both in the attitude of independence with which young women went to the discos and in the styles of dancing themselves. Although I never visited the Barnsdale Club disco myself – I would have felt out of place in terms of age alone and regarded it as an intrusion into the girls' private lives – I did hear about what happened in some detail from the girls themselves. I also got an indication of the kind of interaction which took place when a disco was organized during the field trip to the Yorkshire Dales, which I went on with some of the second years from Barnsdale School. This was rather too much like the respectable school discos for the girls' liking. Apart from the fact that adults were present, there were complaints that the room was too big and no one would start dancing until the lights were turned down. Once under way, however, the girls started dancing with obvious enjoyment either on their own or in groups, while the boys stood at the other end of the room and watched. My field notes record: 'Lesley leaping about . . . Penny, Karen and Pam started doing steps (like 'Shadows' routine). . . . Some boys started moving down to girls' end.' It was only when a slow number was played later that a few of the girls and boys paired off.

The dance routines which some of the girls followed reminded me vividly of my own adolescence, when the Twist, Madison, Mashed Potato and Shake were popular dances. In contrast to the ballroom dances which I went to in my early teens, where I suffered agonies sitting around the edge of the hall waiting to be asked to dance (very similar to the mass-dances described by Geoff Mungham (1976)), I remember the tremendous sense of freedom I experienced when pop music started to be played at dances in the mid-1960s. My girlfriends and I could get into a circle or a long line and dance freely without worrying about having partners, as Mary Ingham also remembers (1981). We used to practice the dance routines in the lunch-hour at school (a girls' direct grant) and had great fun in this girls-only environment. When at mixed-sex dances this enjoyment of being all girls together was still strong. At the same time there was an element of showing ourselves off to the boys who would gather round to watch – as happened with the Barnsdale young people – and perhaps part of our enjoyment was in the unusual freedom this afforded us.

I felt that this double edge was present at the field trip disco. As they danced, the Barnsdale girls were obviously having fun together and seemed to some extent oblivious of the boys' presence; but when the boys moved closer the girls' dancing took on a 'courtship display' element, indicated by slightly self-conscious movements and quick glances at the boys. I would suggest both from my own experience and what the girls told me, that part of young women's enjoyment of dance is in the active yet acceptable sexual expressiveness involved, very different from the passive wallflower syndrome of my early teens. This provides at least a temporary escape from girls' daily subordination, where any form of open sexual display, through dress or behaviour, is regarded as provocative and liable to give girls a bad reputation (Lees 1986).

However, the sensual pleasure young women derive from dancing is not simply directed at men. As I have already suggested, there can be considerable enjoyment in women dancing with and for each other, in an 'open celebration of our own sensuality' (Buonaventura and Smedley 1979: 27). Such a celebration is vividly evoked by Maya Angelou (1981) when she describes a women-only party attended mainly by black African women. As the party got going, many of the women danced to 'approving laughter and applause.' One young woman danced particularly sensually:

> She swiveled and flourished, jostled and vibrated, accompanied by the audience's encouragement and laughter. 'Swing it girl – Swing it.'
> 'Show that thing child – show it'
>
>   (Angelou 1981: 240)

Sensual enjoyment in dance can also be an individual experience, a means of gaining control and a source of fantasy. The central character in Joan Barfoot's *Dancing in the Dark* (1982) dreams of dancing as a liberation from her domestic routine. One of the young women I worked with, Deborah, captured this aspect of dance exactly:

> The most enjoyable thing I found in dancing was the 'free' feeling. You just hear the music and it completely takes over. It's very relaxing as you use every part of your body and move freely. It's really a general 'getting away from it all' feeling. You're in a world of your own which is very enjoyable.

These dimensions of dance were evident at the field–trip disco in the self-absorbed quality of the girls' dancing and the energy of some of their movements. Although very different from the less spontaneous dance routines already described, these aspects also seemed to be rooted in an earlier dance tradition, incorporated and transformed into current dance culture. I was reminded of the wild, improvised movements of hippy dancing in the late 1960s and early 1970s. Records from that era still have the ability to recall the marvellous feeling of abandon, of being 'one' with the music, where the everyday self was suspended and the focus was on the physical sensation. As well as the music, the rather primitive psychedelic light shows of that time contributed to the essential atmosphere. In many ways these were the forerunners of the sophisticated light shows of present-day discos, whose very structure, Angela McRobbie argues (1984), creates the build-up of that semi-trancelike state. This was certainly confirmed by the young women in my research who told me that the Barnsdale Club enabled them to experience these kinds of feelings by creating an atmosphere with the lights, the loud music and the young people themselves 'all crowded up'. The combination was 'just great.'

Disco-dancing: clubs and competitions

By disco-dancing I mean the choreographed dance routines that are more often seen on television or in disco-dancing competitions than in discos themselves. Whereas nationally disco-dancing is a mixed-sex activity, in the industrial town in West Yorkshire where I carried out my research it was still very much a female preserve. In fact, in many of the youth clubs in the area it was the only activity which girls could make their own. Mainly through the efforts of some local dance teachers, disco-dancing had become an area in which young women could excel by building on their basic enjoyment of dancing. The visible manifestation of this achievement was the annual disco-dancing competition which all local youth clubs and groups were eligible to enter.

Through a girls-only club called the Girls Friendly Society (GFS), I became involved with three 13-year-old girls who were working out their own dance for the competition. My observations are drawn mainly from this competition, which I saw both from behind the scenes as I helped the girls to get ready to go on stage, and as part of the audience.

Penny, Pam and Becky had previously won a disco-dancing competition within GFS but had not entered a large competition before. They worked out their dance entirely by themselves; although the women in GFS gave them every encouragement, they did not have the knowledge of dancing to help them with the choreography. For their costumes, the girls adapted dresses which they had already by sewing sequins on the skirts. I was impressed in rehearsal by how well the girls danced and by the way they had put the dance movements together; choreography is a skilled and time-consuming procedure. As amateurs I felt they stood a good chance.

However, no one had anticipated the professionalism of the competition. The girls were completely outclassed by the other groups who entered, and their efforts were made to look home- spun. Most of the other groups were larger in number, had complicated dance routines choreographed by adult specialists who helped at their clubs, and highly elaborate costumes made specially for the occasion. Before

Pam, Penny and Becky even went on stage they were demoralized by the other girls' appearance. Needless to say, they won no prizes and vowed afterwards never to take part in such a competition again.

I had very mixed feelings about the event. On the one hand, I disliked the ultra-competitive atmosphere which it generated. Girls were getting nearly hysterical about whether they had won or not. Those who did win prizes were euphoric, but for those like Becky, Pam and Penny who did not, the night ended in disappointment and tears. There was no real acknowledgement on the part of the organizers of the effort put in by all who entered: they were simply winners or losers.

Another aspect about which I had strong reservations was the sexual stereotype reinforced by some of the groups. The tight, sometimes revealing costumes, and the dance routines with their erotic movements – hips wiggling, legs astride, elements of 'strippers' routines – emphasized the girls as sex objects, which in the pre-teen age group particularly was verging on offensive. The essential difference, it seems to me, between this and the sexual expressiveness of the discos which I saw as positive, was that in the disco-dancing competition the girls were first and foremost 'on show'. This took away what seemed a crucial factor in the discos, the girls' enjoyment of dancing for its own sake and for the liberating effect it could generate. Although I identified an element of sexual display at discos, the important point was that the girls were in control, whereas in the disco- dancing competition there was an underlying commercial exploitation, albeit on a small scale, akin to beauty contests. Two local businesses, namely a record shop and a boutique, which depended on young people's interest in youth culture for their profits, had sponsored the competition, and a (male) director of each firm sat on the judging panel.

However, there were decidedly positive aspects to the competition too. For a start, some of the groups taking part presented non-traditional images of femininity. For example, the winning senior team comprised three Afro-Caribbean girls who both in their appearance – brightly coloured jumpsuits and 'shades' – and their style of dancing, based on breakdancing and 'body-popping', presented an image of young women as active, confident and streetwise. Other dances incorporated the energy and originality of modern dance movements as well as the standard disco-dancing routines, and these were particularly exciting to watch.

The fact that all the contestants were girls also built up a positive feeling to the evening. Seeing young women in the limelight was unusual compared, for instance, to school life. The town hall was packed full of enthusiastic supporters, both girls and boys, waving banners and shouting encouragement to their teams. This added to the sense of real achievement for the girls. Whatever the reality of the results, the fact that Becky, Penny and Pam had taken part in the competition gave them status in the eyes of other girls at school. In that sense, they did get some reward for their efforts even though they did not actually win any prizes.

The reservations I have expressed relate specifically to the competition rather than to disco-dancing itself, which provided a positive occupation for girls' leisure time. As one of the few ways in which girls could find their own space in male-dominated youth clubs, and a rare chance for young women's talents and interests to be encouraged, it was hardly surprising that disco-dancing was being maintained as a girls-only enterprise. Whilst I am keen for boys to take up dancing too, there were already numerous local spheres in which boys could succeed. In many ways, therefore, it seemed reasonable to keep disco-dancing as a predominantly female activity, at least until wider choices and opportunities were made available to young women too.

Dance classes: dancing as a career

There were many points of overlap between disco-dancing as an activity organized at youth clubs, and dancing classes held at local schools of dancing. For example, some of the sessions at youth clubs were run by qualified dance teachers and included modern dance techniques as well as disco-dancing routines. Some of the dancing schools taught disco-dancing and modern dance as well as the more traditional ballet, tap or ballroom dancing.

Both dancing at youth clubs and schools of dancing were essentially all-female preserves and being maintained as such apart from the occasional boys who hardly seemed to count, as Carol said about her dancing classes: 'Well there's three little lads go that's all [laughs], only little boys go, all the rest are girls'. There was also a feeling that only 'little' girls went to dancing classes. By the age of 13, many girls who had been to ballet school when younger had stopped going. Others like Carol still went but described the classes in an embarrassed way as 'babyish' or 'boring', hardly admitting that they went at all. To these girls, dance classes were increasingly out of keeping with their adolescent interests, in spite of the efforts of some schools of dancing to include modern techniques. In contrast, the dance sessions at youth clubs attracted girls who were heavily involved with teenage youth culture. The difference in image was crucial.

Whilst the youth clubs certainly took their dancing seriously, as exemplified by the disco-dancing competition, the schools of dancing were characterized to a much greater extent by professionalism, competitiveness and dedication. Entering for dance exams and competitions in order to gain medals and grades was an important part of the process. However, the expense involved could be prohibitive, as Carol explained: 'You see you have to pay about £5 just to get there on the coach trip, and then you have to pay for the tickets and all this lot, so it's fair expensive.' This tended to exclude many working-class girls carrying on to higher levels. Only those who were seriously interested in taking up dancing as a career carried on at this stage. Deborah, who was 13 when I got to know her, was one of these. Right through her school-life Deborah was determined to become a professional dancer. Perhaps because she was known to be highly talented and because she was aiming at a career in dancing, none of the other girls regarded Deborah's interest as babyish, and she enjoyed talking about it. She was quietly proud of her own achievement in dance and was totally dedicated to it, spending most evenings and Saturday mornings at one dancing school or another. Her own description indicates the extent of her commitment:

> On a Monday I do private lessons which I practise all different solos and that for competitions. Then we do class work practice groups and things for competitions. Then on a Wednesday just do ballet – I'm working towards

my pre-elementary ballet one [exam] – and then on a Thursday we do modern dance grades and then on a Saturday we do point work and normal ballet.

Seeing friends was fitted into remaining evenings or weekends 'when I get time'. What kept Deborah going was her love of dancing and the personal satisfaction she gained from it, as well as the hope of rewards in the future.

Dancing as a potential career has a powerful allure, holding out the promise of glamour and fame, as Julia Pascal describes (1985). Deborah's ambition started at the age of 3½:

> It all started with the 'little girl fantasy'. Seeing the dancers on television with the pretty ballet dresses and the thought of being famous. 'Deborah Thickett: Prima Ballerina.' It sounds great, in bright lights!

My own equivalent fantasy as a girl was of becoming an actress, which shares much of the same appeal. Although ballerina or actress can be seen as conventional feminine career choices, in many ways they represent an unconventional image of womanhood, far removed from the roles of housewife and mother (McRobbie 1984). They offer an escape both from domesticity – this was certainly the appeal of an actress's life to me – and from 'mundane surroundings and an increasingly bleak jobless future' (Konttinen 1984). However, determination and commitment at all levels are needed to turn the dream into a reality.

Some of these apparently contradictory strands were evident at the Gloria Slade School of Dancing which I visited to watch Deborah. Glamour was evident in the figure of Gloria Slade herself, with her blonded hair and heavy make-up, who took the class dressed in a lurex jumpsuit and very high heels. This was a total contrast to the girls themselves, with their severe almost asexual appearance: hair pulled tightly back, black leotards and black ballet shoes. The classical look went hand in hand with serious concentration as the girls went through a series of exercises and barre work which Gloria 'drilled' them in until they perfected each movement. Hard work and discipline were the order of the day. As someone who grew up on Margaret Morris dancing, a form of free expression and eurythmics inspired by Isadora Duncan, ballet positions have always seemed to me constricting and unnatural, and these feelings were renewed by watching the ballet class.

However, Deborah's own experience of ballet was quite different. Whilst she acknowledged that 'it has to have style', she saw nothing constricting in it:

> It's a soft and gentle feeling with elegance and grace. . . . It has always made me feel light. It helps to 'stretch' out all the tension that builds up. It's a peace that nobody can disturb.

Certainly the best dancers in the group such as Deborah were poised and graceful, and had control and confidence in their movements which carried over into their everyday lives.

Becoming a dancer, particularly a professional ballet dancer, is one of the most gruelling and physically demanding careers one could choose. Sirrka-Liisa Konttinen (1984) describes the X-ray test held by the Royal Ballet School to ensure a perfect shape in their prospective pupils. Many dancers become anorexic in their attempts to retain this 'impossible stereotype', as Sirrka-Liisa Konttinen calls it, as accounts like Gelsey Kirkland's also describe (Kirkland 1986), or fail to make the grade at all and end up in the chorus line at seaside holiday shows.

Deborah had already been initiated into the tough reality which awaited her. She was hoping to go to the Royal Ballet School, but was keeping modern dance as an option and had auditioned unsuccessfully for *Annie* and a few other musicals. She had also had an unfortunate experience with a fake agent, who had disappeared with his fee. Luckily for Deborah and her family, the police caught up with him and the money was retrieved. This episode certainly brought home to her the potential for exploitation.

However, for Deborah and for many other girls the allure remained strong. It was not that they were unrealistic about what would be involved, or that they were aware of and yet discounted the harsh realities. Perhaps paradoxically, as Angela McRobbie argues (1984), part of the romantic appeal of becoming a dancer is in the dedication, sacrifice and even pain required to succeed, as well as the potential fame and fortune for those who do make it to the top. As Deborah said:

> My advice to any girls thinking of taking up dancing professionally is to go for it. If you are really serious and really want to do it then it is there but you have to work at it.

Ambition, and pushing oneself to the limits of physical endurance, are attributes traditionally admired in and pursued by men. They were certainly evident in young women like Deborah. Although for most girls the ultimate success in dance may be unattainable, to have such a goal can be seen as a form of resistance and a means of self-fulfilment. Deborah's love of dancing gave her a physical and emotional confidence. She was admired by other girls both because she was talented and because she had a strong sense of purpose.

Deborah finally gave up the idea of dancing as a career two months before she left school. Like Julia Pascal (1985), who had also had ambitions to study at the Royal Ballet School, she would have to have gone 200 miles away from home to train and did not want to leave her family. Unlike Julia Pascal, whose mother put considerable pressure on her to give up her plans, Deborah's mother gave her every encouragement throughout: 'I would probably have given up dancing a long time ago if she had not been behind me.' Deborah herself also became concerned about the insecurity of life as a professional dancer, and saw the demands of that life clashing with the possibility of having a family of her own in the future. Although Deborah did ultimately decide not to become a dancer, she is still carrying it on as an interest. As she wrote to me recently, 'I still love the energetic side of life!'

Dancing into middle age?

Whether through schools of dancing, youth clubs or discos, dancing forms an important part of many young women's lives. Although it is sometimes directed at men, girls enjoy dancing first and foremost for its own sake, as a pleasurable, sensual experience which gives them some control over their own bodies. As Françoise Sergy writes, dance can give women 'an incredibly positive energy

. . . confidence building, balancing and stimulating' (Sergy 1983: 7). Dance can also be liberating in other important ways, as a source of fantasy or a release from everyday constraints.

As can be seen from my own recollections, dance can be a potent source of memories for women, often epitomizing the freedom and enjoyment they experienced in adolescence. The young working-class mothers Dorothy Hobson interviewed described their dancing days with nostalgia and regret (Hobson 1978). Childcare responsibilities and partners' disapproval prevented them from continuing with this interest, as Rosemary Deem also found among women in Milton Keynes (Deem 1986). A poignant comment from one woman who had been a prize-winning disco-dancer in her teens was, 'My husband says I'm too old for dancing – but he just doesn't want me to go!' (Deem 1986: 125). Sirrka-Liisa Konttinen describes how many mothers relive their dreams of becoming a dancer through their daughters, by encouraging them to take up dancing rather than by carrying on dancing themselves (Konttinen 1984).

Nevertheless, there are now many opportunities for women to carry on dancing; these are increasing and becoming more accessible. For example, whilst adult education classes may be frequented more by middle-class than working-class women (Deem 1986), the increasingly popular dance studios and fitness centres attract women from all backgrounds (McRobbie 1984). Although aerobics, keep-fit and yoga classes may be traditional female interests and in some ways reinforce feminine stereotypes (Deem 1986), this does not undermine the fact that they are a positive means by which women can meet together and enjoy themselves. This was certainly true for a modern dance class I went to in Yorkshire, which was predominantly for young mothers and was enjoyed both for its own sake and as a social activity. The classes provided a much-needed night out away from the children, as well as a time to restore energy and fitness and enjoy the company of other women. Classes like these, health clubs and dance studios can also be seen as 'safe' places for women to go, both by husbands worried about their wives meeting other men at discos (Hobson 1978; Deem 1986) and by women themselves who may feel more comfortable in women-only environments (Green, Hebron and Woodward 1985; Deem 1986).

I am aware that, like Angela McRobbie's article which has been such a positive stimulus, what I have presented in this chapter 'resembles more a series of snapshots than a thorough academic thesis' (McRobbie 1984: 130). This has largely been because of the lack of previous research. As with many other areas of young women's experience, the importance of dancing has been largely unacknowledged. There are still many gaps to be filled and further research to be done.

Acknowledgements

My special thanks go to Deborah Thickett for her invaluable contributions, both verbal and written, on the personal importance of dancing to her.

References

Angelou, Maya (1981) *The Heart of a Woman*, London, Virago.

Barfoot, Joan (1982) *Dancing in the Dark*, London, Women's Press.

Buonaventura, Wendy & Smedley, Gail (1979) 'Rebirth of the belly dance', *Spare Rib* 84, July, pp. 26–7.

Deem, Rosemary (1986) *All Work and No Play? The Sociology of Women and Leisure*, Milton Keynes, Open University Press.

Frith, Simon (1978) *The Sociology of Rock*, London, Constable.

Green, Eileen Hebron, Sandra and Woodward, Diana (1985) 'A woman's work', *Sport and Leisure*, July/August, pp. 36–8.

Griffiths, Vivienne (1986) *Using Drama to Get at Gender*, Studies in Sexual Politics No. 9, Sociology Department, University of Manchester.

Hobson, Dorothy (1978) 'Housewives: isolation as oppression', in Women's Studies Group CCCS (eds.) *Women Take Issue: Aspects of Women's Subordination*, London, Hutchinson.

Ingham, Mary (1981) *Now We Are Thirty: Women of the Breakthrough Generation*, London, Methuen.

Kirkland, Gelsey (1986) *Dancing on My Grave*, London, Hamish Hamilton.

Konttinen, Sirrka-Liisa (1984) 'Step by step', notes accompanying photographic exhibition, Side Gallery, North Tyneside.

Lees, Sue (1986) *Losing Out: Sexuality and Adolescent Girls*, London, Hutchinson.

McRobbie, Angela (1984) 'Dance and social fantasy', in Angela McRobbie and Mica Nava (eds.) *Gender and Generation*, London, Macmillan.

Mungham, Geoff (1976) 'Youth in Pursuit of Itself', in Geoff Mungham and Geoff Pearson (eds.) *Working Class Youth Culture*, London, Routledge & Kegan Paul.

Pascal, Julia (1985) 'Prima Ballerina Assoluta', in Liz Heron (ed.) *Truth, Dare or Promise: Girls Growing Up in the Fifties*, London, Virago.

Sergy, Françoise (1983) 'Dance and feminism', *Spare Rib* 137, December, pp. 6–7.

PART 4

The power game

INTRODUCTION

Of all the papers in this collection, the three in this part portray most directly the significant effects of patriarchal relations on women's leisure. If power is the enforcement of ideology, then it is not merely something which people are given, or can possess; it is part of a complex of envalued structures and modes of behaviour which are at the basis of social life. It is therefore not sufficient to maintain that women are disadvantaged by their subordinate position in a patriarchal society in which men possess greater power. It is necessary to examine the ways in which the structures of institutions are legitimated by complementary ideologies of femininity and masculinity and how these further polarize the expected behaviours of the two gender groups.

As Rosemary Deem asked in Chapter 1, how and why are power relations sustained by ideological and material factors, how does this process translate into the leisure sphere, and how does it affect women's opportunities to exercise real choice in leisure?

Part 2 focused on the ways in which ideologies of femininity, coupledom and family roles change during the life-span, and how cultural definitions of appropriate behaviour affect the ability of women to continue with or take up leisure activities in their changing life situations. In Chapter 10 Diana Woodward and Eileen Green focus this discussion more sharply on to the processes whereby social control is exercised between partners in family groups. Many of the issues which they identify relate also to men's leisure, and have been largely ignored by mainstream leisure studies. The sanctions applied to people who dare to challenge or try to adapt the stereotyped social roles which they are expected to play are themselves interesting examples of the enforcement of ideology. The private nature of family life appears to provide a context within which sanctions can be applied more severely than in others, and are reinforced by onlookers from the extended family and neighbourhood.

The issue of 'women's place' (or space) is discussed by Woodward and Green in relation to women's access to public spaces. It is also identified by Judy White as a particular factor which helps to explain why there are so few women in recreation management positions. Not only is the management role viewed as inappropriate for women, but the values and particular skills associated with femininity are ranked less highly than so-called 'male' models of management. Sandra Harding (1986) has argued that the ways in which women gain informal power are invisible in social theory and research, and undervalued in society.

Authority, generally connected with masculinity, is commonly defined as legitimate power. In this context, at least, it is not only the place of women in management which is seen as anomalous, but their aspirations to play roles which are defined as more appropriate for males. Attempts by women to transcend or transform established management practices and procedures are seen as a direct threat to the established social order. White argues that the scarcity of women in decision-making positions in recreation management seriously limits the information available as the basis for decisions. The adoption of alternative models of 'female' management can enrich the delivery of leisure services; provision for women can be met in much more direct and sensitive ways.

In analysing women's use of leisure institutions and organizations, it has been traditional to analyse distributional aspects – that is, which women take part in which activities, at what levels and from which groups in society. Factors which appear to be associated with low or non-participation are then identified as constraints, for example children, lack of higher education, lack of personal mobility. The constraints model is based on the assumption that, if all the constraints can be removed, then there is nothing to prevent women having a full range of leisure opportunity. If they do not take up the opportunity offered, then they are, in some way, 'to blame'. The term 'low or non-participant' thus acquires an element of stigma, akin to the labelling of women as 'recreationally inert', 'sports illiterate' and so on. Such stigmatisation helps to reinforce the hierarchy of men and women which in turn reifies and reinforces patriarchal relations.

While the constraints model is useful in identifying the imbalance of advantage between the sexes, the inequality of resources and the part played by gender-related personal attributes, it also has severe limitations. It tends to ignore the inherent constraints of the institutions whose brief is to offer leisure provision. Neither does it take account of the ways in which women experience these barriers. Thus there is a need to analyse the relational aspects of gender inequality in terms of both women's perceptions of and reactions to leisure provision, and of the underlying ideologies of the provisions made for different social groups. Margaret Talbot makes a preliminary attempt at this kind of analysis, identifying some of the ways in which women's access to leisure can be prevented by gatekeepers and images which in effect serve to keep activities and groups exclusive.

This last chapter underlines the need to consider the relationship between the personal and structural aspects of power – the extent to which women's ability or desire to exert control over their own lives is seen as a threat to social order. Often it is when this kind of challenge is faced that the taken-for-granted aspects of inequality become legitimated by claims that such inequality reflects a 'natural' difference between the sexes and is therefore inevitable and immutable. Gender ideology is thus operationalized and re-emphasizes, for example, the notion that women operate in the private sphere, while men control the public aspects of life. Clearly this idea has significant effects on women's ability to make choices in leisure outside the home, and on the range of opportunities which it is legitimate for them to enjoy within the home. The embodiment of these ideologies within the legal system further highlights the need to make them explicit and to subject them to critical analysis.

Power can be viewed as a collectively developed commodity, with negotiation and bargaining as integral components, resulting in relations of power which are reciprocal and constantly renegotiated. In this sense, power is the ability to act effectively. This clearly implies a willingness and openness on the part of all parties to take part and compromise in the bargaining process, and an awareness that there is a constant shifting of advantage and disadvantage. However, the term 'leisure provision' itself implies 'delivery to' and the unequal power relations of providing 'authorities' and consumers, rather than collective development. Criticism of many aspects of public sector leisure provision as paternalist – provided by people who know what is good, for the benefit (unnegotiated) of others – is relevant here. Where are women in the leisure provision process – active partners, or target (things which people throw things at) groups?

References

Harding, Sandra (1986) *The Science Question in Feminism*, Milton Keynes, Open University Press.

10

'Not tonight, dear!' The social control of women's leisure

DIANA WOODWARD AND EILEEN GREEN

Women's perceptions of leisure as 'time free from constraints' or 'free time when you can do whatever you want' stand in stark contrast to the lack of such time and the absence of unhindered licence to spend it as they wish, which are the daily experience of most of them. In this chapter we will argue that the area of leisure, which is portrayed by patriarchal capitalist ideology as the ultimate in freedom and pleasure, is actually one of the aspects of life in which women's behaviour is the most closely monitored and regulated. The purpose of the chapter is to explore the complex processes of social control which operate to constrain women's (and also men's) freedom at a general level, and more specifically serve to limit their opportunities for free time and access to leisure activities by virtue of their social position. We are concerned both with the particular forms which such regulation takes and with the structural context within which choices about leisure emerge, and decisions and negotiations take place. It is important to examine the web of norms and beliefs which legitimate and sustain gender inequalities in leisure, as they help to explain why such differences are institutionalized parts of the social fabric, and are widely accepted as 'normal'.

Social control and everyday life

Women share a subordinate social position to men in our society, albeit one which is mediated by divisions of social class and race, as well as those of age and marital status. Gender is obviously a key factor in understanding both the form and content of leisure generally in patriarchal capitalist societies, and also the specific influences on the leisure interests, activities and attitudes towards leisure of various groups within society. Since dominant ideologies make a vital contribution towards the maintenance of a patriarchal social system, it is important to understand the links between the production and reproduction of such ideologies and the cultural forms which they assume. Popular images of leisure, particularly those represented in the media and leisure-based publications, promote the reproduction of ideologies of masculinity and femininity, with their representations of gender-appropriate roles and activities, and stimulate the hostility shown to those who do not conform to these stereotyped models.

Sexuality and respectability

The concept of respectability is a key element in the construction and representation of women as portrayed within dominant stereotypes. Ideologies construct
specific aspects of the social world as 'natural' and 'universal', and this is particularly the case for the prevailing ideologies about gender within our culture.
Models of masculinity and femininity are a vital component of the commonsense
knowledge upon which we draw to make sense of our experience and to evaluate
others whom we encounter in the course of our lives. Cultural stereotypes form an
integral part of such ideologies. Representations of 'the male' and 'the female' are
linked to a broader system of signification and to real relations which are historically constituted (Pollock 1977). Gendered stereotypes are social constructions
closely tied in with the interests of dominant social groups, which in this case are
patriarchal and sited within capitalist social relations.

Ideological stereotypes of women in contemporary capitalism divide them into,
on the one hand, those respectable women who are or will be daughters, wives and
mothers, and on the other, women who are beyond the limits of respectability,
that is whores or 'fallen women'. This dual classification represents the majority
of women within a particular stereotype of the nuclear family, and prescribes for
them the roles of housewife and mother. All women are considered to be either
potential housewives and mothers, or sex objects. Class and racial differences are
rendered invisible, except in relation to the supposed deviant minority who are
represented within a parallel stereotype. Such stereotypes are both racist and
reflect the interests of the dominant class.

Recent studies (Hobson 1981; Westwood 1984; Deem 1986), emphasize the
importance of courtship and the early stages of marriage and motherhood in
limiting behaviour in general, and leisure activities in particular, to only those
which are seen as appropriate for married women. The Sheffield study illustrates
this clearly (Green, Hebron and Woodward 1987c). During the stage of 'serious
courting' and the early stages of married life which followed, most women gave up
their own spare time pleasures away from home in favour of couple-based leisure,
or staying at home, 'saving to get married'. This was in vivid contrast to the
leisure activities of male partners which remained substantially unchanged or
sometimes increased in frequency and importance, as in the case of the following
male interviewee:

> Once we were married I was starting to go out a lot more, I started to play
> football again and I was training twice a week, playing football Saturdays
> and Sundays, so that were like four days out of a week really. I were never
> in, that was the main argument, that I was always out.
>
> (quoted in Green, Hebron and Woodward 1987b: 35)

Romance, togetherness and the double standard

For most women who lived in a family situation with male partners, couple-based
leisure seems to be the ideal, reflecting dominant ideologies of romantic love and
'togetherness'. The following quotation from a young mother in the Sheffield
study illustrates the importance of 'special' nights out, events which assumed

particular significance for the women, despite the reluctant participation of most of the men concerned. It was also perceived by the women as providing an opportunity to get closer to their partners, in order to recapture the intimacy of an earlier phase in their relationship:

> Oh yeh, it makes us spend time together, without just being in the house with the kids around us . . . when it's birthdays and anniversaries, seem to go out and you have little heart-to-heart talks and things like that. Because the mood of the moment sweeps you along you know, and you perhaps talk about things that you haven't said for a bit.
>
> (quoted in Green, Hebron and Woodward 1987b: 39)

Despite such sentiments, it is common for both men and women to engage in independent leisure outside the home with members of the same sex. Men are far more likely than women to maintain the patterns of leisure established before marriage and parenthood. Visits to the pub with 'the lads' are both frequent and accepted leisure activities for men, despite objections from female partners. However, the issue of women's independent leisure creates major conflicts, their level varying in relation to the women's choice of companions and leisure venues. 'Respectable' feminine activities such as keep fit, aerobics and flower arranging are approved of, as are outings with female relatives. Outings to pubs or discos unaccompanied by male partners are at best occasionally tolerated, and at worst liable to severe sanctions from men (Deem 1986; Green, Hebron and Woodward 1987a). Unless couples have maintained separate leisure activities from an early stage in their relationship, independent outings can be seen as threatening to both the stability of the partnership and its public profile. As one woman who very rarely went out alone commented, 'Well he doesn't object because it's so rare, and he knows where I am and he knows who I'm with, it's just local. And the same applies with him. If it got any too regular, I think he'd go up the wall and so would I' (Green, Hebron and Woodward 1987b: 41). This public profile of togetherness and domestic harmony is often closely protected by both marriage partners, especially when under scrutiny from outsiders. Sallie Westwood's study illustrates this clearly, particularly in the area of home making. The attitudes of the majority of women at Stitcho (the workplace studied) underlined the fact that

> It was a matter of pride to the women . . . that they cared for their children and their homes as they might have done if they were full-time homemakers. Any criticism seemed cruelly out of place and was interpreted as a criticism of them, not of the men and children in their households and the way that domestic labour was organized.
>
> (Westwood 1984: 169)

This illustrates the fact that most women internalize the idea that womanhood ties them to primary responsibility for the care and well-being of others, in particular male partners and children, but also other dependent or elderly relatives too. Less explicit but arguably more powerful as an unexamined force, is the parallel concept that the woman is equally accountable for making the marriage partnership and associated parenthood 'work' and continue into the land of 'happy ever after' as portrayed in romantic fiction and soap opera. Evidence from studies of domestic violence lend support to this notion (Dobash and Dobash 1980). This is not to say that women are unaware of the hard realities of married life and motherhood, rather that most of us cling to some romantic illusions to gild the raw edges of routine domesticity. Just as the young women assembly-line workers studied by Ruth Cavendish made their lives tolerable by day-dreaming about escape into marriage and the role of housewife (Cavendish 1982), so it can be argued that wives escape from the humdrum reality of housework and insensitive men partners through fictional romance, whose heroes display the sensitivity and tenderness which their own menfolk conspicuously do not.

Patriarchal control of public spaces

Hard-won opportunities to venture into leisure venues such as pubs, although potentially rewarding to the individual and offering opportunities for lively (often female) company, are still flanked by reminders that such places are closely guarded as male territory by the regulars. Sociological accounts of rural pub cultures (Whitehead 1976; Hunt and Satterlee 1987) emphasize the importance of the public house as an arena in which to display masculine bonding behaviour, where patriarchal power is reaffirmed and women are represented as the property of their male relatives. Women entering pubs unaccompanied in the 1980s are subjected to a male hostility which ranges from silent scrutiny to sexual harassment, and is strongly reminiscent of Victorian attitudes towards women's consumption of alcohol in public (Hey 1986).

A considerable body of evidence points to the fact that both the regulation of women's access to public places and their behaviour once they gain entry, are grounded in the question of women's right to occupy particular spaces (Imray and Middleton 1983). Women's proper place has traditionally been seen as the home, with men monopolizing the public arena. By and large women have been discouraged from having a high profile in most areas of public life (Hall 1979) and the example of social relations between men and women in the setting of the pub provides a good illustration of current representations of patriarchal beliefs and values as 'normal'. The teasing and banter engaged in by men, usually directly or indirectly at the expense of women, whether in the form of negative mother-in-law jokes, the ridicule of 'hen-pecked' husbands, or overtly sexual innuendos aimed at female customers and bar staff, constitutes a form of verbal violence against women (Green, Hebron and Woodward 1987a). Such behaviour is generally perceived as acceptable displays of masculinity, but these forms of informal group process are a major source of social control (Whitehead 1976; Smart and Smart 1978) which can be related to the regulation of both female and male sexuality.

Strategies of control exerted by male groups in leisure venues are ultimately just one expression of a process of social control which is constructed with reference to dominant forms of masculinity, and 'acceptable levels of violence'. However, as David Morgan states with particular reference to the limitations of male theorizations of male sexuality, we must be careful not to present a model of male violence which is overly simple and one-dimensional: 'This has the danger of understating the power of patriarchy; the benefits of which are enjoyed by gentle as well as violent men' (Morgan 1987: 192). The paradox suggested by the complex mixture of empathy and distaste which links men indulging in overt macho displays at the bar with those men quietly sipping beer in mixed groups in the lounge, is partially explained with reference to the ways in which all men as a gendered group benefit from the patriarchal inequalities of power which are maintained and reproduced through such social constructions of masculinity.

Independence, intimacy and a sense of 'belonging'

Women's desire for independent leisure outside the home is often perceived as signalling dissatisfaction with family life and perhaps leading to a neglect of the responsibilities of motherhood (Westwood 1984; Green, Hebron and Woodward 1985a). The potential costs in terms of both economic and emotional security of challenging the social norms which shape conventional attitudes towards family life and gender-appropriate behaviour are too great for most women. Some of the women in the Sheffield study reported a high incidence of lengthy and acrimonious negotiations with male partners about their own access to an independent social life. Unsurprisingly, many women simply opted out of the negotiation process altogether:

> It doesn't cause any arguments except that sometimes I just think about it, because, you know, I work with quite a lot of single people, they go out and I think 'well perhaps I could join in . . .' but I don't sort of entertain it any longer.
>
> (quoted in Green, Hebron and Woodward 1987a: 87)

This understandable retreat from open conflict, coupled with deep-seated emotional and economic investments in heterosexual partnerships and associated forms of family life, serves to reinforce the status quo and to protect male leisure usually at the expense of women's free time, autonomy and release from domestic labour and childcare. Although the majority of women interviewed in the Sheffield study felt that leisure was an important and necessary element in their lives, if resources for leisure were short (such as time and money) women's own leisure tended to be a low priority. As one woman said: 'I think a husband's leisure comes first no matter what' (Green Hebron and Woodward, forthcoming). This was a view shared by most of the male partners interviewed, and can be explained with reference to the enduring assumption that leisure is earned through paid work. Women in employment are in a stronger position legitimately to take time for themselves: because their labour in the workplace is visible and generates financial rewards, it therefore 'earns' them some entitlement to autonomous leisure. However, as has been argued elsewhere (Oakley 1974; Wilson 1980), it is unpaid work – housework and childcare – which is the least visible and socially recognized kind of work. It is exhausting, devalued and unremitting, and yet is not widely recognized, as paid work is, as conferring an entitlement to recreational time.

The dominance of representations of family and couple-based leisure as the most rewarding kind (Clarke and Critcher 1986) is reflected in the fact that the majority of women accord it highest priority (Deem 1986; Green, Hebron and Woodward, 1987b), particularly those with small children. Organizing leisure activities and outings with a male partner and/or children is perceived by most women as part of their role as wives and mothers, with the success of the event being measured in terms of the pleasure and satisfaction derived. The 'family outing' is the personification of cereal-packet nuclear family life. Although family life is not the only source of emotional and parental satisfaction, it is a privileged source in modern industrial societies and the needs which it meets are both real and fundamental. As Michele Barrett and Mary McIntosh note, 'affection, security, intimacy, sexual love, parenthood and so on . . . are not artificial. We see these as human needs, not pathological constructs' (Barrett and McIntosh 1982: 133). However they go on to argue that the form in which such needs are currently met is both unsatisfying and anti-social, because it traditionally involves an unequal sexual division of labour, and shifts the burden of domestic provision and caring on to the woman. This burden carries over into the area of leisure, which needs organizing and servicing, a process usually carried out by women. Feminist critiques of the nuclear family (Barrett and McIntosh 1982; Segal 1983; Gittins 1985) focus upon such inequalities and their economic and political underpinnings, and conclude that 'Nobody should have a housewife. Nobody, man, child, invalid or woman needs a long-term "housewife" or has the right to have one' (Barrett and McIntosh 1982: 144).

The continuing trend towards marriage and nuclear family life is buttressed by romantic love and social expectations of coupledom and parenthood. Once enmeshed in the threads of emotional closeness and domestic life, the majority of women experience difficulty in challenging the norms of the institution which they willingly entered, albeit via the process of gender socialization. As Sue Cartledge writes, 'When my desires appeared to conflict with the needs of my husband, I felt responsible for the pain I was causing' (Cartledge 1983: 168). Similarly, women who attempt to exercise their right to independent leisure, experience guilt at 'deserting' their partners and children, especially when male partners signal clear disapproval. This guilt is paradoxically often reinforced by the behaviour and attitudes of other women, in particular female friends and relatives, who adopt more conventional leisure patterns.

Women's networks: autonomy, support and collusion

An important aspect of the social control process discussed above concerns the role of other women in defining and maintaining 'appropriate' behaviour for women. Recent research underlines the importance and extent of support women receive from female friends and kin, both domestically and in the workplace (Delamont 1980; Pollert 1981, Phizacklea 1983, Westwood 1984). However, such female networks can also be powerful reinforcing agents of patriarchy, by policing other women's behaviour.

Independence and support

Young women's desire for independence and enjoyment of the opportunities denied to their mothers is well recorded in feminist studies of family life and paid work (Green and Parry 1982; Pollert 1981; Westwood 1984). While they are single and in employment, women experience a greater degree of freedom than their married counterparts who have children. It is, however, a temporary condition for the majority (see Ch. 3 above for parallel discussion). The group of young, single women interviewed in the Sheffield study were aware that the relatively high degree of autonomy they were experiencing was a transient state largely attributable to their unmarried status: 'I think it's about, it depends whether you're married or not. I could do what I want because I'm single, but if you're married you've got ties and you've got to be in at certain times and things' (Green, Hebron and Woodward 1987b: 72).

This parallels Dorothy Hobson's (1981) work on young married women. The arrival of babies heralds a dramatic shift in both attitudes towards leisure time and the availability of resources (Wimbush 1986). Young mothers experience a narrowing of their opportunities for independent outings and increasingly rely upon other women in similar situations for both support and company. The Sheffield survey indicated that women with children under the age of 5 are the least likely to feel satisfied with the amount of free time they have, and 59 per cent reported finding it too difficult to set time aside for themselves. Female relatives were a major source of support in the areas of social company and babysitting. As one woman said, 'well I think you do need a break from 'em, they go out sometimes for the day, my sister has them or my sister-in-law, and I love that day to myself. Can get done what I meant to do and they're not in the way' (Green, Hebron and Woodward 1987b: 36). Women's own mothers constitute a preferred source of babysitting whether for the women's employment or leisure, but this entails costs in terms of allowing their mothers open access to the daughter's home and/or the right to approve or criticize standards of housework and childcare. This exchange of domestic help can also result in parents, and in particular according to Anne Whitehead (1976), mothers becoming involved in the marital problems of their offspring. Parents typically supported the marital bond when offering advice and/or interference, and exhorted young wives to 'avoid trouble', particularly that associated with challenging domestic norms and demanding freedom for independent leisure. Their influence tends therefore to be a conservative one, upholding the patriarchal status quo.

Struggle, collusion and 'learning to cope'

A large part of the above discussion of women's networks centres upon the contradictory nature of such support networks, highlighting both the struggle for space and independence engaged in by individual women and the ambivalent nature of the advice or other forms of support available from various female groups. From an early age women learn to conform (Belotti 1975), and the habit of not 'getting dirty' or 'causing trouble' learnt so well in childhood serves as a foundation on which to build the coping strategies acquired in later life.

Women are often accused of lacking initiative and being 'their own worst enemies' – accusations which severely underestimate the force of the structural and cultural constraints within which women operate. Learning how to 'cope' may mean the difference between survival and annihilation in situations of extreme poverty and/or violence. And 'coping' can mean anything from juggling the competing demands of paid work and childcare, to the use of avoidance strategies to minimize the likelihood of sexual harassment (Hanmer and Saunders 1983), or other forms of interpersonal violence (Stanko 1987). Such strategies are passed on from one generation of women to another and form an important aspect of female cultures. Older women who have developed coping strategies in order to survive domestic and labour market inequalities generated by patriarchal structures, take (justified) pride in the skilful nature of such strategies (Phizacklea 1983; West 1984). They are passed on to younger women accompanied by cautionary tales about the dangers associated with disturbing 'the balancing act'. Although such attitudes may be characterized as 'colluding' with the status quo of women's gender-based inequality, they also reflect years of often painfully acquired experience. Recent feminist accounts which attempt to challenge the status quo and propose alternatives are often criticized as undermining and negative. This is to misunderstand their political purpose. In the words of Diana Leonard and Mary Ann Speakman:

> Feminist accounts [also] do not say that women are dupes. Quite the contrary. They stress that women choose what to do and that their choices are made within a situation which is not of women's own choosing – within a sexist (and class-based, racist and age-based) society. One way of making the best of such a situation is to go along with it: to play the feminine role (appropriate to one's class, race and age) to the hilt. Another is to try and change it. Both have their problems.
>
> (Leonard and Speakman 1986: 22)

Negotiations within the home about women's leisure

Negotiations with male partners about women's access to the resources needed to enjoy leisure – time free from work and other commitments, the use of physical space, opportunities to do chosen activities, and the availability of companions, equipment and transport – take place within a context of expectations about gender roles. Individuals' perceptions of prevailing norms about being a wife or husband, mother or father, young woman or man, inform these social interactions on how roles should be performed within their own households. They provide a yardstick of presumed commonly accepted standards against which to assess the legitimacy of particular instances of behaviour, whether one's own or a partner's. An unemployed Sheffield man's account of a long-standing disagreement with his wife about his weekly trip to the pub clearly reveals the divergent frames of reference which each of them is using to demonstrate the moral force of their respective positions:

A. 'Don't enjoy yourself', she'll say.
Q. Is that joking, or a bit of seriousness there?
A. Oh, there's a lot of seriousness. I used to like my night out on a Friday, even if we couldn't afford it, you see. And she'd be saying 'Well, bang goes a couple of loaves of bread' or summat like that, you know. She said I really should forfeit going out and think more about what's going on in the house. And I used to say 'Well, every man goes out'. Most men go

out nearly every night of the week. I don't do that, I just do it once, you
see. She used to . . . it's just her tone, you could tell, when she talked to
me, it were different.

(quoted in Green, Hebron and Woodward 1987b: 58)

This kind of dialogue debates not only access to resources but also the legitimacy
of how they are used. The sets of norms which underpin them are not fixed and
immutable but are worked out in the course of a relationship.

The following sections of the chapter examines how gender inequalities operate
within the household to constrain women's leisure opportunities. The
negotiations which take place about women's freedom to have leisure time and
how it is spent, reveal what partners' sets of norms are, about respectable and
socially approved standards of behaviour; and how power, authority and influence are exercised to affect the outcome of these negotiations. The issues to be
examined are, first, women's entitlement to leisure and the means to enjoy it; and
second, access to safe and convenient forms of travel. These areas have been
chosen to illustrate the social processes associated with the acting out of gender-
role norms and control of access to resources.

Women's entitlement to leisure

Women's access to time free for leisure is constrained by their everyday commitments – paid employment, childcare, domestic labour, and the care of frail or
elderly relatives. In the Sheffield study the majority of the women respondents had
little free time during weekday daytimes, and the amount of their evening leisure
time clearly reflected their level of domestic commitments: the single women had
an average of 4.3 hours' free time; childless married women had, on average, 3
hours' free; the mothers of children aged between 5 and 16 years old had 2.3
hours' leisure; and the mothers of under-5s had only 1.9 hours of free time.
Whether or not the women had paid jobs mattered much less than their domestic
responsibilities. The same patterns applied to weekend leisure time (Green,
Hebron and Woodward 1987b, 1987c).

The main reason for this state of affairs is the unequal distribution of domestic
labour within the household. Women's responsibility for domestic work and
childcare is one of the most significant constraints upon leisure, a constraint which
is largely not shared by men. As Michele Barrett notes, 'As is now well known,
even when women work outside the home they normally carry the burden of
household organisation and labour at home as well' (Barrett 1980: 208). Ninety-
seven per cent of the married women in the Sheffield survey reported that they did
most of the housework themselves. Women's paid work, whilst in many cases
providing an essential contribution to household resources, is still widely seen as
being secondary to the work of nurturing the family and providing a pleasant
environment for the male worker to return to.

For many women, children form the centre-point of their domestic responsibilities and caring role. Our findings indicate that having children influences all
areas of life, including leisure. Having children may result in less time and less
money being available for leisure, but the effects are rarely felt equally by men and
women. Because children are deemed to be primarily women's responsibility, it is

women's leisure which is typically most circumscribed by having children, as many of the women in the interviews revealed: one woman voiced sentiments felt by many, in her resentment of her husband's continued commitment to his leisure activities away from home when their children were young: 'I got annoyed with him at times, particularly when I had to stay in and babysit, when the children were really tiny.' She quickly went on to say, 'But I mean it was as much my fault, because I didn't trust anyone else to look after my children so I can't complain too much . . . I wouldn't say there were any real row, it was just sort of I'd have the odd go at him every now and again' (quoted in Green, Hebron and Woodward 1987b: 67).

Many women with young children lack the necessary funds to pay for a regular childminder or babysitter, and in any case may be reluctant to leave their children with 'strangers' except in emergencies. Whilst male partners may be asked to look after children on special occasions, we found no evidence of real shared responsibility for childcare, and several women commented on partners' unreliability as childminders, which can be a major barrier to their independent leisure away from home:

> It's so much hassle, to get everything organized, to do something like that [i.e. to go away on her own]. And when we get babysitters, I always get a babysitter, it's never a case of him getting a babysitter for us. It's sort of my responsibility, which annoys me, because it's as though the kids are my responsibility and not a joint one. . . . The men don't have that same responsibility.
>
> (quoted in Green, Hebron and Woodward 1987b)

One woman who objected to the inequality in this area, commented in answer to a question about disagreements between herself and her partner, 'Yeh, because I'm always playing hell that I've got to stop here and he can, like I said, just go off and do what he wants to do'. Her husband often promised to babysit but rarely fulfilled that promise: 'Well, probably he'll say for the next weekend, "Well you go and go out with your mum on a shopping spree" or something like that, you know, or "You go and see your friend one night and I'll stop in and look after him", that kind of thing, and then he forgets' (quoted in ibid.: 41–2).

Because of the general acceptance of traditional divisions of responsibility by the Sheffield respondents, there was little perception that women might 'need' leisure outside the home to the same degree as men. Thus men's leisure away from home was accorded high priority, in terms of its precedence over competing activities, and spending patterns. Women's leisure was seen as much less important, both by themselves – some made a virtue out of the necessity of spending free time alone at home watching television – and by their partners. Disagreements mainly centred on the amount of time men spent away from home, rather than on their right to spend time in this way, and women reported these conflicts as 'niggles' or 'having a go at him', thereby revealing their feelings of impotence to change their partners' habits: 'I just have a niggle once in a while and I say, "Oh no, not out again?" But really I quite enjoy it when he does go out because it means I can watch what I want to watch without any arguments' (quoted in ibid: 67).

Another area of widespread conflict was over how leisure time would be spent, and with whom. The ideal was clearly for this time to be spent as a couple, or as a family, and preferably away from the home which, for many women was also their primary workplace. The complaints of the mothers referred to above were of their isolation at home in the evenings if their partners were at leisure away from home. The same expectation by many husbands, that if they wanted to have free time at home then they were entitled to expect that their wives should be there with them, constrained many women's leisure activities in the evenings. The choices were either to disregard their husbands' wishes by going out anyway, or to defer to him by staying in. One husband, who had recently started a job after five years' unemployment, could not accept his wife's need to have leisure outside the home, which, because of their young family and low income, was likely to happen during the evening, when he was available to babysit:

Q. How do you feel when you come back and she's not around?

A. Sick, lost somehow, you know. I think what it is, really, is being out of work such a long time and being in the house all day with her, as well as night time, you see. Now I'm out at work I look forward to coming home and spending the nights with her, and then when she goes out like that, it's a bit lonely for me again.

(ibid.: 59).

A number of references in both his interview and his wife's indicate that each is engaged in monitoring and counting the partner's evenings spent out of the home without them. The husband explicitly mentioned his jealousy and concern about her fidelity when his wife goes out with other women, without him. The last occasion of this kind had been two years earlier! Apart from the expense of such 'nights out', this latent hostility makes it difficult for women to negotiate for leisure time to be spent in this way. Another husband – also the father of young children – twice referred to 'letting' his wife go out without him, and implied that she would thereby obtain the opportunity to engage in extramarital liaisons, which, however, she would be unlikely to take because she would know that he would retaliate. Both of these husbands said that their wives had never been in the habit of having regular evenings out at pubs or clubs, or having meals out, because of their youth when they met; never having had much money to spend on leisure and/or the man's unsocial working hours; and more recently, the demands of caring for babies and small children. The dissonance is striking between the husbands' perceptions of their wives as potentially available to other men during evenings out without their partners, and the reality of their wives' extremely restricted opportunities for such leisure, even if this was what they wanted.

The group of middle-class women interviewed who had teenage or older children, were more often able to attain the goal of couple-based leisure, and indeed, most of their free time was spent with their husbands. As leisure patterns were long established, there was little conflict about what to do or with whom:

It's always been sort of an understood thing that we went out together. If he did want to go out on his own, fair enough, I mean, I have had the odd night out as I say, with the leaving parties and that for people at work, I've gone on my own and the same for him, I mean for the stag nights and bachelor do's, he's gone to them. But as I say, by and large, we've done everything together.

(ibid.)

Few disagreements seem to arise over how joint leisure time is spent. In some cases, where there is disagreement, one or other partner is willing to compromise: 'David will say, "shall we go to so and so theatre" you know and I'll say, "Oh I don't think I want to go to that", so he'll say, "Well I'm going if you're not", so then I usually say "Well I'll come too then" ' (ibid.: 67). Others reported having 'niggled' at their husbands or manipulating them: 'This is where you get round to manipulating each other. I mean, if I really wanted to do something, I would do something and I'd get him to . . . I don't think I could really have done it without him agreeing' (ibid.: 68). She acknowledges, however, that it would be difficult for her to engage in independent activities without his consent.

So far we have considered how the unequal sexual division of domestic labour reduces women's time and energy for leisure, as well as making it their responsibility to organize substitute childcare. Whilst norms about gender roles influence ideas about women's and men's needs for leisure away from home and their entitlement to it, this emphasis on social and cultural practices should not distract attention from the material inequalities in women's and men's leisure opportunities. Access to money to spend on travel to and from external leisure venues and the use of a car are, for women, important facilitators of autonomous leisure.

Gender, mobility patterns and leisure opportunities

Although there has been a fivefold increase in car ownership since the 1950s (Central Statistical Office 1981), this improved access to private transport facilities has been unevenly distributed between social groups, approximately in relation to their level of affluence. Households whose heads are in professional or managerial jobs are three times as likely to have one or more cars available for their use than households whose heads are in unskilled manual jobs (ibid.). However, as with other measures of prosperity it should not be assumed that all members of a household share equal access to these resources. The Sheffield study found, as others have done (Pahl 1983, 1984), that in general women tend to spend less on leisure than their male partners, but some groups of women had easier access to personal spending money for leisure or travel than others. Women employed full time, those with no children and young women, had control over larger sums of money for their own use than women who were financially dependent on male partners, who had young children, were lone parents or had unemployed husbands. Even women who are in employment are, in the context of the Sheffield labour market, likely to be poorly paid (Sheffield Low Pay Campaign 1985).

The economic subordination of women influences the balance of power within the households of married couples, which has major implications for women's access to the material resources they need for autonomous leisure. The control of household assets may largely determine how women can spend their spare time, particularly if they have no personal income. Studies of mobility patterns reveal similar patterns of gender inequality, as do those of the political economy of household units; women have less money to spend on travel, and are much more likely to use low-cost but slow means of travel, such as buses and walking, than men. Men are much more likely to make journeys by car; to have access to a car for more of the time, especially during the day; and are twice as likely to hold a driving licence (Pickup 1981; Graham 1984; GLC Women's Committee 1984–85).

In the Sheffield study a fifth of the women respondents said that not having the use of a car was a major problem for their access to leisure, and for another fifth it was a lesser problem (Green, Hebron and Woodward 1987b). The mothers of young children were especially prone to travel difficulties. Well under half of them were able to drive, and in any case few had access to a car in the daytime when they most needed it. This affects decisions about whether to make journeys at all, unless they are essential. As Rachael Dixey and Margaret Talbot point out:

> Distance is measured in different ways by people with unequal levels of mobility. On public transport distance is measured by the time taken to reach a destination, the number of bus changes, the cost of fares, modified by the extent of knowledge of the route and destination. Thus twenty minutes in a car for a middle class woman with children safely strapped to the back seat is translated into 1 ½ hours for the woman who travels by bus, one change of bus, adult and children's fares, the extra effort of boarding children and pushchairs, plus the time taken waiting for the bus to arrive.
>
> (Dixey with Talbot 1982: 31)

Not surprisingly, the inconvenience of using public transport means that many women, particularly those with young children, prefer to walk. Women make twice as many trips on foot as men, particularly to shop or to get to work or school (GLC Women's Committee 1984–5, Pamphlet No. 4).

Interviews with members of car-owning households bring to light some of the processes of negotiation within the home which give rise to these significant gender differences in mobility patterns. Some of the 'justifications' for the priority accorded to men's access to the family car are accepted as legitimate by the women whose access to it is thereby reduced. In the context of the prevailing importance attached to the male breadwinner's role, it is not surprising that men's journeys to and from work are seen as the first claim on use of the car (Hillman, Henderson and Whalley 1974). The widespread view that cars, being mechanical objects, fall within men's sphere of interest and competence rather than women's makes it easy to persuade many women that they lack the skills and aptitude for learning to drive, or have no need to learn because their husband, boyfriend or father will drive them.

One couple interviewed in the Sheffield study, who had 'retired' prematurely after both being made redundant, made considerable use of their car for leisure. They not only made almost daily trips to the local countryside when the weather made it possible and occasionally went to drink at country pubs, but also used the car as a site for leisure. While the husband umpires cricket matches in the summer the wife sits in the car, watching the game and doing her knitting! All these trips appear to be initiated by the husband, with the wife's willing accession. She could not drive, and offered the interviewer an elaborate rationale for this which, as she recognized whilst she was saying it, sounded implausible:

Q. Do you drive, yourself?
A. No, I've never got into it at all. Only ever had one try and that was it. I really couldn't reach the pedals properly and I thought it would be too much of a strain. Although I've got two sisters and they both drive. One sister, she has to go out in the firm's car, but she says she's got into a way of doing it even though she's not much taller than me. She says 'I can manage now I know how to', even though it's a really big car that she drives, but she manages. And my other sister, she drives.

But even when women were able to drive, their access to the 'family' car often depended on having to ask a partner for it – which allows him the opportunity to refuse, should he so wish. As one woman said feelingly: 'It's his car. I borrow it. Do you know what I mean? We're supposed to share it, it's our car but I always have to ask 'Can I have the car?' which I don't think is really fair. And if two things clash, you can guess who finishes up on the bus!' (Green, Hebron and Woodward 1987c: 28).

Conclusion

In this chapter we have explored the social processes through which women's access to leisure is constructed, defined and regulated. Although leisure is generally perceived in terms of hedonism, pleasure and freedom, in practice norms about femininity, respectability and motherhood operate as powerful constraints on women's licence to engage in leisure activities. Prevailing ideologies about appropriate behaviour are enforced through social control mechanisms ranging from verbal hostility, ridicule and unwanted comments with sexual connotations, through to the threat of or actual use of physical violence against women. These controls operate both privately within relationships and in the public arena. Individual men are able to exercise control over the activities of 'their' women in this way, and women as a whole experience circumscriptions on their freedom of movement because of their fears of encountering male hostility in leisure venues or on the streets. The long-established nature of these controls, for example the opprobrium experienced by women who entered pubs alone in Victorian times, and the history of marriage – even violent marriages – as a 'private' relationship largely closed to external scrutiny and involvement, make them accepted and legitimated by custom, and supported by an integrated system of norms and values about women's respectability.

An analysis of how dominant ideologies of gender difference inform both private and public behaviour reveal considerable consequent inequalities in women's and men's leisure opportunities. The concept of social control linked to patriarchal power systems is a useful way of exploring and explaining how these inequalities are sustained. The best prospect for promoting women's recreational opportunities seems, in the light of this work, to be in promoting greater autonomy and power for women within relationships and in the wider society, so that these discriminatory attitudes and behaviour become anachronistic and socially unacceptable. In the meantime, policy-makers within leisure and recreation may need to 'work round' the effects of such inequalities, in relation to the pricing and time-tabling of use of their facilities, the development of women-only sessions, and the introduction of a much wider scale of transportation to and from leisure venues.

References

Barrett, Michele (1980) *Women's Oppression Today*, London, Verso.

Barrett, Michele and McIntosh, Mary (1982) *The Anti-Social Family*, London, Verso.

Belotti, Elena (1975) *Little Girls*, Leeds, Writers and Readers' Publishing Co-operative.

Cavendish, Ruth (1982) *Women on the Line*, London, Routledge & Kegan Paul.

Cartledge, Sue (1983) 'Duty and desire: creating a feminist morality', in Sue Cartledge and Joanna Ryan (eds.) *Sex and Love: New Thoughts on Old Contradictions*, London, The Women's Press.

Central Statistical Office (1981) *Social Trends*, no. 12, London, HMSO.

Clarke, John and Critcher, Chas (1986) *The Devil Makes Work: Leisure in Capitalist Britain*, London, Macmillan.

Deem, Rosemary (1986) *All Work and No Play? The Sociology of Women's Leisure*, Milton Keynes, Open University Press.

Delamont, Sara (1980) *The Sociology of Women*, London, Allen and Unwin.

Dixey, Rachael with Talbot, Margaret (1982) *Women, Leisure and Bingo*, Leeds, Trinity and All Saints' College.

Dobash, Rebecca and Dobash, Russell (1980) *Violence against Wives: A Case against the Patriarchy*, London, Open Books.

Gittins, Diana (1985) *The Family in Question: Changing Households and Familiar Ideologies*, London, Macmillan.

Graham, Hilary (1984) *Women, Health and the Family*, Brighton, Wheatsheaf Books.

GLC Women's Committee (1984–5) *Women on the Move: GLC Survey on Women and Transport*, Pamphlet no. 3, 'Safety, harassment and violence'; Pamphlet no. 4, 'Differences between women's needs'; Pamphlet no. 5, 'Ideas for action'.

Green, Eileen and Parry, Janet (1982) 'Women, part-time work and the hidden costs of caring', paper presented to the BSA Conference, April, University of Manchester.

Green, Eileen and Woodward, Diana (1986) 'Gender relations and women's leisure patterns', in Alan Tomlinson (ed.) *Leisure and Social Relations: Some Theoretical and Methodological Issues*, Leisure Studies Association.

Green, Eileen Hebron, Sandra and Woodward, Diana (1985) 'Everyday life and women's leisure: ideologies of domesticity and processes of social control', paper presented to the *Conference on Everyday Life*: *Leisure and Culture*, Centre for Leisure Studies, University of Tilburg, Holland.

(1987a) 'Women, leisure and social control', in Jalna Hanmer and Mary Maynard (eds.) *Women, Violence and Social Control*, London, Macmillan.

(1987b) *Women's Leisure in Sheffield: A Research Report*, Sheffield City Polytechnic.

(1987c) *Gender and Leisure: A Study of Women's Leisure in Sheffield*, London, Sports Council.

(forthcoming) *Women and Leisure*, London, Macmillan.

Hall, Catherine (1979) 'The early formation of Victorian domestic ideology', in Sandra Burman (ed.) *Fit Work for Women*, Beckenham, Croom Helm.

Hanmer, Jalna and Maynard, Mary (eds.) (1987) *Women, Violence and Social Control*, London, Macmillan.

Hanmer, Jalna and Saunders, Sheila (1983) 'Blowing the cover of the protective male: a community study of violence to women' in Eva Gamarnikow *et al.* (eds.) *The Public and the Private*, London, Heinemann.

Hey, Valerie (1986) *Patriarchy and Pub Culture*, London, Tavistock.

Hillman, Martin Henderson, I. and Whalley, Ann (1974) *Mobility and Accessibility in the Outer Metropolitan Area*, London, Political and Economic Planning

Hobson, Dorothy (1981) 'Now that I'm married . . .', in Angela McRobbie and Trisha McCabe (eds.) *Feminism for Girls*, London, Routledge & Kegan Paul.

Hunt, Geoffrey and Satterlee, Sandra (forthcoming) 'Darts, drink and the pub: the culture of female drinking', *Sociological Review*.

Imray, Linda and Middleton, Audrey (1983) 'Public and private: marking the boundaries' in Eva Gamarnikow *et al.* (eds.) *The Public and the Private*, London, Heinemann.

Leonard, Diana and Speakman, Mary Ann (1986) 'Women in the family: companions or caretakers?' in Veronica Beechey and Elizabeth Whitelegg (eds.) *Women in Britain Today*, Milton Keynes, Open University Press.

Morgan, David (1987) 'Masculinity and violence', in Jalna Hanmer and Mary Maynard (eds.) *Women Violence and Social Control*, London, Macmillan.

Oakley, Anne (1974) *The Sociology of Housework*, Oxford, Martin Robertson.

Pahl, Jan (1983) 'The control and allocation of money and the structuring of inequality within marriage', *Sociological Review* 31 (2):

   (1984) 'The control and allocation of money within the family', paper presented to the *Second International Interdisciplinary Congress on Women*, Groningen, Holland.

Phizacklea, Annie (ed.) (1983) *One Way Ticket: Migration and Female Labour*, London, Routledge & Kegan Paul.

Pickup, Laurie (1981) *Housewives' Mobility and Travel Patterns*, Transport and Road Research Laboratory, Report LR 871.

Pollert, Anna (1981) *Girls, Wives, Factory Lives*, London, Macmillan.

Pollock, Griselda (1977) 'Whats wrong with images of women', *Screen Education* no. 24.

Segal, Lynne (1983), (ed.) *What is to be done about the family?* Harmondsworth, Penguin.

Sheffield Low Pay Campaign (1985) *Are You Low Paid?* campaign leaflet, Sheffield, SLPC.

Smart, Carol and Smart, Barry (eds.) (1978) *Women, Sexuality and Social Control*, London, Routledge & Kegan Paul.

Stanko, Elizabeth (1985) *Intimate Intrusions: Women's Experience of Male Violence*, London, Routledge & Kegan Paul.

   (1987) 'Typical violence, normal precaution: men, women and interpersonal violence in England, Wales, Scotland and the USA', in Jalna Hanmer and Mary Maynard (eds.) *Women, Violence and Social Control*, London, Macmillan.

West, Jackie (1982) (ed.) *Women, Work and the Labour Market*, London, Routledge & Kegan Paul.

Westwood, Sallie (1984) *All Day Every Day: Factory and Family Life in the Making of Women's Lives*, London, Pluto.

Wilson, Elizabeth (1980) *Only Halfway to Paradise*, London, Tavistock.

Wimbush, Erica (1986) *Women, Leisure and Wellbeing*, Centre for Leisure Research, Dunfermline College, Edinburgh.

Whitehead, Anne (1976) 'Sexual antagonism in Herefordshire', in Diana Leonard, Diana Barker and Sheila Allen (eds.) *Dependence and Exploitation in Work and Marriage*, London, Longman.

11

Women in leisure service management

JUDY WHITE

Women have been slowly becoming aware that their particular wants and needs are not being met by a variety of public agencies. Some startling discoveries have been unearthed, not least of which are the lack of congruence between recreational activities which many women enjoy, and the resources available for that enjoyment. Being bottom of the list of priorities is familiar to ethnic minorities and disabled people too, who also have to suffer the strange indignities of policies and programmes being instituted by those who have not thought to involve the potential user in policy development. Physical activities are enjoyed for the social support they provide as much as for 'feeling good'; having a facilitator who understands some of the complexities of feeling is essential. Such a woman is frequently identified by her customers as a great mediator and counsellor, whilst her superiors tend to be either patronizing, dismissive, suspicious, jealous or otherwise marginalizing. They might identify her skills as being vital in the job she is doing, but they rarely consider the application of these skills to other managerial situations.

Leisure services management is a 'growth' profession. It has become respectable and regularized. It still reflects its origins, based on male team sports, cleanliness and fresh air, handed to it a century ago in the form of playing fields, swimming baths and parks. The managerial structures are overwhelmingly masculine, with male attitudes and values. The central concerns of leisure services are developing much more quickly than the profession is responding. Financial pressures from central government and the widening of competitive tendering are forcing re-evaluation of the service. In many instances this re-evaluation is based on the central core as it has always existed, with few taking the risk of examining the service from fundamental principles. A re-evaluation carried out by senior management is unlikely to consider the position of women managers or their potential contribution unless there are women in senior management positions. As this chapter argues, there are few such women, and their loneliness and perceived 'aberration' does not overly help when looking at ways in which women managers become powerful in leisure management.

There are areas of the leisure service which men have identified as 'women's' – play leadership and libraries being two. Men have tended to encourage only women to go into those branches which they consider more peripheral. The rest of the departmental structures appear to be centred around male values and to exclude women as an important factor in setting the objectives, style and tone of the department. Too frequently, in most departments, women's management attributes are devalued or ignored as having anything distinctive to contribute to improving the internal effectiveness of the department, to the delivery of services to the public and to developing innovative ways of working with customers which recognize the varying needs and wants of different sections of the public. This chapter looks at where women managers are in professions, with particular reference to leisure, and postulates why they are where they are. It discusses ways in which women's power has been suppressed and how women could work towards increasing their power and influence in organizations, and the benefits which could accrue to men, women and the organization by working androgynously. A final section illustrates work I and other trainers have carried out with women leisure managers. This aims to encourage women's understanding of the effects of socialization processes on their self-concept and their managerial attributes, and to give them skills to increase their power and self confidence in their lives.

Statistical evidence: where women managers are

Cooper and Davidson (1982) showed that whilst male managers represent 10 per cent of all men in employment, women managers represent under 5 per cent of all women in employment. They also disclosed that the percentage decreases as women climb up the traditional hierarchy, with more than twice the percentage of men occupying senior management positions.

In 1980 the General Household Survey found that 29 per cent of men's jobs were in the five main managerial and professional occupational orders, whilst Martin and Roberts (1984) interviewing 3,000 working women in the same year established that there were only 19 per cent of women's jobs in the same orders – and most of these were in the caring professions of education, health and welfare. Comparing this with the situation fifteen years earlier, Sheila Rothwell commented drily that 'apart from the declining proportion in manual occupations, it is striking how little has changed' (Rothwell 1985: 80).

However, using figures from the professional institutions, there are indications that change is beginning to be noticeable in the younger, newly qualified professionals, where the proportion of women is growing rapidly. For example, only 10 per cent of members of the Institute of Chartered Secretaries over 30 are women, but 30 per cent of those under 30. The Institute of Leisure and Amenity Management, the main professional body for the public leisure service, appeared in 1985 to have about 10 per cent of its membership who were women, although it was impossible to find accurate figures of either their number or distribution by age. It is clear that more women are entering the leisure service as graduate trainees, as well as via postgraduate education. What is still unresearched is the level of entry of qualified women compared with equally qualified men, as well as any substantive work on their career aspirations, and comparative progress through the hierarchy of the public leisure service.

It is depressingly true that even where women outnumber men in a profession –

as in health administration, teaching or banking – men occupy the bulk of the managerial positions. Women in personnel, for example, might be expected to be holding considerable proportions of management posts; in 1982, 58 per cent of men were employed at personnel manager level or above, compared with only 30 per cent of women.

A survey by the Local Authorities' Conditions of Service Advisory Board (1983) of recreation managers employed by local authorities in England and Wales in 1983 found that only 8 per cent of the total respondents (63 per cent of all authorities) were women. The survey excluded libraries, museums, art galleries and catering, which might have increased the total for women, but it did illustrate the substantial differences between parts of the service. For example, women managers in the tourism and conference sector formed 35 per cent of the total numbers of managers, 18 per cent of those in exhibitions, 16 per cent of those in theatres and concert halls, 12 per cent of those in National Parks, 10 per cent of those in sports and leisure centres and only 3 per cent of those in playing fields and 2 per cent in parks and open spaces. Although there was no breakdown available by age and sex, it appears that many more women than men managers are under 40, and that most of them fall into supervisory or lower managerial grades, with men taking the higher administrative and policy-related grades.

The segregation of responsibility in this vertical fashion is not unique to or unusual in leisure. Hakim's (1981) major analysis of vertical and horizontal job segregation in Britain since 1900 found the level of occupational concentration of women and men to have remained broadly constant. But vertical segregation is increasing. This is particularly evident from a 1973 survey by Hunt (1975) which showed that half of all establishments surveyed employed no women at all in the categories of manager or supervisor.

There seems to be little difference between industries in which few women are employed and those employing a lot, such as the Civil Service, banks, teaching, the personnel service or NHS. In banks in four European countries, research established that between 32 per cent and 55 per cent of all banking employees were female, but 96 per cent of managers were male. In the UK Civil Service, over 96 per cent of Assistant Secretary posts and above were held by men in 1982, although men only formed 52 per cent of all Civil Service (non-industrial) staff (Corby 1983).

It appears most likely that this sort of vertical segregation accounts for the sex differences in earnings. Overall, only one in forty of the top earners nationally are women. The Cooper and Davidson study of women managers in the late 1970s found that women managers earned an average of £6,000 to £8,000 per annum, whilst the male executives' salary range was £8,000 to £10,000. They indicated that whatever the management level, men were still earning more than their women equivalents. It is striking how many characteristics are common to both men and women managers; for example, the majority of both men and women managers had continuous work patterns with no break, had worked for the same length of time in their existing organization, had been for an average of five years in their present job, and worked for an average of 3.7 organizations. However, it is significant that the women managers were less likely to be married than the men (57 to 75 per cent) and more likely to be divorced or separated (15 to 8 per cent).

The figures available for women with dependent children do not discriminate between types of employee.

So the major differences illustrated by research are in status and salary. This applies to all organizations and professions and appears to be changing only slowly if at all. In the twelve years since the Equal Opportunities Commission was established, women still only earn 74 per cent of salaries paid to men, and only occupy 2.5 per cent of the directorships in the country. In 1975 it was estimated that 9.7 per cent of top management jobs were held by women; by 1987 there was a marginal improvement to 10.4 per cent. At the 'very top' of business, women are holding their own: a recent survey by the British Institute of Management (quoted by Garran Patterson 1987) shows that women directors got bigger pay rises than their male colleagues – 9.4 per cent compared to 7.8 per cent. Female directors now average £41,000 per annum compared to £45,800 for men.

Two other statistics are also worth noting. An increasing number of women are working for themselves; they represent 25 per cent of all self-employed. A quarter of small businesses in the United Kingdom are owned and run by women. More small businesses founded by women are likely to survive than those founded by men. More women in self-employment are married and have dependent children than in employment in general (74 to 39 per cent). The attractions of small businesses to women can be that women have more control over their lives, more flexibility to combine their roles, and to structure their working hours themselves.

Management as a male concept

Most research to date, whether in the United Kingdom or the United States, supports the idea that in general terms women do not have as many 'managerial characteristics' as men. Both women and men managers believe that 'successful managers' have characteristics, temperaments and attributes most commonly attributed to men. The 'masculinity' characteristics include leadership ability; competition; self-confidence; objectivity; aggressiveness; forcefulness; ambitiousness; desire for responsibility. 'Femininity' characteristics are intuition and employee-centred behaviours such as understanding, helpfulness, humanitarian values and awareness of other people's feelings. Some characteristics are not perceived as being gender related – especially competence, intelligence, persistence, tact and creativity.

This perceived similarity between the characteristics of successful managers and men in general increases the likelihood of a man rather than a woman being selected for or promoted to a managerial position. A woman's self-image incorporates some of the female sex-role stereotypes, generally as a result of long conditioning, and this influences a woman's job behaviour. Women who perceive the close resemblance between 'preferred' management characteristics and those of men are often encouraged to suppress showing many managerial job attributes to maintain their feminine self-image. But there is a double bind inherent in this behaviour which, although women may recognize, they may be unwilling or unable to do much about by themselves or individually.

Another reason for women to be reticent and hesitant is that they have recognized that most organizations still value instrumental behaviour above expressive behaviour. The characteristics of instrumental behaviour are overwhelmingly concerned with exchanging information by using data to increase power and control; it is generally planned and future oriented, predictable, certainly clear, agreed upon and negotiated. It avoids surprise at all costs. It is perceived as virtually congruent with 'masculine' behaviour. Expressive behaviour is sometimes called 'subjective'; it is characterized by using feelings, being spontaneous without any planning or predictability, by being ambiguous, flexible and surprising. It is identified as being primarily 'feminine' and of less import than 'masculine' behaviours. How can women work to change these perceptions?

There are at least four ways:

1. Endeavouring not to get marginalized into jobs/positions which only use (or expect the use of) 'feminine' characteristics (this is a particular problem for leisure).
2. Learning about the 'masculine' behaviours which are advantageous to use in developing a balanced management style, which takes equal account of the strengths of expressive and instrumental characteristics; this might be something such as tempering expressive feelings with the use of logic and analysis.
3. Self-promotion within their organization by becoming more visible and entrepreneurial.
4. Making opinions clearly known without backing down in the face of possible disagreement.

Leisure management by women is particularly prone to being pigeonholed into the feminine, expressive behaviour categories. Many of the long-standing, traditional sports were primarily perceived as (and indeed developed) for men, were organized and governed and managed by men. All they needed from women was their support to maintain the status quo. It is only since the rise of sports and activities classified as women's that men have accepted the legitimacy of women managers at all in some leisure areas – but on their (the men's) terms. So they have encouraged women to develop in spheres which they can accept as appropriate and in pursuits which they consider need an expressive treatment, such as play leadership, aerobics, dance, drama, popmobility, schools librarianship. Not only does this display the male bias of understanding of the nature of management but also of the nature of women. It is not enough to equate 'women managers' with 'women's activities' or 'interests'. This is not to deny that there are situations and occasions in which sympathetic and appropriately trained people of the same gender as the client/customers are essential – that is that both women and men might need separateness. But to isolate or segregate women is to deny the wholeness of their potential (although of course from a male perspective it may be safer . . .).

Women management theorists such as Alice Sargent (1981) are now arguing that

> Managers who develop a combination of masculine and feminine behaviours will be able to employ a full range of management styles as they work to *develop and empower* as well as to *lead and evaluate* employees.
>
> (Sargent 1981: 38, emphasis added)

Developing styles is not enough by itself. It is as important to change managerial and organizational attitudes to what are appropriate management systems for developing the attributes of women as managers.

Power, women and organizations

All organizational power is positional power, but relative in its strength. Many women often have particular problems in acquiring and using power in organizations. Men tend not to perceive women as having political resources and correctly assume that women find them difficult to acquire because they are held and controlled by men and men are reluctant to let women 'infiltrate' them. Authority and expertise power are also problematic for women. Formal authority is vested in key decision-making groups whose rules are understood and made by them; it is very difficult for outsiders to infiltrate such groups.

Membership of these groups is restricted in leisure services situations to the senior officers and the administrative and finance officers and advisors – who are almost invariably men. It is more than likely that this group will share common experiences, values and understandings from their backgrounds and work situations. They will have more in common with each other than with many of the women who work for them. Some of these women hold expertise power: they will have knowledge and information and experience which the senior managers may need to use and draw on for policy development and implementation. The expertise varies from skills such as familiarity and dexterity with word-processing (which are still identified as important support skills rather than managerial skills and so associated with administrative staff) to knowledge of coaching women in women's sports and developing programmes of physical activities designed to attract particular groups of women (which although seen as essential by many top managers, are still seen as essentially female, and therefore of less weight than 'mainstream', 'bread and butter' activities which assume that the client group and those serving them will be male).

Women managers have found it difficult to persuade their male colleagues that even if their expertise is primarily situated in women's experience, that this is transferable to other situations. They have a different language and vocabulary which also distances them from many men as much as it unites them. They have still to develop expertise in transferring skills from their particular situation to larger, more general ones. Even when they are 'experienced' managers, many women have spent much of their professional lives in functional areas identified as their strongholds. As already illustrated in the figures quoted above, few are working in sectors which have been traditionally associated with the mainstream areas for career development. Few women have yet progressed from management of a single facility, such as a library, swimming pool, adult education centre or community centre, into area management of a group of facilities and activities, or overall management of a group of similar units, or into policy-centred posts. Remaining in one functional area, or those closely associated with each other, is a handicap.

Mobility within a single authority to gain experience of contrasting types of facility management is an option many women would like to undertake but horizontal movement within leisure services has not been encouraged. It has been expected that managers will move upward as well as across the hierarchy, which frequently means changing authority. For many women this is not a realistic option if they are in a conventional, settled partnership. They will find it difficult to co-ordinate career changes, even if their partner understands the need for them. The existence of children who are still resident in the parental home adds a further complication.

Ryan and Fritchie (1982) identified four types of power which women managers need to be adept at recognizing. They are primarily political resources – authority, expertise, resource control and interpersonal skill. Women middle managers undergoing management development courses illustrate that even when they have formal authority – to make decisions, other than trivial ones, without other people's permission, to supervise staff, to have inputs into policy changes – their senior (male) manager often contrives to subvert it, dilute it or make their contribution appear to be less important. Subversion may be interpreted as deliberate and provocative. Dilution and downgrading may be more subtle and unrecognized by the male manager, as he has become conditioned into believing that it is appropriate behaviour and what is expected of him by his male peers, whose managerial styles will also reflect their lack of recognition of the need to reinforce and develop the confidence of their women subordinates.

Resource control generally covers access to finance, non-trivial information, promotion, training senior managers and operational or administrative facilities such as computers. All of it is available by right to senior managers; parts of it are claimed by middle managers either by right or by long-term use. But within each section or department there tend to be individual managers who are adept at ensuring their control over key resources and at stopping others gaining access and therefore power. This is something in which women are becoming increasingly adept. They are also questioning the ways in which resources are controlled and are developing methods of sharing information and resources so that they are not centralized onto one person. This is a characteristic often observed amongst groups of women, in training contexts as well as in their employment. They are generous of their information and of their genuine desire to include others in creating methods for change, for improved service delivery for example, in ways to which men are unaccustomed. They are not jealous of their power or strength; they understand that sharing can be empowering.

This characteristic is connected to their primary power base grounded in interpersonal skills. Women are seen to be on good terms with a number of people in their authority across different departments and hierarchical levels; they are more likely to have people confiding in them. But this power base is generally limited to the personal, not the political scene. Women are less likely to be on good working terms with powerful people, even if they know them. Women managers are also less likely to speak in meetings than their male peers; they find it more difficult to make people take their views seriously, either in informal or formal situations. Being interrupted and discounted are situations frequently recounted by women managers on training courses. They are angry, not resigned, about such behaviour. They know that they are much more adept at being 'active listeners', at listening to others' viewpoints and giving them space and support to do so. They also know that as they have less practice than their male colleagues, they have less confidence in their ability to hold the attention of a group or larger audience. Many women feel that whilst they are eager to help to change and develop themselves, and that they have valuable contributions to make to help managers understand more broadly what the nature of management is, men are resisting such change in the belief that they can only lose power and therefore credibility as a result.

But women in leisure management question the assumption behind this. Management should be a universal skill, transferable and explicable in a great range of contexts. Leisure is concerned with people's ability to lead fulfilled lives. It is incumbent on those working in it to recognize that the service can only be enriched by encouraging a multifaceted approach which sees the contributions from women, ethnic groups and the disadvantaged as positive developments not negative ones.

Androgyny, women and organizations

Ideas about the development of androgynous organizations and ways of working seem to be useful pegs on which to hang questions about changing management philosophies. Most of the ideas seem to contain self-evident truths. The challenges come when we attempt to turn these truths into changing organizations so that the balance between the needs of male and female is more equal:

> An androgynous organisation is one that strives to develop its people at the same time that it increases its productivity, and not to do either to the exclusion of the other. An androgynous person is one who strives to attain a balance in all relationships.
>
> (Sargent 1981: 7)

> It is fatal to be a woman or a man pure and simple; one must be woman-manly or man-womanly. Some collaboration has to take place between the woman and the man before the act of creation can be accomplished. The whole of the mind must be wide open if we are to get the sense that the writer is communicating experience with perfect fullness.
>
> (Woolf 1929: 99)

Both women and men need to consider what types of change are needed and the processes by which they can take place. Women need to be particularly alert to areas of change over which they have control and influence. Men need to be persuaded that the skills of dealing with people, of expressing and accepting emotions, of nurturing and supporting colleagues and subordinates, of encouraging interactions between bosses and subordinates and between leaders and members of work teams, are desirable for their own sake but are also instrumental in increasing organizational efficiency and effectiveness. These types of 'feminine' behaviours must not continue to be marginalized or discounted by both women and men. It is difficult to see how deep-seated cultural beliefs can be quickly altered, or overturned. Many women live with the realization that they will not gather the fruit of the seeds they are now sowing; that the slowness and painfulness they are enduring will eventually force re-examination and realignment of ideas. But these realizations make it often hard to bear. It is not only older, established women – who are acting as role models for younger women behind them in the leisure service – who feel isolated, desperate and sometimes disbelief that they can be instruments of change. Many of the younger women, also aware of the pace of change, feel misunderstood and on their own, and resent being seen as the 'femininist vanguards for change whose aim is to destroy male colleagues', as has been described to me by a woman middle manager. Others have more supportive and empathizing colleagues who have recognized that they have much to learn from women managers as well as much to teach – but they are still very unsure what can be changed and how. It is bound to remain hard for women to retain their 'feminine' characteristics as they progress through organizations which reward them for their 'masculine' characteristics.

Their role is a threefold one: to develop themselves as managers; to influence others on the contribution which an androgynous approach, drawing on the strengths of each kinds of characteristic, can make to organization vitality; and to develop new patterns, structures and ways of working which will enable the organization to function more fairly for men and women. It is unrealistic to expect all aspiring managers to want to, or to be able to, adopt all of these roles. Women have the right not to act as torchbearers or role models; they must, however, be given the right to knowledge, and choice based on that knowledge.

Men's attitudes to women managers

A central dilemma for women managers is how far they will have to go in developing the 'masculine' traits which are presently perceived as making successful managers in general. Do women need to incorporate aggressive and competitive behaviour in order to make others believe in their potential and grant them the confidence and resources to achieve success? Developing 'masculine' managerial characteristics in the past has often been at the expense of the 'feminine' ones. 'Success' has only been attainable in a male-dominated organization by aspiring to copy male models and to submerge the female attributes. So many 'successful' women managers are surrogate men. In the words of Natasha Josefowitz:

> I have not seen the plays in town
>   only the computer printouts
> I have not read the latest books
>   only the Wall Street Journal
> I have not heard birds sing this year
>   only the ringing of phones
> I have not taken a walk anywhere
>   but from the parking lot to my office
> I have not shared a feeling in years
>   but my thoughts are known to all
> I have not listened to my own needs
>   but what I want I get
> I have not shed a tear in ages
>   I have arrived
> Is this where I was going?

(Josefowitz 1983: 3)

Work done for the US Department of the Navy by Hinsdale and Johnson (1978) and in the United Kingdom by Hunt (1975) both found that when asking men managers about managerial characteristics, 'the extent to which managers believed every attribute was more likely to be found in men rather than in women was most striking – almost shattering (Rothwell 1985: 85). Sheila Rothwell commented: 'the fact that women are likely to have children and leave is still used as the major justification for not training or promoting women' (Rothwell 1985: 84). She quotes Bennet and Carter (1983):

> A bank manager said; 'The only way we could place the same kind of reliability on a woman as on a man is if a woman came to us and said she had been sterilised, that would prove she was really serious about her career.'

The MSC survey, 'No Barriers Here?' (1981) illuminated the belief amongst many British male managers that they and their organizations are not discriminatory. Some of this belief is due to ignorance of the effects of their attitudes to gender roles, and of the double bind in which women can be placed, which has been referred to earlier in this chapter. If an aspiring woman manager does not appear to have typical male management characteristics, she will not be accepted. If she does appear to have them, she might also be rejected as the male manager might suspect that she is 'odd', as she does not conform to his idea of her gender role. Those women in the higher echelons of management who act as surrogate men are counter-productive to helping other women to develop their own models of managerial roles. The fact that such women are so rare complicates the issues for their female subordinates, who have many fewer role models on whom to base their development than the male middle manager.

Women's attitudes to their development

Work at Ashridge Management College (1980) is one of the many pieces of evidence pointing to women's own ambivalence about themselves or other women as managers. Women most commonly requested confidence-building and assertion training, to help themselves to see themselves as decision-takers and as equal partners to men managers. It seems that younger women are becoming less uncertain of themselves as potential managers, but they remain quite unaware of, or perhaps more realistically, are kept unaware of, the subtleties of organizational politics which enable them to develop opportunities for promotion. The Ashridge finding that women's lack of promotion and advancement is a result of their own attitudes and behaviour is echoed by many women. Whilst this cannot be ignored, too many men appear to find it a convenient explanation and excuse for their own behaviour, allowing them a reason for not changing their attitudes and for pursuing the status quo.

Women have stress developing from two directions – from the discomfort of their ill-fitting roles as stereotypical women and from uncertainty of what type of manager they are. Many choose not to fight to become more masculine and in so doing deny many of their most important attributes. Instead, they choose to work either in an organization in which they have the opportunity to develop their own style in their own way, often through their own business; or to develop partnerships with their male colleagues in which each individual is able to contribute their own skills toward a more androgynous style of management.

The role of training for developing new management competence

The need for more management training for women is slowly being recognized. This should encompass training which looks at the effects of gender-role attitudes on themselves, on men and on their management organizations. It is also important to recognize a similar need for men to examine these areas. Most training is still technical, and even behavioural courses tend not to work in this area of concern. Much management development is stressing the need to develop the particular caring and counselling skills of individuals, to eliminate weaknesses and develop strengths useful for promoting creativity. But despite acknowledging that current changes in personnel policies are in accord with developing women's aspirations, this does not mean that they will necessarily continue to happen. A period of change is unstable – it can just as easily lead to retrenchment of attitudes as to their development into new experimental or sharing realms. It needs careful thought and planning, to avoid accidents or sporadic change, and to develop the most useful alliances and types of training programme in the most appropriate areas.

Few women attend 'mixed' management courses for women and men. One survey undertaken by Ashridge found that all the men on courses were there because their companies had sent them, while the (few) women had all had to request it by themselves. Such findings could be mirrored by those institutions working with local authority managers. Women are also discouraged themselves from attending courses as the content of many are not relevant to their situations. There can also be covert sexism in the unconscious assumption of male values in the course structure, design and content, and more overt sexism in the teaching material, behaviour and the propensity of other course members to treat women patronisingly, with suspicion, or to ignore them. Such problems tend to reinforce women's assumptions that management is not appropriate to them, not that the programmes are inappropriate.

In devising training programmes specifically for women, Elaine James (1986) has argued that they need to start in a different place from men's, as much of the knowledge and many of the skills that women may be expected to contribute to management courses will not be reflected in the normal management training framework:

> There is a need to explore femininity, masculinity and management, and through the exploration, to create a framework within which women can apply their own understandings and experiences of the world, and to gain confidence in the ways in which they can best contribute as managers.
>
> (James 1986: 73)

The Local Government Training Board pilot training programme started from the premise that much of the existing management training literature and programmes assumes implicitly that the user is male, white and is comfortable with a world which both illustrates and underlines the centrality of male attitudes and values to that world. Women in management find many of these attitudes, values and experiences alien and disturbing, as they do not seem to relate to their own. They also appear to neglect or completely ignore the realities of women's holistic views of their lives, which causes them to have to attempt to deal with pressures and stresses in a more integrative way than their partners or male colleagues. Further, women's life experiences are generally different from men's, and the woman's way of dealing with them quite distinct. She has different preoccupations and priorities, and commonly perceives them in different ways:

> She needs the opportunity to take one step back from the world of management, in order to be able to analyse and to understand its mode of operation, and the range of qualities that she can bring to bear on its functioning.
>
> (James 1986: 74)

In the public and private leisure service, Elaine James identified some of the considerable problems of stereotyped notions of masculinity and femininity, and the types of activity which are 'acceptable' for women to work in or enjoy. In providing training, trainers need to be aware of the problems of being a female manager *per se*, and of working in a male-centred and structured environment, which is also overwhelmingly male in its customer orientation and culture. She was concerned that women should be given more opportunities to develop their management skills on a broad basis, and eventually the Local Government Training Board agreed to fund a pilot programme, for two years, for training a group of women from the leisure services with middle-management potential, but lacking training or skills awareness to improve their position. I am retained as consultant trainer in the programme.

The justification for separate management training for women can only be validated if women managers attend them in higher numbers than mainstream management courses and if they feel that the women's courses provide them with both a better understanding of themselves and an improved capability to change and develop management attitudes into more androgynous channels. The Local Government Training Board had little research to show how many women had attended their other 'general' management programmes, but there was an overwhelming response to both the first and second pilot programmes. For each programme the sixteen places offered were oversubscribed ten times. All of the thirty-two women offered places accepted places and all attended all the modules (except for one being forced to drop out due to illness).

The programmes have two important concepts which they use as starting-points. The first is that whilst women recognize much more clearly than men the holistic nature of their lives, they are aware that the socialization which they have undergone creates a tension between many societal expectations of them as wives and mothers and their employed role as managers where they were expected to take on stereotypical 'masculine' roles. The second is that many of women managers' 'managerial' problems are a result of their lack of appropriate skills to cope in an alien and uncomfortable environment in which most of their male colleagues are unwilling and unable to share their skills. These two concepts were thoroughly discussed at the start of the programme so that the participants could realize that the environment encouraged openness, honesty, support and mutual understanding in a non-threatening atmosphere. Only then did the programme explore specific management skills which emphasize androgynous values and encourage the strengthening of existing feminine skills, to help improve management effectiveness. The emphasis on feminine skills was deliberate; it was designed to show that they are as valuable as men's in developing committed and sympathetic managers.

Much of the diagnostic module of the programme examines what management is and how the masculine model which has been dominant in leisure service provides stress for women who have their own sets of ideas and attitudes which they feel are also appropriate to management. The participants found it difficult but rewarding to explore how their feminine attitudes and viewpoints affected their relationship to management processes, and how socialization processes also affected men. They became much more aware of the strength and usefulness of many of their 'feminine' characteristics and were helped to find ways to increase them. As Elaine James says, these programmes are 'not about identifying and accepting masculine managerial behaviour as the one acceptable standard, and then providing the participants with the skills and knowledge to be accepted in terms of that norm', they are about 'looking at management as a range of behaviours both masculine and feminine in nature, to which women were equally as capable of bringing a useful contribution as men' (James 1986: 76). We wanted to help facilitate the women to identify and examine their feminine behaviours which they had been encouraged, usually unconsciously, to develop to fit into the male model of what they should do and who they should be, and then to work on them to see how they might be converted into characteristics which could be used as positive management attributes.

The 'success' of the courses can be measured by the sea-change in many of the participants' self-perceptions, and their greatly increased understanding, skills and confidence to challenge male norms and to exemplify alternative attitudes and ways of working. These alternative attitudes are not competitive or exclusive but can only be successful if the women taking them on board are confident of their ability to take power and to share it. They have identified the skills themselves, and the programmes have given the techniques to develop them. The enhanced self-confidence and self-belief is illustrated by the pleasure felt by several participants in tackling a problem which previously they had regarded as intractable or too risky. Several (at least eight) women have considered applying for more senior management positions, and three have gained them. The majority of the participants now have a much clearer idea about the scale of change needed to redress the balance of power. They also have the motivation and the skills to do something about it.

References

Ashridge Management College (1980) *Employee Potential: Issues in the Development of Women*, London, IPM.

Bennet, Yves and Carter, Dawn (1983) *Day Release for Girls*, Manchester, EOC.

Cooper, Cary Lynn and Davidson, Marilyn (1982) *High Pressure Working: Lives of Women Managers*, London, Fontana.

Corby, S. (1983) 'Women in the civil service', *Personnel Management*, February.

Green, Eileen, Hebron, Sandra and Woodward, Diana (1987) *Women's Leisure in Sheffield: A research report*, Department of Applied Social Studies, Sheffield City Polytechnic.

Hakim, Catherine (1981) 'Job segregation' *Employment Gazette*, London, December.

Hinsdale, K. and Johnson, J. D. (1978) *Masculinity, Femininity and Androgyny: What Really Works at Work?* ONR Technical Report No. 2, US Office of Naval Research, Washington, DC.

Hunt, Ann (1975) *Management Attitudes and Practices towards Women at Work*, London, HMSO.

James, Elaine (1986) 'Management development and women in leisure and recreation', *Local Government Policy Making* 13(3), December.

Josefowitz, Natasha (1983) *Is This Where I Was Going?* Bromley, Columbus Books.

Local Authorities' Conditions of Service Advisory Board (1983) *Recreation Managers' Survey*, June 1983 for Local Government Training Board (available from Local Government Training Board).

Manpower Services Commission (1981) *No Barriers Here?* London, MSC.

Martin, Joan and Roberts, Ceridwen (1984) *Women and Employment: A Lifetime Perspective*, report of the 1980 Department of Employment/OPCS Women and Employment Survey, London, HMSO.

Patterson, G. (1987) 'The world of working women', in *Moneycare*, August/September, pp. 6–11.

Rothwell, Sheila (1985) 'Is management a masculine role?' *Management Education and Development* 16 (2): 79–98.

Ryan, Michael and Fritchie, Rennie (1982) *Career Life Planning for Women Managers*, London, Manpower Services Commission.

Sargent, Alice (1981) *The Androgynous Manager*, New York, American Management Associations.

Woolf, Virginia (1929) *A Room of One's Own*, London, The Hogarth Press.

12

'Their own worst enemy'?
Women and leisure provision

MARGARET TALBOT

The conventional wisdom in the provision of leisure services for women is embodied in the phrase 'getting more women into' leisure – a phrase which implies that it is women who must change *their* behaviour rather than the providers critically analysing what is provided in the light of women's needs and wants. After hearing two presentations on provision for women, a speaker from the floor at the Recreation Management Seminar commented:

> Perhaps you ought to be changing the attitudes of women themselves who have their own particular views of what they do and what they want to do. Quite often that does not conform to recreation at all.
>
> (Sports Council 1984:182)

This comment, from a practising recreation manager, reveals that commonly accepted notions of institutionalized leisure provision are often implicitly male defined. Making provision for women is still seen as marginal, 'special' and problematic. The traditional forms of provision, dominated by men and boys, particularly in the public sector, make few concessions to reflect that women constitute over 50 per cent of the population; their needs are still seen as separate, different from and even residual to so-called 'mainstream' provision.

This point was first brought home to me when I was playing first-class club hockey. We were the only women's team to be playing on one of the local authority pitches, where every Saturday there were eight home teams. It was noticeable that our team (and our visitors) were the only ones to be denied showers: we shared one (cold) tap and an outside lavatory, which was frequently blocked and, in mid-winter, frozen and unusable. When the club protested, on the grounds that we paid the same rent as the men and, indeed, would have been willing to pay more for better facilities, we were told that we did not 'need' showers like the men, because we would not get dirty or sweaty! This puzzled us; in general, we were fitter, being a premier club, with very talented players, and our physical output was higher than on the neighbouring football pitches, where the skill level and the standard of play left much to be desired. The differential in facility provision might not have been so important to us, if the football players had not behaved at the end of their matches as if our game did not exist – they walked across our pitch

while play was still in progress. The same kind of behaviour by sportsmen was apparent in the sports centre, where indoor hockey league matches were held. While
female players waited until five-a-side football was finished, the five-a-side players
following the hockey session invariably walked into the sports hall before the end of
the final match. It was a real-life confirmation of Paul Willis's proposition that:

> it is quite likely that a team of high ability women will be better, even in so-
> called masculine qualities, than a low ability men's team. And yet, the
> meanest local, 5th division, male works team gets more respect, in popular
> consciousness, than a women's national team.
>
> (Willis 1974: 25)

These experiences serve not merely to illustrate that some sportsmen lack good
manners, but that at all levels, from the casual recreation participant, through dedicated clubs and societies, to public and even private providers, there is the inherent
and unquestioned notion that in some way women's leisure is marginal and not as
important as men's.

Women who do succeed in utilizing the existing structures and provisions do so,
on the whole, not on their own terms but on terms pre-defined by the dominant
(male) user groups. Margaret Andersen's observation about the power relationships and inequalities within academic institutions applies equally well to sport and
leisure contexts:

> A closer look at institutions where scholarship is created reveals that there are
> unequal distributions of resources within them, power relationships between
> dominant and subordinate groups, beliefs and attitudes that define the work
> of some as more legitimate than that of others, and socialisation processes by
> which newcomers are taught the ways of the system. And just as in other insti-
> tutions, for those who do not conform, a variety of sanctions can be applied,
> ranging from ridicule to exclusion.
>
> (Andersen 1983: 224)

The providers claim that they alone cannot change the social context in which we
live. But they seldom examine their own practices and structures, over which they
do have control, thereby maintaining and perpetuating the very social constraints
which they claim that they wish to change. When the nature of the constraints
operating against women taking part in leisure activities is considered, it is so often
from the point of view of helping women to 'break out' of the fine mesh of personal
and social constraints surrounding them, in order to 'free themselves' for participation. Providers fail to see the other layer of mesh in the social filter – that which
surrounds, to a greater or lesser degree, all our institutions, including our leisure
institutions.

> Societies have generated their own rules, culturally determined, for making
> boundaries on the ground, and have divided the social into spheres, levels and
> territories with invisible fences and platforms to be scaled by abstract ladders
> and crossed by intangible bridges with as much trepidation as on a plank over
> a raging torrent.
>
> (Ardener 1981: 11–12)

This chapter attempts to outline some of the ways in which the institutions of leisure exclude or inhibit female participation, and especially preclude the holding of equal power by female members – where they are allowed to be members. All leisure activities, including so-called 'institutionalized' leisure activities and informal ones (however casual to the observer), are hedged around and influenced by major social institutions and social practices. The major institutions in society – the law, the economy, the world of work, education and the media – serve to protect the means by which a full leisure franchise for women is withheld, and the dominant groups' interests are protected. These processes act, not only against the ability of women to exercise the freedom which leisure is said to represent, but also against other groups in society, for example, disabled people, members of ethnic minorities, elderly people and the poor. Women have responded in various ways, and some of their strategies will be discussed.

Women, organizations and leisure provision

Clearly, the nature of the various forms of leisure provision, and the institutions which provide them, have different effects on the extent to which women can benefit from them, and on women's attempts to carve out some degree of control. All, however, share the institutional features which commonly reinforce prevailing ideologies of provision and which exclude or inhibit women from controlling their own leisure lives. Institutionalized leisure, whether provided by public or private sector, is characterized by elements which set apart such provision from spontaneous and unplanned leisure which is the product of their participants' activities.

First, institutions are, by their very nature, continuous: they survive beyond the occurrences of the activity which they represent and provide, through structured, rule and role governed organizations, often possessing significant bureaucracies. Positions which involve decision- and policy-making are crucial to the survival of the institutions, and occupance of such positions confers power. Most of these powerful positions in leisure provision, both in formal and in informal organizations, are occupied by men. The employment and reward practices of many of the leisure providers continue to exclude or prevent women from holding positions of power. Judy White has discussed this issue in more detail in Chapter 11.

Kari Fasting and Mari-Kristin Sisjord (1986) have analysed the processes of the exercise of verbal power in Norwegian sports organizations, and the ways in which these affect policy and decision-making. They note that, while women are underrepresented proportionally in the General Assembly, their limited verbal participation in meetings served to make them even more invisible, and they were less likely to speak on important organizational matters which affected positions of power within the organization. Summarizing the evidence from organizational analyses, they point out that women behave more passively than men in mixed situations; that they speak less often and for less time; and that they do not speak as often on policy issues. They conclude that it will be difficult for women to influence organizations in any significant way unless they are better represented within the organizations; contribute more to central issues; and do not continue to allow men to dominate the verbal interchange.

Herein lies a double-bind situation: it seems that women can only begin to achieve parity with men in organizations when they adopt and practise the very male procedures and strategies which the female culture would criticize. This course of action supports the expectations of leisure providers that what they are providing is appropriate, and that it is the non-user or non-participant who is at fault. Fasting and Sisjord pose two main alternatives: either for women to establish their own sex-separated organizations, or to get more women elected within the existing organizations and change things from within. Even when women achieve the means to affect others (*power*), they are not always in a position to use it (*influence*), and their influence may not always be successful in achieving *control*. A further danger in the second alternative is that when the power of the gatekeepers is so great, women will be forced to adopt those values and attitudes which they most wish to change, in order to succeed within the system. When women choose not to risk this danger, and decline the chance of filling positions of power, it is at this point that they are so often described as 'their own worst enemies'.

Facing such dilemmas, it is not surprising that women who reject ultra competitive tactics in order to succeed within organizations, instead choose to form separate and exclusively female groups, in order to be able to practise the values and procedures which they see as appropriate. The separatist alternative of forming all-female organizations is also problematic, because of the unequal ways in which male and female activities are valued and attributed status.

The danger of women being obliged to adopt the prevailing ideology within organizations has been noted by Rosabeth Moss Kanter (1977), in her analysis of the network of organizational relationships and sex roles in large North American corporations. She maintains that

> no study of human behavior can any longer be considered complete that ignores the special roles, positions and constraints affecting women in the public arena.
>
> (Kanter 1977: 8)

> Women populate organisations, but they practically never run them.
>
> (ibid.: 16)

She points out that the rational management model is infused with a 'masculine ethic' which results in the stratification of organizations by sex. The skills associated with management (see Ch.11) are also considered to belong to men, while the support skills of clerical work, cleaning and servicing in general are considered to be essentially female in nature; indeed, any questioning of the assignation of females to these roles is often met by the assertion that females are better at these jobs than men! This tendency to naturalize culturally ascribed roles is readily observable in both institutionalized and more informal leisure organizations; women are assigned positions, both in paid and voluntary situations, of low uncertainty, routine and little autonomy, often associated with 'expert', rather than decision-making, responsibilities. Kanter cites a quotation by Moore: 'The corporation seems to seek an arrangement which is surely an anomaly in human society, that of homosexual reproduction' (Moore 1962; cited in Kanter 1977: 47). This comment is uncomfortably close to the ways in which leisure organizations reproduce their processes and structures for the benefit of the dominant groups, whether the leisure activity is offered on a voluntary, grant- or rate-aided, commercial or private basis. The prevailing assumption is that what is offered for and by men is natural, normal and standard. When this assumption is challenged, there is often genuine surprise and resentment:

> Institutionalised sexism is harder to identify since it is a result of rules, regulations, and traditions that may not result directly from the decisions of one or more sexists. But the rules, regulations and traditions end up supporting a sexist ideology.
>
> (Frieze *et al.* 1978: 13)

The questioning of these practices leads to an involuntary questioning of hitherto inviolate and taken-for-granted customs, and the possibility of the dominant group losing status or privilege. In the case of many recreation providers, it constitutes a risk that performance previously regarded as successful and 'good practice' may lose its currency because of new criteria for critique. It is important that both the questioners and those whose decisions are being questioned understand the political and psychological significance of these implications of change, and that they are considered alongside strategic changes which may be considered. It is also worth remembering that criticism may also be engendered from women who have conformed to the expected practices and who do not see why changes should be made for other women. For this latter group of women, and the providers concerned, it should be remembered that discrimination implies negative feelings towards a group or individual, which may be based on stereotyped or erroneous judgements; and that such feelings are often inflexible and not easily changed, even in the face of new and contradictory information. Thus rules which ignore the different life experiences of men and women may be continued in wilfully blind adherence to 'normal' practice. Social norms remain 'envalued'. Women can react to this in various ways, as they have done in asserting control, to a greater or lesser degree, over their own leisure experiences.

This complex situation also explains why there is so often a divergence in understandings between providers who are genuinely attempting to make space for women in their services or facilities, and women who perceive their provisions as hostile, unsympathetic, or just plain irrelevant to their lives:

> I stood outside the door [of a community centre] and I was shaking. I didn't have the courage to come in . . . I thought, if I go in, they won't talk to me and I won't talk to them. I walked away again. I couldn't go in, but the following week I came back again.
>
> (Dixey with Talbot 1982: 24)

> It's a man's place, a place where all the fellows go. Women can go in but it's mostly for men.
>
> (ibid.: 68)

One genuine difficulty for managers and policy-makers is that women's negative reactions to the social settings and the structures of mainstream leisure provision rarely reach public awareness; they are experienced individually and privately, and it takes more than survey data on admissions or audience figures to identify why women do not 'take advantage' of the facilities and services which are made available to them. The effects of the behaviour and perceptions of the 'gate-keepers' of leisure facilities, and of the existing participants and users, on the willingness of non-participants to enter them, is an area of research which would provide useful data for all providers and policy-makers who are interested in increasing participation in leisure activities. Valerie Hey (1987) and Anne Whitehead (1976) have described women's experiences and position in pubs and pub culture in terms of patriarchy and sexual antagonisms. Isobel Emmett suggested as far back as 1971 that it would be

> a fruitful sociological exercise to investigate such filtering devices: to explore their mechanisms and the diverse forms they take in different social groups and in relation to different leisure facilities. . . . No piece of ground used for leisure is merely a physical place: it is always a social entity too – the filters are always there.
>
> (Emmett 1971: 7–8)

In the absence of such data, in situations where managers have set aside time or space which is in heavy demand from existing users, specifically for women, with the result that women do not use them, it is perhaps not surprising that the conclusion is so often, 'Women are their own worst enemies – even when we try to cater for them, they don't use the facilities and services': and even, not unseldom, 'Women just don't want recreation (or bands in the park, or mother and toddler sessions, etc.)'. When the manager has also gone to the trouble of providing a crèche, the popular panacea for women's participation, his (*sic*) antipathy to the notion of making special provision for women grows even more. Even when data is available, it may be ignored or only partially used. For example, when female development officers are employed by local authority recreation departments, it is often the case that only minor adaptations in provision are tolerated; it seems less easy for providers to contemplate more radical changes which would genuinely test their commitment towards women as a client group: 'the vast majority of Authorities have failed to recognise the need for women/girls recreation provision' (Macksmith and Stewart 1986: 61).

Legal framework

However, notwithstanding genuine problems of communication between provider and potential client, there is a further structural problem in any attempt at changing provision practices. The structures and practices of many leisure institutions which inhibit or exclude women are, in many instances, actually protected by law. The Sex Discrimination Act 1975 made sex discrimination unlawful 'in employment, training and related matters, in education, in the provision of goods, facilities and services, and in the disposal and management of premises'. At first sight, the terms of the Act appear to cover leisure provision in all its contexts. However, there are notable exceptions in the Act which have important effects on leisure, especially in the voluntary sector.

Most importantly, the terms of the Act do not cover voluntary, non-profit-making organizations. Since in Britain an enormous proportion of leisure activities are carried on in voluntary, one-activity clubs, many of these clubs can (and do) continue to practise legal sex discrimination. This exception has meant that women are treated less favourably than, for example, members of ethnic minorities under the terms of the Race Relations Act, whose terms do not embody such an exception.

The Equal Opportunities Commission has received nearly 2,000 complaints about the unequal status and treatment of women members of private members' clubs. It has therefore suggested in its consultative document (1986) that voluntary clubs with mixed membership during the three years preceding the consultative document should be brought within the scope of the Act. This would mean, for example, that working-men's clubs – which at present legally exclude women from full membership rights and are directed to do so by their governing body, the Clubs and Institutes Union – would be brought within the terms of the Act. If this change were to be implemented, then ERICCA (Equal Rights in Clubs Campaign for Action) would achieve its objective of full membership rights for women – including equal access to snooker facilities, exclusion from which prompted the forming of the action group. The importance of this extension of equal opportunity, especially for working-class women, is difficult to overestimate.

However, this EOC suggestion would allow all private clubs and voluntary organizations which have never admitted female members, to continue to exclude them. The effect of this proposal would be to allow those organizations which have successfully resisted female membership through obduracy or power, or both, to continue to do so. Given that private members' clubs receive a considerable amount of government finance in one form or another (e.g. grant aid, rate relief, etc.), it seems wrong indeed that these established power structures, which play such an important part in the leisure life of Britain, should be exempt from the terms of the Act. Indeed, this partial reform could be seen to penalize unduly those clubs which have at least allowed women to use their facilities – albeit on an unequal basis or under unacceptable conditions, or because women's consumer power or services are required by the club.

The legal protection of single-sex clubs and organizations is, however, not always to the detriment of women and girls. It is equally legal for clubs to set up and maintain an all-female membership and, indeed, such groups provide important leisure opportunities for many, especially Asian women and girls. The removal of such protection, while possibly allowing access for women to organizations with facilities which they might like to use, would also open up membership of currently all-female organizations to men, with a concomitant loss of an important arena of female power and control over leisure provision. This is a real dilemma. Legal precedents in other countries (e.g. the Title IX amendment to the US Constitution) do seem to indicate that when single-sex organizations lose their legal protection there has been a significant reduction in the number of women in positions of responsibility and executive power, even in organizations which formerly have been all female. The purpose of the Equal Opportunities Commission's suggestions to change the terms of the Act with regard to clubs which have admitted women on unequal conditions of membership, is to force such organizations to grant women full membership rather than 'associate' membership fees with only limited membership privileges and rights. Even so, some women have pointed out that if this happens, they will, of course, be expected to make the same membership payments as their male counterparts: equity in these cases refers to both rights and responsibilities!

The Sex Discrimination Act also has an important weakness with regard to employment practices. This affects leisure provision, and the job opportunities available for women in the leisure industries and services. Where considerations of 'decency or privacy' require a job to be held by a man (or woman), such a job is also an exception to the Act. In practice, this allows some organizations to refuse to employ women or to provide facilities for women clients. As David Pannick (1983) has commented with regard to this practice in sports provision, 'Privacy is therefore a rationalisation of invidious discrimination'. (Pannick 1983: 43). It is also worth noting that sex differentiation is not illegal under the terms of the Act, so long as provision may be held to be equal – this is the old defence that men and women are equal, but different. However, the effects of the differential social valuing of men's and women's activities means that in practice such provision will not be equal. Furthermore, the onus to prove inequality or discrimination rests with the complainant, as it does with regard to all the forms of sex discrimination within the Act: to take on established power structures from a position of relative weakness is a course of action which is fraught with problems for potential complainants, in both economic and emotional terms. Most complainants have fewer resources than the institutions whose practices they are challenging, and therefore have a great deal more to lose than their case; the odds are stacked against them. The legal system thus plays an important part in the perpetuation of discriminatory practices in leisure provision, as in other areas of life.

Images and perceptions

A less easy area to identify institutional sexism is in the portrayal of images, using symbols to reinforce them, which serve as reference points for organizations' practices and procedures, and act as guides for the conditions under which people are accepted into them, or allowed roles within them.

For example, Dorothy Hobson has described how the media reinforce and reify the lack of power of female consumers of the media, by the images and assumptions which are presented to them:

> It is the message and the information about the world which are rejected not because they are not understood, as is sometimes suggested, but precisely because they *are* understood, and because such an understanding induces in the viewer a feeling of powerlessness and overwhelming despair at the world which is being re-presented to her.
>
> (Hobson 1983: 94)

The reinforcement of the image of the female consumer as powerless and unable to control her own life, including her leisure life, must have important effects on the attitudes of both providers and consumers. This stereotype is often bitterly resented. The women in the Armley study (Dixey with Talbot 1982) clearly distinguished between having the television or radio on and actually choosing to watch or listen to a programme; normally it was merely an accompaniment to other activities. Many women severely criticized the content of programmes which they felt bore no relationship to their own lives. Given the fact that television occupied approximately one-third of their leisure time, these women showed little enthusiasm for it; it served as the means by which they passed time at home, but it was not seen in the same light as other leisure activities which were more consciously chosen. Gillian Skirrow, in urging women to make their views known more clearly to television programmers, likens television to

> an ideal mother, a source of constant nourishment always ready to communicate with us. For this reason we may feel particularly betrayed when television misrecognises us.
>
> (Skirrow 1987: 12)

The television series *Putting Women in the Picture* (BBC 1987) attempted to question why women were less visible than men on television, except in a narrow range of stereotypical roles, and to examine how women might contribute positively to the ways in which television is presented. One group of strategies suggested in the accompanying information pack centres on more women actually being employed in television, especially in decision-making positions. This is a strategy adopted in various leisure provision contexts, and one which is affected by common features related to the sexual division of labour and the structure of organizations.

In this connection it is interesting that the hotel and catering industries have aroused criticism by the Low Pay Unit that employment of women is based on stereotypes; the notion that women work only for 'pin money', and the ghettoizing of women into a narrow range of low-status, low-paid jobs. This confirms Kanter's (1977) general point that women occupy positions in, but do not control, organizations, with regard to this leisure industry. Indeed, there is often a requirement, not always unwritten, for women workers in hotels and catering to conform to a feminine stereotype for the 'benefit' of customers.

> female staff would only be offered the chance to re-apply for their jobs if they could fit into a size 10, 12 or 14 uniform.
>
> Most of the women workers were long-serving middle aged women – first-class waitresses, extremely popular with the regular customers, but not fitting with the dolly-bird fantasies of the Berni Inns management.
>
> (Byrne 1986: 19)

This particular case is by no means unique in this industry and illustrates clearly unacceptable inequalities in conditions of employment in a leisure industry for men and women. It is also clear that such differences, although more subtly expressed, are implicit in the employment practices of many leisure providers, whether in the commercial or public sectors. The relative powerlessness of women workers, especially those working part time, contributes to the unchallenged continuation of these practices. Union leaders, too, sometimes see women as 'their own worst enemy' with regard to their apparent reluctance to join and become active in, occupational unions and professional bodies. Anna Coote (1980) has described some of the barriers encountered by women in attempting to come to terms with their need to acquire more labour power; the main problem is not that men set out to exclude women, but that the structures they have set up to protect their interests cannot accommodate the needs of women. Like leisure institutions, labour institutions themselves exclude a large group of potential members because of unquestioning adherence to male-defined practices and structures.

Employment practices in the leisure industries reflect those in the general labour market, and limit the opportunities for women to achieve full potential in this important growth area of employment. There are further effects which limit women's ability to take advantage of the leisure opportunities which are, on the face of it, open to them. If leisure facilities and services are exclusively or predominantly staffed by men, this further reinforces women's (and men's) perceptions that the activities concerned are being provided for men. Role models are crucial to the development of sex roles, for both boys and girls. Absence of women in the leisure provision process must have important effects on the development of attitudes to both male and female leisure participation.

Attitude change is another area over which leisure providers and employers themselves claim they have no control. Even in the Action Sport programme (a scheme designed to make provision for groups who traditionally participated in sport less than others) it was found that stereotyped attitudes were held by many staff, even though they were recruited on to the scheme knowing the philosophy behind it:

> Without explicitly saying so, some trivialise or virtually dismiss the idea of women's involvement in sport: it is fine for women to come along 'if they've got the time to waste'.
>
> (Glyptis *et al*. 1985: 17)

Attitudes are also central to the informal relations between men and women, which affect all organizations, but are most crucial in the voluntary sector of leisure provision, since provision within this sector is based on an ideology of consumer control. Unfortunately, there is relatively little recent research work on the ways in which men and women relate to each other in the leisure context of voluntary social groups. Paul Hoggett and Jeff Bishop (1985), while examining the social organization of leisure in the voluntary sector, apparently found it difficult to break out of the male-defined subcultural contexts through which they interpreted what they observed. They recommended that further research should be carried out which examines the relationship of leisure subcultures with class, gender, race and 'other structural variables' (Hoggett and Bishop 1985: 106): the description of gender as merely one of a number of structural variables helps to explain their failure to make more than passing reference to the distinctively different experiences of women within voluntary sector clubs and organizations. This weakness is symptomatic of so many analyses of contemporary leisure.

This weakness in theory and research methodology has also been evident in work on youth subcultures, which has been criticized as intrinsically male (see

McRobbie 1980). Leisure is one area which provides a fertile ground for critique of this androcentrism. Even Ken Roberts (1983) has described young people's leisure as 'engendered', although the provision for young people's leisure by the youth service and by voluntary organizations has tended to assume that its main purpose is to present young men and boys with alternatives to anti-social behaviour and delinquency. Girls and young women in this context of provision have been seen as problematic or marginal. The National Organization for Work with Girls and Young Women is a response to 'The male dominated youth service hierarchy, the harassment by young men and male colleagues, and the entrenchment of their sexist attitudes' (National Association of Youth Clubs 1985: 18). The problem approach underlying much of public sector leisure provision is another contributory factor in the lack of provision for women and girls, who are rarely defined as a problem group or a danger to society.

It has been argued that providers in the commercial sector are forced, by definition, to cater more sensitively for female consumers, if they are to stay in business. There is some evidence to support this, and there are instances, for example in the case of bingo, where women, as the primary consumers (see Dixey 1983), do have some effect on the form and delivery of provision, albeit within the framework of mainly male ownership and management. However, Yvonne Roberts (1985) has argued that middle-aged women in particular are not even recognized as consumers, even by those with products to sell. Images of women are presented in advertising which are antipathetic to this group of potential buyers, many of whom are in stable work and have considerable personal disposable income. The danger in the commercial sector is that women, like other potential consumer groups, will be seen as merely another sector of the market to exploit, rather than meeting their needs. Donald Cowell and Carol Octon (1979) argue that marketing in leisure simply has not taken sufficient notice of women's needs:

> This of course may be in part the fault of the leisure provider who has not identified the female market in sufficient detail and with significant discrimination to reach them and hence has generated blanket marketing strategies based on 'the housewife', 'the mother', with little regard for the differences within those groups and hence the very specific marketing mixes which are required.
>
> (Cowell and Octon 1979: 18)

Public providers and policy-makers seem to have taken even longer to appreciate that women do not constitute a single 'target group', and that more sensitive treatment is necessary than simply labelling women as 'under-participant', 'recreationally inert', 'sports illiterate' or 'disadvantaged'. The current provision practices and structures are so entrenched and institutionalized that making change is tantamount to revolution; there appears to be almost a moral value implicit in the provision of certain activities to certain groups of people. To change such provision to make 'special' provision for women is thus inevitably to change the status quo, and change to existing practices is seen by the groups in power or those who currently benefit, as a threat.

Strategies for change

To change such structures is to understand and to value aspects of women's culture. Berit As (1975) stressed the need to begin by making female culture visible by analysing the common values shared by many women and, later, by identifying the extent to which these have been adopted by men. It is also important to identify the extent to which female culture is reactive to, or dependent upon, men's culture and institutions.

Clearly, women are not merely the passive recipients of the discriminatory practices of social institutions. They themselves, at various times, have devised a variety of ways of carving out some degree of control over time, spaces, facilities and procedures for the leisure activities which they value and wish to pursue. These strategies are, in themselves, illustrative of the particular forms of hegemony in operation when the strategies were developed. There has been little or no research work on the ways in which women's leisure activities, in both all-female and mixed-sex groups, relate to the dominance of patriarchy surrounding and pervading leisure institutions and organizations. Figure 1 is an attempt to present diagrammatically some of the strategies for control adopted by women, and their relationship to the 'malestream' of leisure structures.

Traditional female and familial ideologies have, for some groups of women, formed the basis of exclusively female groups, controlled by women, around foci defined as 'female'. Organizations like the Women's Institute, the League of Health and Beauty and mother and toddler groups, are examples of the ability of women to overcome personal constraints such as lack of time and self-confidence, to set up areas of female autonomy which are, nevertheless, framed by patriarchal society. Such groups depend for their survival on the continued adherence by women to relatively narrowly defined sex roles and behaviour, and their continuing to value the ideologies which underpin them. Such groups, resourced by the voluntary effort and contributions of members, are commonly tolerated and supported by patriarchal society, because they pose no threat to the dominant group. Indeed, their existence serves to reinforce and confirm the polarity of sex roles in leisure behaviour. This category of female leisure groups is commonly based on the assumption that women's 'spare time' should be filled by learning or elaborating aspects of domestic ideology like 'homemaking', the care and nurture of others, 'good works' and improving one's physical appearance. Activities tend to be presented as expressive rather than productive, and voluntary rather than committed. While they may serve as useful support systems for many women, they also serve to perpetuate and preserve the hegemony of patriarchal relations in leisure and in society in general.

A second category of strategies are those adopted by women who have been able to overcome both personal and role constraints, to express a wish to take part in activities offered by organizations which are traditionally controlled by men. Some women are able to do no more than express the wish to participate, because they lack the resources necessary to overcome the structural constraints which form the linkage between all potential participants and activities – mobility, personal income, personal freedom/autonomy, skills and so on. However, even successful negotiation of these important barriers does not guarantee entry to leisure institutions.

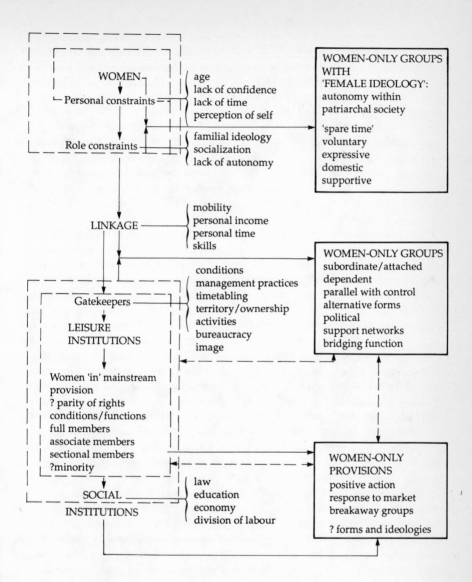

Figure 1.   Women and leisure provision: constraints and strategies

The analysis of power is inescapable when discussing the issue of equality of access to and control of leisure opportunity. Yael Azmon (1981) suggests that one should take into account the production of material values as well as non-material ones, and the ways in which these values are converted from the private sphere, in which so many of women's activities take place, into the public sphere. She suggests that the main barriers to this conversion taking place successfully for women are the existence of gatekeepers: examples would be pricing policies, lack of provision for children, and sexual harassment of women who criticize these practices. These mechanisms control the conversion of values produced by women, and the way in which women's values are stereotyped back into the private sphere but not accepted into the public sphere. She points out that even when women achieve political power, this is not necessarily accompanied by social recognition of their power, and often they are not assigned to positions of real authority: 'In other words, male dominance is self-protecting' (Azmon 1981: 557).

Thus, while some women are able to overcome the personal constraints, role expectations and structural elements of the social filter, they may be prevented from participation by the 'gatekeepers' to which reference has already been made. Gatekeepers may adopt a variety of exclusionary practices – restrictive or exclusive membership, antipathetic images, unreachable pricing, sexual harassment, or lack of parity of access or facility. In such circumstances some women decide to form groups or organizations of their own, sometimes with distinctively female cultures, parallel to the male structures. They may be dependent upon the male institutions only for wishing to copy their activities, although many female groups of this kind find themselves dependent on the male group for access to essential spaces or expertise. Women's sports groups are a good example of this type of group; many lack total autonomy because they lack the same power to acquire physical resources. Golf clubs commonly have 'ladies' sections', which are not only dependent upon but are often subordinate to the main male membership – 'lady members must give way at the tee to full members' is by no means an uncommon rule. The extent to which such female groups can control the norms and values of their activities is directly related to the extent to which they depend on the male group for facilities and other benefits.

Some women's groups formed as a reaction to male domination of leisure activities have even devised alternative *forms* of activity and procedures in conscious rejection of male-defined norms and values. They may also be committed to political change, as a direct result of exclusionary practices of the dominant group, like ERICCA (Equal Rights in Clubs Campaign for Action), which is working towards not only parity in membership of working men's clubs for women but changing the nature and even the name of the clubs. Some groups serve as 'sisterhoods', important support networks for women facing the same problems; some, like the Women's Sports Foundation, have even been set up expressly for that purpose, as well as to try to change the status quo. Women-only groups serve to provide status for their members, and experience of holding positions of responsibility which may be precluded in mixed-sex organizations. Other all-female groups function as a transitory stage for some women in helping them to acquire, in a sheltered situation, the skills, knowledge and/or confidence to take their place in mainstream provision.

Indeed, some of the leisure institutions themselves have recognized this last need, and the more sensitive providers in both public and private sectors have set up women-only sessions to encourage women who feel more comfortable in single-sex settings to take part. (It is perhaps cynical to ask whether the prime motive at times is not so much to cater expressly for the needs of women, but to fill expensive facilities at off peak times.) It is not known how successful these bridging operations are: do women who have played a full part in all-female groups continue to do so when transplanted into mixed groups? And does their participation continue in the same or adapted form?

Such categorization is a crude attempt to describe some of the strategies adopted by women to establish some degree of control over their own leisure opportunities. There is little published work which has analysed these processes, or on the social relations between men and women within the same leisure institutions. Where women are at least nominally admitted, it is necessary to analyse what conditions they must fulfil. As 'full' members, do they enjoy real parity of privilege and rights, in access to facilities, ability to make contributions to change and personal auton-omy within the organization? Or are there conditions imposed on their member-ship - for example, the expectation that they will service male members' activities through refreshments or use of facilities at inconvenient times? Or are they minority members who are expected to accede to established procedures, even if they are dis-advantageous to women? Members of ladies' sections within the organizations are sometimes expected to perform functions and operate in distinctively different ways to the main section, and are often subservient to it. What forms of autonomy and power do female members enjoy, and how are these framed and mediated by the social relations within the organization?

Another fundamental question still to be answered is the influence of differential social valuing on the ability of women to attract the kinds of resources which are needed to subsidize their leisure activities. What are the effects of the tendency to see women's activities, even when separate and controlled by them, as less important and carrying less status than men's? Can the experiences of some previously all-female groups in retaining some degree of control when male membership is per-mitted also form the basis for an analysis of social relations between men and women in leisure organizations?

References

Andersen, Margaret L. (1983) *Thinking about Women*, New York, Macmillan.

Ardener, Shirley (1981) 'Ground rules and social maps for women: an introduction', in Shirley Ardener (ed.) *Women and Space*, Beckenham, Croom Helm.

As, Berit (1975) 'On female culture: an attempt to formulate a theory of women's solidarity and action', *Acta Sociologica* 18: 142–61.

Azmon, Yael (1981) 'Sex, power and authority', *British Journal of Sociology* 32(4): 547–59.

British Broadcasting Corporation (1987) *Putting Women in the Picture*.

Byrne, Dominic (ed.) (1986) *Waiting for Change? Working in Hotel and Catering*, Low Pay Pam-phlet No. 42, Low Pay Unit/Hotel and Catering Workers Union.

Coote, Anna (1980) 'Powerlessness - and how to fight it', *New Statesman*, 7 November 1980, pp. 8–11.

Cowell, Donald and Octon, Carol (1979) 'Marketing leisure services to women', paper presented at MEG Conference, Bristol Polytechnic, 9–12 July.

Dixey, Rachael (1983) 'The playing of bingo: industry, market and working-class culture', in Alan Tomlinson (ed.) *Leisure and Popular Cultural Forms*, Brighton Polytechnic, Chelsea School of Human Movement.

Dixey, Rachael with Talbot, Margaret (1982) *Women, Leisure and Bingo*, Leeds, Trinity and All Saints' College.

Emmett, Isobel (1971) 'The social filter in the leisure field', *Recreation News Supplement*, Countryside Commission, July 1971.

Equal Opportunities Commission (1986) *Legislating for Change? Review of the Sex Discrimination Legislation*, a consultative document, Manchester.

Fasting, Kari and Sisjord, Mari-Kristin (1986) 'Gender, verbal behaviour and power in sports organisations', *Scandinavian Journal of Sports Science* 8(2): 81–5.

Frieze, I. H., Parsons, J. E., Johnson, P. B., Ruble, D. N. and Zellman, G. L. (1978) *Women and Sex Roles: A Social Psychological Perspective*, New York, N.W.Norton.

Glyptis, Sue, Kay, Teresa and Murray, Michele (1985) *Working with Women and Girls*, Birmingham, Sports Council (West Midlands).

Hey, Valerie (1987) *Patriarchy and Pub Culture*, London, Tavistock.

Hobson, Dorothy (1983) 'Watching television: viewing with the audience', in Alan Tomlinson (ed.) *Leisure and Popular Cultural Forms*, Brighton Polytechnic, Chelsea School of Human Movement.

Hoggett, Paul and Bishop, Jeff (1985) *The Social Organisation of Leisure: A Study of Groups in Their Voluntary Sector Context*, London, Sports Council/Economic and Social Research Council.

Home Office (1978) *Sex Discrimination: A Guide to the Sex Discrimination Act 1975*, London, HMSO.

Kanter, Rosabeth Moss (1977) *Men and Women of the Corporation*, New York, Basic Books.

McRobbie, Angela (1980) 'Settling accounts with subcultures: a feminist critique', *Screen Education* 34.

Macksmith, Anne and Stewart, Doug (1986) *Women and Recreation: A Survey of Existing Local Authorities and Provision*, Planning and Research Section, Recreation and Arts Department, Leicester City Council.

Moore, Wilbert (1962) *The Conduct of the Corporation*, New York, Random House.

National Association of Youth Clubs (1985) *Working with Girls*, March/April.

Pannick, David (1983) *Sex Discrimination in Sport*, Manchester, Equal Opportunities Commission.

Roberts, Ken (1983) *Youth and Leisure*, London, Allen & Unwin.

Roberts, Yvonne (1985) 'Invisible women', *Sunday Times* 3 November, p. 37.

Skirrow, Gillian (1987) 'Television and us', in British Broadcasting Corporation (ed.) *Putting Women in the Picture*, Information Pack, London, BBC.

Sports Council (1984) *Participation: Taking Up the Challenge*, Recreation Management Seminar Proceedings, London, Sports Council.

Whitehead, Anne (1976) 'Sexual antagonism in Herefordshire?', in Diana Leonard and Sheila Allen (eds.) *Dependence and Exploitation in Work and Marriage*, London, Longman.

Willis, Paul (1974) 'Women in sport', *Working Papers in Cultural Studies* 5, Centre for Contemporary Cultural Studies, University of Birmingham, pp. 21–36.

Conclusions

The papers in this reader have been collected in an attempt to go beyond the 'add women and stir' approach to understanding women's leisure. While knowledge about distributional aspects of women's leisure behaviour has been useful to demonstrate inequalities in opportunities and services, the information available about the relations between men and women, between leisure organizations and women, and between women's perceptions of provision and providers' perceptions of women, has been far from complete. It has been discouraging that when such information has been available, it has often been ghettoized by, for example, conference organizers, policy-makers and non-feminist academics – selective deafness appears to be endemic!

Traditional leisure studies has tended to be based on established theoretical approaches and methodologies which assume a definition of leisure which is related and residual to a full-time, paid job. Proponents of this perspective can either ignore women because they do not 'fit in' to the apparently neat models which have been produced, or assume that they will be appropriate to the experience of those women who, 'like men', also have full-time, paid jobs: those women who do not fit this model continue to be seen as marginal or invisible.

Herein lies unnecessary limitation of insight and understanding, not only of women's experiences, but of other people who do not work in full-time, paid jobs outside the home, and therefore do not fit the prevailing model; for example severely disabled people, retired people, unemployed people. The implicit definition of work as a full-time paid job has long been criticized by feminist writers as devaluing the work which women do in the home, especially housework and child and elderly relative care. But it also marginalizes the people whose lives simply are not divided in this structured way – those with religious vocations, full-time students, schoolchildren, people working in the black economy – all of whom work, but are rarely the focus of study because the definition of their leisure is seen as problematic. Women were once dismissed as 'extraneous noise' by a researcher embarking on a study of leisure around retirement!

The sociology of leisure has leant heavily on the sociology of work. This has reinforced some of the problems outlined above, since the sociology of work has itself been criticized as androcentric, élitist (in occupational terms) and inapplicable to women's experience. Roslyn Feldberg and Evelyn Nakano Glenn (1984) argue that the 'job model' has been applied principally to men, while the 'gender model' has been applied principally to women, and they argue that this sex-segregation of approach seriously distorts understanding of both men's and women's life experiences.

Of course, feminist writers are not alone in having criticized this rather simplistic view of work–leisure relationships, and its limitations to understanding the full range of people's experience. Indeed, it is increasingly obvious that the model applies to only a minority of the population. And yet critical thinking appears rarely to be radical enough. John Kelly identifies some of the parameters which demonstrate that 'the most realistic model is "pluralistic" ' (Kelly 1983: 28). Yet he seems unable to break out of the assumption that men's experience is the yardstick against which to measure women's: 'Women, in most leisure settings, are expected to behave rather differently from men' (ibid.: 38). While he goes on to discuss the ways in which social structures limit and shape women's behaviour (and this may be a necessary stage in his own education!), he fails to see the need to shift his focus of enquiry to women themselves – they are just an interesting aberration to his main discussion points. Gender, in this perspective, is seen as merely another social structural factor, and is not in any way associated with gender relations, complementary relationships, negotiations or the forms of hegemony and power which are integral to patriarchal society. He is, in fact, studying 'sex as a variable' rather than 'women as people' (Acker 1981: 79).

Similarly, Fred Best claims that he asks radical questions about the place and timing of work in people's lives, and yet he leaves unasked, questions about the gender-related patterns of work and duties:

> For women, the intertwining of years commonly spent in home keeping, child rearing and 'job employment' complicate the computation of lifetime scheduling options. Among the most viable rescheduling options for women might be to lengthen the worklife to 32 years such that 15 of the total working years would be spent on part time workweeks of 20 hours.
>
> (Best 1980: 13)

In an approach which claims to be 'radical', it is interesting that Best describes women as 'complicating' an unquestioned device for understanding life at different stages; and he appears not to see (or does he prefer to ignore?) the 'viable option' of men sharing responsibility for childcare and homework, and thereby preventing the need for women's paid work life to be extended as he suggests! While he goes on to criticize the rigid division of paid and unpaid work, and argues that both men and women are changing their values towards a more integrated view of life, he gives no consideration to the kinds of changes in ideological and material factors which would be necessary for this to happen, especially the need for equal *valuing* of men's and women's work, and the taking of equal responsibility for childcare and homework.

Kelly and Best (along with so many others) thus miss the opportunity which is identified by Rosemary Deem in the first chapter of this collection – to look critically at how masculinity constrains and shapes men's leisure, and thereby boys' enculturation for future leisure; and how class, age and race shape views of what 'being a man' means at different stages of life and in different cultural groups, and how this affects their leisure opportunities and behaviour.

More importantly for the purposes of this book, the assumption that women with full time, paid jobs also 'fit' the male model, seriously distorts understanding of the full range of perceptions and meanings which women attribute to their experiences. It is essential that they be allowed to speak for themselves, rather than being 'taken on board' rather like stowaways who, when discovered, continue the voyage under strict control and conditions applied by the (male) crew!

> we must ask what counts as knowledge. Our experiences as women in an androcentric world must differ from those of men who clearly do not live in a gynocentric cosmos. What has counted as knowledge, until recently, has been based not on *human* experience but essentially on male experience seen through male eyes. Our knowledge of the social world and social life, and possibly even the natural world, is distorted so that often this 'knowledge' does not make sense to women.
>
> (Hall 1985: 26)

It is with this awareness of the implicit masculinism of much of leisure studies, that we wished to collect contributions which challenged assumptions about the applicability of theoretical models to women's experiences, and which gave accounts which focused centrally on women's perceptions and experiences. We do not believe that this reader is a summation of this hope, but it is at least an attempt to demonstrate how enriching and critical such contributions can be, not only in understanding women's leisure, but also the experiences of men. In this way, we are presenting not merely a critique of existing research and theory, but in reconceptualizing leisure, we are contributing to the progress of leisure studies.

Our approach has therefore, even within a feminist framework, been pluralist. We do not see feminism as a narrow approach, but as one which should encompass the myriad of experiences which women may have. This is not to argue that we should never be critical about women's experiences, since this would lead us into another strait-jacket of exclusive, smug and stereotyped belief. It is essential to be critical about the overarching structures and ideologies surrounding and shaping women's lives, in order that we may begin to understand (but not necessarily accept) the reasons for choices. For example, identifying the ideology of femininity which underpins and helps to structure a sports form like modern rhythmic gymnastics or synchronized swimming is not to deny or decry the technical, physical and aesthetic achievements of the women and girls who take part in them, but to understand why women see such activities as realistic opportunities for physical involvement and success, while rejecting others. Such analysis also helps us to explain how such activities are valued and supported by male-dominated power structures.

We have thus tried to value alternative views within feminist frameworks. We and our contributors share the belief that women are central to enquiry, and that all the knowledge gained relates and is directly applicable to theoretical understanding and to policy issues:

> good sociology is necessarily feminist
>
> (Fildes 1985: 109)

But we do not see that it is necessary for all of us to agree, as feminists, on all issues, especially those related to use of different areas of theory, methodologies and strategies for change. We do not believe that this in any way weakens our case. On the contrary, the fact that women researchers and writers who promulgate a variety of realities of experience, and recognize a range of social worlds, can collaborate in such a coherent and supportive way, underlines the validity and essential importance of the perspective which is shared, and the enriching potential of debate and discussion around a central shared belief. As editors, we have learnt and benefited from the generosity of our contributors' willingness to share their insights, uncertainties and process.

What we have tried to do is to illuminate the 'sociography' of leisure which has given us information about *patterns* of participation in various leisure activities, with cameo pictures which give some insights into the *meanings and interactions* surrounding women's leisure in a patriarchal society. In this way, we have tried to be positive rather than positivist (Stanley and Wise 1983) in our interpretation of women's experiences. While it is important to identify, through the sociography, the nature of inequities and inequalities, it is more difficult to learn how such inequalities become taken for granted and legitimated within various ideologies. This insight then allows a fuller appreciation of the achievement of those women who have managed to carve out some degree of control in their own leisure choices, and even in some cases to subvert apparently overwhelming personal and structural constraints because of the commitment and meaning with which they imbue their activities.

Collections of readings necessarily involve making choices. It has not been possible to include all aspects of or approaches to the study of women and leisure within one volume. There are other lines of enquiry which would repay further analysis, and feminist approaches in other fields of study which might also provide useful understandings of this subject area.

Feminist writing within cultural studies has established the need to recognize the distinctively female experiences of the transition from child to adult, and from school to post-school life. The influence of these experiences on the leisure 'enculturation' of girls and women, in terms of the contexts to which they are exposed, the skills which are passed on, and the frameworks in which they learn to live, would provide useful information which would augment the rather more mechanistic data collected in sex-role socialization research. Angela McRobbie (1978), for instance, suggests that girls' leisure behaviour is less influenced by entering the world of work, than by their relationships with men (see also McIntosh *et al.* 1981).

The point that 'youth culture' is in fact no such thing, but a series of different social worlds for different young people distinguished by gender, class and race, highlights a central problem. Some social research assumes one, or at least a consensus, reality, for named groups. Policy based on this therefore ignores the ways in which members of groups may experience membership in different ways. For example, to speak of 'family recreation' is to embody an ideology of the family which presupposes certain roles and positions, with associated behaviours. It ignores the differences in shared experiences; in access to and control of family resources; in dependence; in priority and primacy of domestic negotiation processes; in the amount of time spent in the home; in social contacts outside the family or in the extended family; and in personal resources – relative freedoms!

And yet so much leisure policy is based on this ideological form of group identification. The notion of target groups is a case in point; the danger is that when groups are identified and targeted, new stereotypes may be substituted for old, and if targets are not met, the pathology of leisure provision will tend to label members of the target group as 'difficult' or even deviant. A critical re-evaluation of the common and distinguishing characteristics of the constituents of named target groups seems to be a rare occurrence.

Leisure research which focuses on women's lives reveals many other aspects of the need to observe and analyse more sensitively. The importance to women of what many other people would call vicarious experience, especially with children, shows that appreciation of the different social worlds inhabited by the direct participant and the onlooker or supporter reveals a whole range of experience which is masked by the usual descriptions of 'active' or 'passive'. The less publicly visible elements of women's lives are often the most important, and better research methods and procedures are needed to take account of them. The privacy of much of women's time is a barrier to researchers which it is difficult to overcome, especially where that privacy is an inherent part of the leisure experience. The respect for such privacy often prevents feminist researchers intruding, but it also leaves gaps in our knowledge which are crucial, and which we can fill only through more indirect observation, and techniques like retrospective autobiography.

Similarly, traditional research perspectives and methods fail to take account of the extent to which women's activities are concurrent. Given the centrality of free time as a component in leisure definitions and concepts, it is significant that it has been seen primarily as a unilinear and continuous resource. We need much more understanding of the intermittent nature of much of women's free time, and how pleasurable activities or contexts mediate or enable disliked obligations. Ken Roberts (1981) has suggested that this 'fusion' of women's activities is an area from which men might learn. While many women would contest the notion of 'fusion' and substitute 'conditions', this also ignores the tendency for many women to do the opposite with pleasurable or easily identifiable leisure activities: many women refer to their inability merely to sit and watch television or listen to the radio – they feel they must be 'doing' something, like knitting or mending (see Dixey with Talbot 1982; Wimbush 1986). It is as if they feel that they must justify moments of quiet or relaxation with some productive activity.

The perceptions of activities as leisure-like or work-like is an element of a holistic approach to leisure which still requires further investigation and analysis. The political danger of this approach for women, however, is that people who operate within structural constraints do find ways of making their lives meaningful, and this may result in a kind of determinism which allows structural inequalities to continue. For example, the use of satisfaction measures among people whose experiences have taught them to expect little, and therefore whose aspirations are low, reveals little about their potential to enjoy a range of alternative experiences. It has been suggested previously (see Talbot 1979) that a more accurate measure of life satisfaction for women might be their aspirations for their daughters.

The distinction between productive and non-productive work is a further dimension which might throw light on the ways in which women's work is valued, and consequently how they value themselves, and how their 'right' to leisure is evaluated. The tendency to equate men with instrumental (or useful) aspects of life, and women with expressive elements, further begs the question of whether women possess leisure, and shows the limiting effects of polarized sex roles on both gender groups.

There has been relatively little longitudinal research in leisure studies; we therefore have limited knowledge and understanding of the processes and influences surrounding decisions to take up or to give up different leisure activities through life. For example, the leisure sociography gives us some clues about the important influence of young children on their mothers' opportunities for leisure outside the home, but we know less about the ways in which women come to terms with changing sets of obligations, and the ways in which priorities change within family groups. This example also highlights another aspect of women's lives which deserves further consideration in terms of its effects on leisure: women's perceptions of duty and obligation, especially to family members, are important potential influences on women's use of time and their freedom to decide how to use it.

Feminists have drawn attention to the very real constraints on women's freedom applied by fear of harm or harassment in public places. The intricate processes of identification with places and spaces are difficult to isolate, although some of the work which has been done in social anthropology and human geography could inform future approaches in leisure studies. Shirley Ardener (1981) has collected contributions which relate time, people and space: public and private spaces, and the part women play in constituting and defining them, are seen as fundamental to the conduct of social life. The findings of social anthropology also question the universality of gender roles: 'the special relationship between *women and space* in one community may be set alongside the relationship of *men and space* in a second community' (Ardener 1981: 27). Ardener goes on to discuss the effects of boundaries, the appreciation of space and physical mobility, and the body practices of different cultures, on women's lives. Her description of physical space and our perceptions as 'mutually affecting spheres of reality' (ibid.: 32) is a potentially useful concept in helping to understand the construction of women's mental maps of leisure facilities and opportunities.

Similarly, Don Parkes and Nigel Thrift (1980) discuss the ways in which time and space interact in people's perceptions to become 'places', which are multidimensional, personalized and phenomenological entities. The analysis of leisure as time and space within leisure studies has tended to be restricted to timetabling of specific facilities! Parkes' and Thrift's distinction between locational and experiential elements of time and space, all interacting within a social system providing various kinds of information, provides a helpful model for examining individuals' reactions to both physical and human aspects of their environment.

Such approaches underline the desirability of embedding the study of women's leisure in their whole life experience; otherwise they make only limited sense. Acceptance of this precludes the dualism implicit in the traditional work–leisure model. While this framework makes leisure studies more flexible and relevant to more people, no one, and least of all feminist researchers, would argue that the removal of this structural 'safety net' makes research and theory-making any easier. Indeed, one of the benefits of producing this reader together has been the support we have gained from each other's generosity in exposing our uncertainties and difficulties and in sharing the acknowledgement that what we have produced is only one imperfect stage in a long and ongoing process. There is no claim for absolute truth; we have dealt only in 'relative freedoms'.

References

Acker, Sandra (1981) 'No-woman's land: British sociology of education 1960–1979', *Sociological Review* 29(1).

Ardener, Shirley (1981) *Women and Space*, Beckenham, Croom Helm.

Best, Fred (1980) *Flexible Life Scheduling: Breaking the Education–Work-Retirement Lockstep*, New York, Praeger.

Dixey, Rachael with Talbot, Margaret (1982) *Women, Leisure and Bingo*, Leeds, Trinity and All Saints' College.

Feldberg, Roslyn and Glenn, Evelyn Nakano (1984) 'Male and female: job versus gender models in the sociology of work', in Janet Siltanen and Michele Stanworth, (eds.) *Women and the Public Sphere*, London, Hutchinson.

Fildes, Sara (1985) 'Women and society', in Michael Haralambos (ed.) *Developments in Sociology: An Annual Review*, London, Causeway Press.

Hall, M. Ann (1985) 'Knowledge and gender: epistemological questions in the social analysis of sport', *Sociology of Sport Journal* 2(1). pp. 25–42.

Kelly, John (1983) *Leisure Identities and Interactions*, London, Allen & Unwin.

McIntosh, Sue *et al.* (1981) 'Women and leisure', in Alan Tomlinson (ed.) *Leisure and Social Control*, Brighton Polytechnic, Chelsea School of Human Movement.

McRobbie, Angela (1978) 'Working class girls and the culture of femininity', in CCCS Women's Studies Group (ed.) *Women Take Issue: Aspects of Women's Subordination*, London, Hutchinson.

Parkes, Don and Thrift, Nigel (1980) *Times, Spaces and Places: A Chronogeographic Perspective*, Chichester, John Wiley & Sons.

Roberts, Ken (1981) 'Leisure and gender', paper presented to seminar on Women, Sport and Leisure, Open University, Milton Keynes, 26 June.

Stanley, Liz and Wise, Sue (1983) *Breaking Out: Feminist Consciousness and Feminist Research*, London, Routledge & Kegan Paul.

Talbot, Margaret (1979) *Women and Leisure*, London, Sports Council/Social Science Research Council.

Wimbush, Erica (1986) *Women, Leisure and Well-Being*, Edinburgh, Centre for Leisure Research, Dunfermline College.

Author index

Abenstern, Michelle, 27
Acker, Sandra, 178
Allan, Graham, 79, 83
Allat, Patricia, 34
Amos, V., xix, 50
Andersen, Margaret, 162
Anderson, Michael, 75, 76
Ang, Ien, xx, xxi
Angelou, Maya, 118
Ardener, Shirley, 162, 182
As, Berit, 172
Ashridge Management College, 156, 157
Azmon, Yael, 174

Barfoot, Joan, 118
Barrett, Michele, 136, 139
Bell, Colin, 14
Bell, Lady Florence, 94
Belotti, Elena, 137
Bennett, Tony, 88
Bennett, Yves, 156
Bentley, K., xvii
Best, Fred, 178
Beuret, Kris, 52
Bishop, Jeff, 170
Blum, Arlene, 106
Booker, Chris, 93, 94
Borish, Linda, xviii
Bowles, Gloria, 6
Brackenridge, Celia, 8, 114
Brake, Mike, 38
Brown, George, 73
Brunsdon, Charlotte, xx
Bryan, Beverley, xvii, 41
Buonaventura, Wendy, 118
Burch, W. R., 7
Burnett, John, 24

Burns, Tom, 5
Burrage, Hilary, xviii
Buxton Smither, G., 112
Byrne, Dominic, 169

Calder, Angus, 27
Carrington, Bruce, xvii
Carter, Dawn, 156
Cartledge, Sue, 136
Cavendish, Ruth, 134
Central Statistical Office, xix, 142
Centre for Contemporary Cultural
    Studies, xix, 4, 6
Chambers, Deborah, 8, 10, 11, 15
Cheek, Neil, 7
Chivers, Terry, xvii
Clarke, John, xvii, xix, 1, 6, 9, 11, 14,
    135
Cole, John, 30
Comaneci, Nadia, 111, 112
Cooper, Carylynn, 148, 149
Coote, Anna, 170
Corby, S., 149
Cornish, D. B., 100
Cornwell, Jocelyn, 83
Cowell, Donald, 171
Coyle, Angela, 10, 76
Critcher, Chas, xvii, xix, 1, 6, 9, 11, 14,
    135

Dadzie, Stella, xvii, 41
Damouni, Kathy, 112
Davidson, Marilyn, 148, 149
Deem, Rosemary, xiii, xv, xix, xx, 1, 4,
    6, 7, 10, 11, 12, 13, 14, 30, 34, 49,
    124, 127, 132, 133, 135, 178
Delamont, Sara, 136

Dennis, Norman, 96
Dixey, Rachael, 3, 8, 12, 88, 91, 109,
    110, 143, 165, 168, 171, 181
Dobbin, Ian, 100
Downes, D. M., 92
Driberg, Tom, 24
Dumazedier, Joffre, 7
Dunning, Eric, 6
Dyer, Ken, xviii

Edgell, Stephen, 42
Emmett, Isobel, 166
Equal Opportunities Commission, 167

Fasting, Kari, 163
Feldberg, Roslyn, 178
Ferris, Liz, 8
Fildes, Sarah, 179
Finch, Janet, 83
Fletcher, Sheila, xvii, 7, 20
Ford Smith, Honor, 28
Frieze, I. H., 165
Fritchie, R., 153
Frith, Simon, 117
Fulcher, Margaret, 28

Garber, Jenny, 53, 54
Gatehouse, 28, 30
General Household Survey, 3
Gershuny, Jay, 10, 13
Gillott, Jackie, 112
Gittins, Diana, 41, 136
Glenn, Evelynn Nakano, 178
Glyptis, Sue, 8, 107, 170
Goody, Jack, 97
Graham, Hilary, 6, 11, 33, 143
Graydon, Jan, xviii, 7, 8
Greater London Council Women's
    Committee, 143
Green, Eileen, xvii, 3, 7, 8, 13, 14, 20,
    34, 35, 37–48, 79, 124, 127, 132,
    133, 134, 135, 136, 137, 139, 140,
    143, 144
Green, T. S., xvii
Gregory, Sarah, 12, 107
Griffin, Chris, xix, 7, 8, 9, 39, 49, 51, 52,
    54, 55, 56, 180
Griffiths, Viv, xvii, 8, 35, 39, 40, 50, 51,
    52, 54, 56, 88, 116

Hakim, Catherine, 149
Hall, Catherine, 134
Hall, M. Ann, 8, 179
Hall, Stuart, 6, 38

Hanmer, Jalna, 13, 138
Harding, Sandra, 128
Hargreaves, Jennifer, xviii
Harris, Dorothy, 102
Harris, T., 73
Hearn, Jeff, 43, 46
Hebron, Sandra, 3, 7, 8, 13, 14, 20, 34,
    35, 37–48, 79, 124, 132, 133, 134,
    135, 137, 139, 140, 143, 144
Hegarty, S., xvii
Hemmings, Sue, 79
Henderson, I., 143
Henriques, Fernando, 96
Heron, Liz, 61
Hey, Valerie, 134, 166
Hillman, Martin, 143
Hinsdale, K., 156
Hobson, Dorothy, 7, 8, 39, 49, 124, 132,
    137, 168, 180
Hoggart, Richard, 96
Hoggett, Paul, 170
Hudson, Derek, 19
Hunt, Ann, 149, 156
Hunt, Geoffrey, 134
Hunt, Pauline, 42

Imray, Linda, 79, 134
Ingham, Mary, 118

Jamdagni, L., xix, 50
James, Elaine, 157, 158, 159
Jefferson, Tony, 6, 38
Jenkins, Clive, 10
Johnson, J. D., 156
Johnson, P. B., 165
Johnson, Richard, 6
Jones, Sally, 10, 13
Josefowitz, Natasha, 155

Kanter, Rosabeth Moss, 164, 169
Kaplan, Max, 7
Kay, Tessa, 107, 170
Keil, Teresa, 34
Kelly, John, 178
King, Billie Jean, 104
Kinston, Maxine Hong, 28
Kirkland, Gelsey, 123
Klein, Duelli, 6
Konttinen, Sirrka-Liisa, 122, 123, 124
Kuper, Leo, 94

Lahr, John, 24
Last, Nella, 25, 26
Leaman, Oliver, xviii, 9

Leather, Liz, 113
Lees, Sue, 51, 53, 54, 55, 56, 118
Lenskyj, Helen, xv
Leonard, Diana, 39, 52, 56, 138
Lewis, Jane, 7
Liddington, Jill, 7
Llewellyn Davis, Margaret, xvii, 7, 73
Local Authorities Conditions of Service
    Advisory Board, 149
Long, Jonathan, 80

MacDonald, Barbara, 90
Macksmith, Anne, 166
Makings, Lynn, 52, 53
Malos, Ellen, 6, 13
Manpower Services Commission, 156
Mason, Jennifer, 2, 14, 35, 75, 76, 78, 82
Mass Observation Archive, 25ff
Martin, Jean, 10, 33, 34, 77, 148
Martin, Robert, 10
Matthews, William, 24
Mayall, David, 24
Maynard, Mary, 6, 13
McCabe, Trish, 7, 8, 49, 180
McInnes, Hamish, 8
McIntosh, Mary, 136
McIntosh, Sue, 7, 8, 49, 180
McKee, Lorna, 14
McKibbin, Ross, 94
McRobbie, Angela, xix, 49, 50, 52, 53,
    54, 115, 116, 117, 119, 122, 123,
    124, 171, 180
Meller, Helen, 95
Middleton, Audrey, 79, 134
Milner, Marion, 27
Mirza, N., 50
Mitchison, Naomi, 23, 25, 26
Moffat, Gwen, 110, 111
Moore, Wilbert, 164
Morgan, David, 134
Morley, David, xx
Mungham, Geoff, 117, 118
Murcott, Ann, 82
Murphy, Michael, 75
Murphy, Philip, 6
Murray, Michele, 107, 170

National Association of Youth Clubs, 171
Nava, Mica, 51
Norris, Jill, 7

Oakley, Anne, xv, 103, 135
Octon, Carol, 171

Office of Population Census Surveys, 76
Overman, S. J., xvii

Pahl, Jan, 2, 142
Pahl, Ray, 5
Pannick, David, 168
Parker, Stan, 5, 7, 9, 11, 75, 77
Parkes, Don, 182
Parmar, P., xix, 50
Parry, Janet, 136
Parsons, J. E., 165
Pascal, Julia, 122, 123
Patmore, Alan, 8
Patterson, Garran, 150
Peiss, Kathy, xvii
Phillipson, Chris, 77
Phizacklea, Annie, 136, 138
Pickup, Laurie, 143
Piercy, Madge, 105, 106
Pollert, Anna, 136
Pollock, Griselda, 132
Ponsonby, Arthur, 24
Prakasa, Rao, xvii

Radway, Janice, xx
Rapoport, Rhona, 6, 15, 33, 39, 40, 75
Rapoport, Robert, 6, 15, 33, 39, 40, 75
Rich, Cynthia, 79
Rich, Doris, 97
Roberts, Ceridwen, 10, 33, 34, 77, 148
Roberts, Ken, 7, 9, 171, 181
Roberts, Yvonne, 171
Rodnitzy, Jerry, 37
Rojek, Chris, 1, 9
Rothwell, Sheila, 148, 156
Rowbotham, Sheila, 7
Ruble, D. N., 165
Runfola, Ross, xviii
Ryan, M., 153

Sabo, Donald, xviii
Salaman, Graeme, 10
Sargent, Alice, 151, 154
Satterlee, Saundra, 134
Saunders, Sheila, 138
Scafe, Suzanne, xvii, 41
Scraton, Sheila, xviii, 7, 8, 105
Seacole, Mrs, 24
Segal, Lynne, 136
Sergy, Francoise, 123, 124
Sfeir, Leila, xvii
Sharpe, Sue, xix, 11, 12, 61
Sheffield Low Pay Campaign, 142
Sheridan, Dorothy, 27

Sherman, Barrie, 10
Shoebridge, Michele, xvii
Sisjord, Mari-Kristin, 163
Sistren Theatre Collective, 28, 29
Skirrow, Gillian, 168
Slaughter, Clifford, 96
Smart, Barry, 134
Smart, Carol, 134
Smedley, Wendy, 118
Smith, Cyril, 7
Smith, Lesley, S., 154
Smith, Michael, 7
Soja, Edward, 97
Spackman, Mary Ann, 138
Sports Council, 161
Spring-Rice, Margery, xviii, 100
Stacey, Margaret, 12
Stanko, Elizabeth, 138
Stanley, Liz, xiii, xv, xvi, xvii, 2, 4, 6, 7,
    8, 9, 13, 19, 180
Stewart, Doug, 166
Stockdale, Janet, 3
Szinovacz, M., 77
Szurek, Jane, 73

Talbot, Margaret, xviii, xix, 3, 7, 8, 12,
    13, 88, 91, 103, 109, 110, 128, 143,
    165, 168, 181
Taylor, M. J., xvii
Theberge, Nancy, xviii
Thomas, W. I., 19
Thompson, Edward, 5, 11
Thrift, Nigel, 182
Tolson, Andrew, 42

Veal, Tony, 9

Vicinus, Martha, 7
Vincent, David, 24

Wallace, Clare, 5
Wallace, Jean, 10
West, Jackie, 138
Westwood, Sallie, 43, 52, 132, 133, 135,
    136
Whalley, Ann, 143
Whitbread, Helena, 24
White, Judy, 128, 163
Whitehead, Anne, 79, 134, 137, 166
Williams, Trevor, xvii
Willis, Paul, 162
Wilson, Amrit, xvii, 28, 40
Wilson, Dierdrie, 54
Wilson, Elizabeth, 135
Wilson, Paul, 28
Wimbush, Erica, 2, 7, 8, 10, 11, 12, 14,
    34, 35, 42, 60, 74, 80, 137, 181
Winship, Janice, xx
Wise, Sue, 180
Woodward, Diana, xvii, 3, 7, 8, 13, 14,
    20, 34, 35, 37, 39, 40, 45, 79, 124,
    127, 132, 133, 134, 135, 137, 139,
    140, 143, 144
Woolf, Virginia, 21, 23ff, 73, 154
Wyatt, Sally, 11

Yeandle, Susan, 12, 14
Young, Iris, 103
Youth Work Unit, 51

Zaniecki, Florian, 19
Zellman. G. L., 165

Subject index

Action Sport, 107, 170
adolescence, xviii, 33, 38, 40, 48–59, 111, 112, 117, 118
adolescent girls, 48–59, 112, 115–25
adult children, 78ff, 84
adult dependants, 6, 10, 78
adult education, xv, 65, 66, 124, 152
aerobics, 124, 133, 151
Afro-Caribbean girls/women, 41, 48, 50, 52, 54, 103, 116, 117, 118, 120
age, xiv, xix, 3, 6, 9, 14, 29, 38, 79, 93, 103, 109, 138, 173
ageing, 29, 33, 43, 110
agency, 35, 87
Air Cadets, 57–8
alcohol, 14, 62
androcentrism, xvii, 170, 171, 177, 178
androgyny, 147, 154–5, 159
'Annie', 123
Asian girls/women, 28, 40, 43, 48, 50, 52, 54, 103, 116, 167
'at-homeness', 96
authority, 128, 152, 174
autobiographies, 2, 19, 20ff, 181
autonomy, freedom, independence, xv, xvi, 35, 40, 43, 45, 51, 56, 58, 61, 67, 68, 70, 81, 82, 135–6, 137, 142, 144, 163, 164, 172, 173, 175

'baby talk', 66
babysitting see childcare
badminton, 42, 83, 103–14
ballet, 115, 121, 122
Barrow in Furness, 26
bereavement, 37, 70, 110
betting, 93
bingo, xvi, 3, 8, 12, 87, 88, 91–101, 171

biographies, 103
birdwatching, 80
Birmingham, 8
black people, 18, 28
black women, xvii, 7, 24, 28, 41, 43, 54, 103
Blackpool, 27
body-popping, 120
Bolton, 26
books, 88
boyfriends, 35, 39–41, 48, 52–3, 54, 117
break-dancing, 120
British Institute of Management, 150
British Sociological Association, 8

capitalism, 9, 131, 132
cards, 96
caring networks, 96
caring roles, 6, 10, 35, 68, 73, 75, 77, 82, 133, 136, 139, 172, 177
CB radio, 53, 54
Centre for Contemporary Cultural Studies, xix
chance, 95
charities, 80
child rearing, 178
childbirth/bearing, xviii, 33, 60, 75, 104, 110
childcare, xix, 6, 10, 13, 35, 41, 43, 46, 50, 60–74, 75, 77, 78, 84, 108, 135, 137, 138, 139, 140, 141, 142, 177, 178
children, xix, 2, 3, 7, 11, 12, 14, 22, 26, 27, 33, 34, 35, 37, 41, 43, 44, 45, 60–74, 75, 76, 77, 94, 96, 103, 105, 108, 109, 128, 133, 139, 141, 143, 153, 174, 181, 182

children's activities, 109
church *see* religion
cinema, 49, 55, 94, 98
class, xiv, xvi, xix, 3, 6, 9,12, 15, 29, 34,
    38, 41, 42, 49, 50, 64, 67, 69, 71, 93,
    100, 101, 131, 132, 138, 170
class, women and, 23, 93
climbing, 106, 110–11
clubs, 13, 45, 51, 56, 57–8, 80, 93, 94ff,
    105, 113, 116ff, 141, 167
Clubs and Institutes Union, 167
coffee mornings, 64–6
college, 56
commercial leisure, xix, xx, 91–101, 171
community/ies, xv, 2, 3, 12, 36, 73, 94,
    96, 113
community centres, xvi, 64, 65, 152, 165
community groups/work, 13, 69, 88
community studies, xv, 2, 3, 12, 91
companionship, 44, 94ff
conflict, 133, 135, 136, 137, 138, 140,
    141, 144
constraints, xiv, xvii, xix, 3, 34, 37, 45,
    48, 49ff, 58, 64, 65, 67, 68, 73, 76,
    83, 84, 88, 92, 102, 103, 107, 113,
    116, 124, 128, 131, 137, 141, 144,
    162, 172, 173, 174, 180, 181, 182
consumers, women as, xx, 88, 129, 170,
    171
context, xv, xvi, xx, 2, 3, 6, 9, 12, 13, 18,
    19, 36, 37, 49, 88, 127, 131, 162
control, xv, 13, 54, 56, 61, 87, 88, 97,
    102, 106, 113, 117, 118, 120, 122,
    123, 128, 142, 162, 163, 165, 167,
    169, 172, 174, 175, 180
cooking, 12, 46, 66, 82
Cooperative Women's Guild, 73
countryside, 55, 143
couples, coupledom, 2, 35, 37, 38–47, 62,
    75, 76ff, 107, 127, 132ff, 141
courtship, xvi, 37, 38–41, 117, 118, 132
creches, 65, 66, 71, 166
cricket, 112, 143
Cullwick, Hannah, diaries of, 19ff
cultural studies, xv, xix, 3, 6, 12, 87, 180
culture, xiv, xv, xvi, xvii, xviii, xx, 19,
    40, 95, 100
culture of bedroom, 48, 53–4
cycling, 14

dance/dancing, xv, xvi, xvii, xxi, 49, 53,
    57, 66, 87, 88, 95, 115–25, 151
dance, ballroom, 118, 121
dance choreography, 119

dance culture, 117, 119
dance studios, 123, 124
dance, tap, 121
dancing as a career, 88, 115–25
dancing competitions, 88, 115, 119–21
dancing schools, 121ff
determinism, 107, 113, 181
deviant/delinquent girls/women, 54, 99
diaries, 2, 19ff
disabled people, 147, 163, 177
discos/disco dancing, xvi, 49, 51, 55, 56,
    58, 87, 88, 115–25, 133
disengagement, 77ff
divorce/splitting up, 33, 37, 43–6, 70, 77,
    110
domestic service, 20, 23
domestic work/labour, xiv, xviii, xix, 6,
    11, 13, 20, 22, 26, 34, 41, 46, 49,
    50–1, 54, 57, 58, 60, 63, 67, 68, 72,
    75, 78, 82, 83, 108, 134, 135, 137,
    139, 142, 177
'dossing out', 48–59
drama, 151
drinking, 91, 134–5, 143
Duncan, Isadora, 122
duty, 104, 182

earnings, sex differences, 81, 149
eating, eating out, 79, 141
economy, 101, 163, 173
Edinburgh, xiii, 8, 14, 42, 60ff
education, xv, xvi, xviii, 99, 128, 163, 173
elderly people, 28, 163
elderly women, 96ff
employment *see* work
employment practices, 168, 170
empowerment, xiii, 28, 29, 36
equal opportunities, 8, 103, 164, 167,
    174, 175
Equal Opportunities Commission, 150,
    167
Equal Rights in Clubs Campaign for
    Action, 167, 174
ethnicity, ethnic minorities, xiv, xvii, 29,
    34, 38, 40, 49, 60, 147, 163
ethnocentrism, xvii, 103
ethnographic methods, 25, 178
exploitation, 123

facilities, 110, 172
'*Fame*', 117
family, family life, xiv, xvi, xix, xx, 33,
    34, 35, 37, 38–47, 49, 50, 64, 65, 70,

103, 106, 107, 127, 135, 136, 144,
  182
family ideology, 50, 63, 65, 69, 70, 173,
  180
family leisure/sports participation, 37, 41,
  106, 135, 141, 180
fashion, 48, 53, 56, 57, 117
Federation of Worker Writers and
  Community Publishers, 30
female domestic circles, 63
femininity, xvi, xviii, 42, 87, 88, 102,
  103, 105, 114, 117, 120, 124, 127,
  128, 131, 132, 144, 150ff, 157, 158,
  178
feminism/feminist approaches, xiii, xiv,
  xv, xix, xx, 1, 2, 3, 5, 6, 7, 8, 9, 10,
  12, 14, 19, 23, 36, 37, 54, 88, 102,
  103, 106, 115, 116, 138, 177, 178,
  179, 180, 182, 183
feminist leisure studies, xxi, 5–15, 18, 20,
  27, 183
fiction, xix, xx, xxi, 3
Field, Joanna, 27
films, 38, 117
fitness, xviii, 104, 105, 124
'Flashdance', 117
flower arranging, 42, 133
football pools, 99
friends/friendships, xiii, xx, xxi, 2, 3, 10,
  12, 20, 35, 39, 40, 45, 48, 49ff, 60,
  62, 64, 66, 67, 68, 72, 105, 115, 117ff
fund raising activities, 73, 80

gambling, 93ff
game(s), 48, 53, 58, 91, 95
gardening, 81
Gatehouse Project, 28, 30
gatekeeping, 128, 164, 166, 173, 174
gay people, 18, 24
gender, xiv, xvi, xix, xx, 1, 3, 6, 9, 12,
  13, 14, 35, 36, 38, 49, 68, 87, 101,
  127, 128, 131, 132, 135, 138, 142,
  150, 170, 178, 182
gender relations, xiii, xvi, 1, 2, 6, 9, 10,
  13–14, 35, 76, 87, 134, 170
General Household Survey, 3
girls, xviii, xix, 8, 88
Girls Friendly Society, 58–9, 119ff
going out, 54, 55, 62
golf, 174
gossip, xxi, 65
government, xviii, 147
grandchildren, 75, 78
grandmothers, 71, 99

guilt, 136
gymnastics, 112

Hackney, 28, 29
health, xiv, xviii, 2, 8, 60, 69, 73, 78, 79,
  82, 83, 96
health clubs/clinics, 64, 124
health education, xviii
health studies, xv, xviii
hegemony, xiv, 3, 92, 172, 178
heterosexual partnerships/relationships,
  18, 33, 35, 37, 38–47
history/historical approaches, xiv, xv, xvi,
  xvii, xviii, 2, 5, 7, 11, 18–30, 91, 94
hockey, 103–14, 161–2
holidays, xix, 5, 11, 22, 27, 55, 99
holistic approaches, xv, 3, 12, 158, 181,
  182
home, 76, 80, 81ff, 133, 141, 169
home work, 62, 178
hotel and catering industries, 169
housewives, 8, 9, 132, 136, 171
housework *see* domestic labour
housing, 94, 99
husbands, xx, 2, 6, 11, 12, 14, 24, 26, 27,
  35, 41, 42, 44, 45, 61, 64, 66, 69, 70,
  75–85, 94, 106, 108, 109, 124, 136,
  141

ideology/ies, xiii, xvi, xviii, xx, 14, 34, 36,
  37, 38, 46, 61, 69, 87, 94, 105, 127,
  128, 131, 144, 163, 164, 170, 172,
  173, 174, 178
income, money, xiv, xv, 68, 78, 80, 141,
  142, 172, 173
individuals, 19, 21
inequality, xiv, xv, xvi, 3, 102, 128, 131,
  135, 136, 138, 139, 143, 144, 162,
  167, 169, 177, 180, 181
influence, 164
informal economy, 5
Institute of Chartered Secretaries, 148
Institute of Leisure and Amenity
  Management, 148
institutions, 102, 127, 128, 148ff, 151–4,
  154–5, 161–76
international sportswomen, 103

joint leisure (couple's), 37, 40, 43, 44, *see
  also* family leisure

keep-fit, 42, 66, 108, 124, 133
King, Billie-Jean, 104
kinship, 105

knitting, 11, 54, 96, 144, 181

labour market, xv
Last, Nella, diary of, 25–6
law, legal system, xvi, 129, 163, 166–8, 173
leadership, 112
League of Health and Beauty, 172
Leeds, 3, 12, 91ff
legitimation, 87, 104, 128, 138
leisure(d) society, 10
leisure management, xvi, 107, 113, 127–9, 145, 147–60, 161–76
leisure services, 161–76
leisure studies, xiv, xv, xxi, 1, 6, 7, 8, 9, 12, 13, 14, 102, 177, 178, 182
Leisure Studies Association, 8
lesbian women, 24
libraries, 147, 149, 151, 152
life course/life-cycle, xvi, 6, 15, 33, 35, 36, 38, 39, 41, 43, 75, 76, 127
lifestyles, xv, 2, 3, 5, 6, 12, 35, 36, 41, 62, 69, 71
literature, 23
Liverpool University, 8
Local Government Training Board, 157, 158
lone parents, 33, 34, 44, 65, 142
Loughborough University, 8
Low Pay Unit, 169
luck, 97

Madison, 118
magazines, xix, xx, 38, 53, 56, 88
male approval, 42, 68
male domination of spaces, 51, 53, 57, 134–5
management, 147–60
marketing, 171
marriage, 76, 132, 134, 137, 144
married women, 34, 137, 139
masculine values, xvii-xviii, 15, 147ff, 150–2, 155, 156, 164, 178
masculinity, 6, 42, 43, 103, 127, 128, 131, 132, 134–5, 147, 150, 155–6, 157, 158, 177, 178
Mashed Potato, 118
Mass Observation Archive, 2, 21, 25–7
meanings of leisure, xiv, xx, 2, 3, 8, 12–13, 29, 34, 35, 60, 92, 101, 110, 115, 178, 180, 181
Mecca, 95
media, xvi, xviii, xx, 48, 88, 115, 131, 163, 168

mending, 181
men's attitudes, 7, 14, 46, 83, 144, 155–6, 161–2, 170
men's leisure, 14, 34, 40, 63, 94, 127, 132, 134–5, 140, 162, 178
methodology, 1, 2, 3, 6, 26, 170, 180, 181
middle aged women, 109, 171
middle class girls/women, 23, 25, 42, 51, 64, 65, 66, 68, 80, 100, 141, 143
Milton Keynes, 13, 124
Mitchison, Naomi, diary of, 23, 25–6
mobility, xv, xix, 128, 142–4, 152, 172, 173, 182
modern dance, 120, 122, 123, 124
modern rhythmic gymnastics, 178
money *see* income
moral panic, 88
Morris, Margaret, 122
mother(s), 2, 8, 12, 35, 36, 58, 60–74, 108, 115, 122, 123, 124, 136, 137, 181, 182
mother and toddler groups, 64, 166, 172
motherhood, 33, 60–74, 108, 132, 134, 135, 144, 169
mother's circles, 64–7, 70
motivation, 104, 105
Munby, Arthur, diaries of, 19ff
museums, 149
music, xxi, 41, 53, 118, 119
Muslim women, xvii
myths, 28, 29, 87–9, 92, 99, 105

National Childbirth Trust, 65
National Organization for Work with Girls and Young Women, 171
National Parks, 149
negotiation, 14, 35, 68, 69, 76, 77ff, 81–4, 107, 108, 129, 131, 135, 138–9, 141, 143, 172, 180
netball, 112
New York, xvii
newspapers, 38
non-feminist approaches, 9–10
nurseries, 64–6

older women, xix, 35, 75–85, 110, 111, 138
oppression, xiii, xvi, 5, 6
oral history, 21, 24, 27–30
organizations *see* institutions
Orton, Joe, 24ff
outings, xix, 65, 133, 135, 137

painting, 80

parental fears, 51ff
parenthood, 60
parents, xix, 33, 35, 48, 53, 108, 137
parity, *see* equal opportunities
parks, 56
parties, 49, 52, 56, 58, 64, 65, 118
partners/male partners, xv, xix, 3, 12, 14,
    22, 34, 35, 37–47, 65, 69, 107, 108,
    113, 127, 132, 133, 135, 138–9, 141,
    153
patriarchy/patriarchal relations, xiv, xv,
    xvi, xx, xxi, 8, 9, 10, 13, 34, 42, 102,
    127, 128, 131, 132, 134–5, 136, 137,
    144, 172, 173, 178, 180
peak experience, 102
pensions, 77
physical education, xvii, xviii, 7, 8, 9,
    103, 105, 116
physical exercise/activity/recreation, xviii,
    88, 147, 152, 178
play, xviii, 64
play leadership, 147, 151
playgroups, 64, 65
'playing out', 48–59
pluralism, 178
policy, 145, 147ff, 163, 165, 166, 171,
    177, 180, 181
politics, xiii, xiv, xv, xxi, 174
pop music, 115, 118
popmobility, 151
popular culture, xix, xx, 3, 37, 88, 95,
    100
poor people, poverty, 100, 137, 163
positivism, 180
power, xvi, xviii, 2, 6, 8, 9, 13–14, 15,
    35, 92, 98, 127–9, 134, 144, 145,
    147ff, 151–4, 159, 162, 163, 164,
    167, 168, 169, 174, 175, 178
pregnancy, 33, 60, 110, 111
pricing, 173, 174
private/public, 174, 182
public transport, 13, 49, 80, 97, 142–4
pubs, 12, 13, 14, 49, 57, 79, 94, 96, 97,
    98, 110, 133, 134–5, 141, 143, 144,
    166
punk, 48, 116, 117

qualitative research, 2, 3, 6, 84, 91ff
quantitative research, 3, 6, 91ff

race, xix, 3, 9, 12, 14, 29, 38, 49, 50, 131,
    132, 138, 170
racism, xvii, 134
radio, 88, 92, 169, 181

reading, xx, 3, 54, 63, 81, 91, 96
records, 49, 53, 54, 56, 120
recovery, 107, 110
recreation management *see* leisure
    management
recreational participation, xiv, xv
recreationally active mothers, 61, 68
redundancy, 33, 81
relatives, relations, xv, 14, 44, 66, 67, 70,
    133, 137, 177
religion, 80, 88, 99, 110, 177
resistance, 123
resources, 135, 138, 139, 143, 147, 153,
    172, 175
respectability, 132ff, 144
retired people, 177
retirement, 33, 34, 35, 75–85
riding, 80, 109
ritual, 88, 97ff, 106
Rochdale, 27, 30
role models, 170
romance, xix, xx, 39, 117ff, 132–4, 136
Royal Ballet School, 122, 123
running, 108

Sackville-West, Vita, 23ff
safety, 51, 88, 97
sailing, 80
salary, 150
Salford University, 19
sanctions, 162
Saturday jobs, 56
Saturday Night Fever, 117
school, xviii, xix, 2, 33, 48ff, 54, 55, 56,
    62, 64, 66, 103, 105, 113, 116, 117,
    120
school leavers, 9
school sport, 103, 105, 112
Scottish women, 60–74
Seacole, Mrs, 24ff
segregation, 149ff, 164
self employment, 150
self expression, 104, 115
self image, 87, 102, 117, 148, 150, 173
sensuality, 118
Sergy, Françoise, 123
servants, 21, 22, 23, 25
sewing, 12, 66
sex differentiation, 9, 168
Sex Discrimination Act, 166–8
sex stereotyping, 115ff, 123, 124, 132ff,
    150ff, 165, 169, 174, 178, 181,
sexism, 9, 13, 37, 79, 93, 138, 157, 165,
    168

sexual division of labour, 10, 13, 35, 41, 108, 136, 169, 173
sexual harassment, xv, 9, 134–5, 138, 174, 182
sexuality, xvi, xx, 7, 48, 87, 88, 132ff
Shake, 118
Sheffield, 3, 8, 13, 14, 34, 35, 38–47, 131–46
shift work, 11
shops, shopping, 56, 57, 64, 67, 83, 84, 107
single parents *see* lone parents
single sex clubs, 167–8
single women, 3, 35, 39, 46, 137, 139
sisterhood, xxi
Sistren Theatre Collective, 28, 29
skating, 109
skills, 102, 112, 114, 147, 154, 159, 164, 172, 173, 174
Smyth, Ethel, 23
soap operas, xix, xx
sociability, 91, 95ff
social change, 19, 29, 93
social control, 3, 7, 40, 79, 127, 131–46
social filter, 162, 174
social isolation, xxi, 35, 44, 58, 60, 63, 66, 71, 141
social networks, xvi, xxi, 35, 44, 60, 62, 63, 64, 65, 66, 68, 72, 73, 94, 97, 107
sociology of leisure, 5, 10–15
sociology of sport, 14
sociology of work, 5, 177
space(s), 81ff, 127, 134–5, 172, 182
spending, 98
sport, xiv, xv, xvi, xvii, xviii, 1, 2, 3, 6, 7, 8, 9, 13, 15, 80, 83, 87, 88, 102–14, 147, 151, 161–2, 168, 174
sport, governing bodies of, xviii, 102
sports centres, 55, 103ff, 149ff, 162
Sports Council/Social Science Research Council Joint Panel, 7
sports leadership, 8
Spotland poorhouse diaries, 30
St John's Ambulance Cadets, 56
strategies, 84, 137ff, 163, 172–5, 180
street culture, 49ff
stress, 156, 159
structural determinism, 87
style, 88, 117, 148, 151, 156
subordination of women, xiii, xiv, xv, 3, 5, 10, 118, 127, 131
success, 105, 112, 113, 123, 150, 178
support systems, networks, 12, 35, 40, 60, 66, 68, 70, 71, 73, 84, 108, 136, 137, 173, 174
surveys, xiv, 3, 34, 100
Sussex University, 21
Swansea, 39
swimming, 49, 55, 66, 80, 109, 152
synchronized swimming, 178

table tennis, 51
talking, 51, 53, 54, 55, 56, 64, 65, 66, 67, 70, 73
target groups, 181
television, xix, xx, 11, 38, 51, 53, 63, 81, 88, 91, 115, 117, 119, 122, 140, 169, 181
Ten Hour Act, 5
Territorial Army, 104
territoriality, 97, 162, 173
theatre, 80, 142, 149
theory, 18, 19
time, 11, 73, 76, 81, 82, 172, 182
time budgets, 1, 11
time, women's conceptions/use of, 11, 12, 74ff
tiredness, 12, 61
Title IX, 167
trades unions, 170
training, role of, 157–9
trampolining, 51
transitions *see* Part 2
transport, 50, 51, 68, 71, 79, 142–4, 145
Twist, 118

unemployed women, 3, 10, 27, 53, 57, 58
unemployment, 5, 25, 34, 35, 42, 48, 50, 138, 141, 142, 143, 177
unpaid/voluntary work, xv, xvi, 1, 2, 5, 10, 12, 38, 76, 178
upper class women, 22, 23, 100

Victorian working women, 21
video, xx, 88
violence, 9, 13, 79, 134, 137, 144
visiting, 64, 65
voluntary organizations, 73, 166, 167, 170

Waldon, Phyllis, 27
well-being, xiv, 2, 8, 12, 60, 67, 78, 79, 104
winning, 95, 98, 105, 120
wives, role of, 136
women/girls-only activities, 40, 41, 42, 57, 88, 99, 116, 118, 120ff, 175

women/girls-only groups, 57, 64–7, 70, 72, 80, 87, 108, 115ff, 164, 167, 172, 173, 174, 175
women managers, 127–8, 147–60
Women's Cooperative Guild, xvii
women's dual role, 10, 64ff
Women's Institute, 73, 80, 172
women's nights out, 40, 41, 42, 67
women's right to leisure, 14, 42, 43, 63, 67, 108, 133, 135, 136, 139–42, 182
Women's Sports Foundation, 8, 174
Women's Voluntary Service, 26
Woolf, Virginia, diaries of, 21ff, 73
work, paid work, xiv, xv, xvi, xix, 1, 2, 3, 5, 6, 7, 9, 10, 11, 12, 18, 19, 20, 27, 29, 33, 34, 35, 38, 42, 48, 60, 62, 67, 69, 75, 76ff, 93, 103, 135, 136, 137, 138, 139, 142, 148ff, 163, 177, 178, 180, 182
working class people, 23, 24, 29, 38, 42, 49, 91ff
working class women/girls, xviii, 2, 3, 5, 20, 21, 23, 48, 58, 65, 67, 68, 72, 80, 84, 88, 121, 124, 167
working men's clubs, 94, 116, 167, 174
workmates, 67
writing, xv

yoga, 124
Yorkshire, 2, 48–59, 103–14, 115–25
young women, xix, xx, 2, 8, 35, 38, 40, 48–59, 115–25, 137, 142
youth clubs, 49, 50, 51, 56, 57ff, 115ff
youth culture, 38, 39, 50, 115ff, 170, 180